The Material Child

Contents

Photographs of teenagers in Kyoto and Osaka by Yara Sellin, 1994

Preface to the Paperback Edition

The years we call the teens are not created the same or marked by the same events everywhere. Teenagers identified in America today as being at risk and teens designated in Japan as being at promise were the focus of the study on which this book is based. Their experiences differ greatly, as do their images. The first characteristic of the Japanese teens that caught my eye, in contrast to their American counterparts, was invisibility. My first trip to Japan in 1963 revealed a nation full of energy and change as it prepared for the Tokyo Olympics: construction of subways, buildings, and roads; a vital sense of modern development; the edge of the economic boom. But there were no "teenagers," in the American sense of the word. In the 1980s Thomas Rohlen could still say that one can call a high schooler *kodomo*, or child, with impunity. This comment alerted me to an interesting cultural gap in life-course categories. Is a teenager in Japan treated like a "child"? What sets the teen apart from younger "children" and adults, if anything, beyond the age-grading of the schools and the obvious biological changes? How is adolescence marked in Japan, and what are the implications for adulthood and Japanese society at large?

In January 1993, on Coming of Age Day, the Japanese media ran a small story about change in youth culture. On Coming of Age Day those who have turned twenty during the past year don their best kimonos and suits and go with their families to visit the nearest temple or shrine and perhaps out to eat. But a new ceremony has begun to mark this day as well: a visit to a love hotel with one's significant other. Love hotels, places where private, clean rooms with sometimes fantastic decor and luxury are rented by the hour for married or unmarried lovers, have been quick to cash in on the "young adult" market. To encourage these holiday visits they provide special package deals, which often include the services of a professional kimono dresser, who helps the young woman in and out of her formal kimono, a skill now said to be lacking in the younger generation. Ah, then, the American audience might say, they aren't so different from our youngsters after all; faddish commercialism, to say nothing of sexual experimentation and rebellion, has arrived in Japan, too!

But to read this, and to cite the prevalence of blue jeans, fast food, rock music, and peer pressure as evidence that Japanese teenagers are learning from the West, is to misconstrue these trends. The question that really begs to be asked is "Who is this *cheenayja* (a recent term borrowed to fill the gap) now appearing in Japan?" It has become evident that the construction of this newly defined lifestyle is at least in part the product of affluence and marketing. Yet it is clearly not a case of convergence alone—not evidence of Japanese society becoming more American as economic development progresses—nor is it mimicry, the result of copying Western ways, that has produced this phenomenon in Japan. To document and analyze this trend I examine the efforts and goals of the institutions surrounding the teens, the lives of the teens themselves, and the relationship between the two.

Methodology

Between 1988 and 1991 I conducted a series of interviews with media and marketing researchers and economists, editors, promotion agents for popular music stars, clinical psychologists, academic researchers, parents, teachers, and journalists writing

The Material Child

COMING OF AGE IN
JAPAN AND AMERICA

MERRY WHITE

UNIVERSITY OF CALIFORNIA PRESS

Berkeley · Los Angeles · London

University of California Press
Berkeley and Los Angeles, California

University of California Press, Ltd.
London, England

First Paperback Printing 1994

This edition is reprinted by arrangement with
The Free Press, A Division of Macmillan, Inc.

Library of Congress Cataloging-in-Publication Data

White, Merry I., 1941–
    The material child : coming of age in Japan and America / Merry White.
        p.   cm.
    Originally published: New York : Free Press ; Toronto : Maxwell Macmillian Canada ; New York : Maxwell Macmillan International, c1993.
    Includes bibliographical references and index.
    ISBN 0-520-08940-5 (pbk. : alk. paper)
    1. Teenagers—United States—Social conditions.   2. Teenagers—Japan—Social conditions.   I. Title.
HQ796.W4727   1994
305.23′5′0973—dc20   94-10639
                                                     CIP

Printed in the United States of America

1   2   3   4   5   6   7   8   9   10

The paper used in this publication meets the minimum requirements of American National Standard for Information Sciences—Permanence of Paper for Printed Library Materials, ANSI Z39.48–1984. ⊗

To

HENRY, LISA, OLIVE, SIMON, AND ZOE
Mille Grazie

on life course or consumer style. At the same time, I also conducted interviews with fifty adolescents, selected from a broader group of one hundred who completed a background questionnaire. The fifty were chosen to represent diversity in region, age, sex, and socioeconomic status. The interviewees were from Tokyo, Osaka, Yokohama, Gumma Prefecture, Chiba, and Hiroshima, which included major urban and suburban areas as well as smaller provincial cities and towns. The participants ranged in age from thirteen to seventeen at the first interview and seventeen through twenty-one by the end of the study. There were equal numbers of males and females in the sample, though not within every age group. Family background varied from elite professional and managerial families with high levels of education to families in which the parents finished their education at the high-school level.

The adolescents interviewed were visited at least three times, and other kinds of data were gathered during the three-year research period. First, all participants were asked to keep diaries in which they wrote their experiences and feelings day by day for brief periods of time during the study. These journals proved to be a valuable resource, as informants used them to describe their homes, family issues, school experiences, the trajectories of friendships and romances, and observations about Japan and the wider world. These musings were often accompanied by their own cartoons, diagrams, graphic displays of mood, details of clothing and trendy gear, and even songs and poems of their own composition. Additionally, participants were asked to fill out simple time budgets on selected weekend days, indicating, hour by hour, what they were doing, where they were doing it, and with whom. Finally, each was asked to prepare a self-introduction of a more formal nature, a *sakubun* or essay, in which he or she wrote a profile of himself or herself.

Interviews with the young people covered the same areas (family, school, friendship, sexuality, popular culture, the larger world, and the future) as the surveys regularly conducted by market researchers. Japanese market research is driven, in part, by the immediate concerns of clients who need to know the potential of a given product, fashion, or pop star. But long-term research is also conducted over a period of several years, covering a wide range of attitudes, habits, and behavior from teen cohorts. Market researchers also construct teen focus groups, which meet regularly in many parts of Japan. These focus groups both test products and ideas (for example, reactions to advertising) and initiate ideas for products and concepts. The researchers also operate "hotlines" for teens to call with suggestions.

Although my study was not intended to be a verification of the marketers' sense of their audience, it informally confirmed my view that marketing surveys do produce accurate and multifaceted profiles of contemporary teenagers. There is an inherent contradiction, however, in that commissioned research often reveals what the marketers want to know: that there is a homogeneous cohort of adolescents ready to buy a given product. For efficiency and profit, consumer industries prefer a relatively undifferentiated market: the more of a single product they can sell, the better. However, what their researchers also tell them is that teens are in fact very diverse in terms of their styles, tastes, and ability to pay. In response to these facts, recently the Japanese youth-centered media, fashion, and other producers have differentiated their product lines, and in this interactive and symbiotic relationship have further amplified teens' awareness of difference.

In America, I conducted interviews with a smaller group of thirty teenagers in a range of environments, rural to urban, and from different socioeconomic backgrounds. In several areas teens also wrote personal essays similar to the *sakubun* written by their Japanese counterparts. Additionally, I conducted interviews with academic and marketing experts on American teenagers. As the study is intended to be a "mirrored" portrait of Japanese teenagers rather than a full comparative study, the American and Japanese treatments are not fully parallel.

Some Further Thoughts

The American teen appeared in the public and mercantile consciousness during the affluence of the 1950s and has continued to have a high profile for several demographic, social, and economic reasons ever since. The American Baby Boom generation, followed by the Baby Bust and at least one Baby Boom echo cohort, have, in America as well as in Japan, encouraged new models, and new consumer desires, with each marked and targeted youth "tribe." But the numbers in an age cohort alone do not make a sense of "generation," "culture," or shared values and community, however much the media would like to construct these notions (as in their recent attempt to construct the *shinjinrui,* or "new breed," image of individuated, affluent, even selfish consumers in their early twenties). What counts, of course, are shared historical and institutional experiences, such as school, or developmental events like puberty.

What have these Japanese young people shared in terms of history, and what are they likely to face in the future? Born as they were into relative affluence, most have not known real deprivation, and none have known, as their grandparents did, the crisis of war and the struggle of reconstruction. Those with aspirations and resources can consider a future reasonably similar to the lives of their parents, but unlike their parents rarely will they surpass the standard of living of their natal homes. For example, whereas their parents may have been able to buy a house by the time they were in their forties, because of increasing land values young people today cannot take for granted land and home ownership. Unlike most of their parents, however, they can aspire to travel and to have more free time for leisure activities. Furthermore, they have more independent years between finishing their schooling and starting a family, which gives them time to establish a professional identity and greater freedom to explore themselves.

This self-exploration includes sexuality. Teens now have more opportunities to engage in sexual activity than young people did just fifteen or twenty years ago—and they are much more likely to take advantage of them. As noted in Chapter 7, a young person now twenty years old would likely have been a virgin at fifteen, but his or her younger cousin who is now fifteen is likely to have already had sexual experience. This change in sexual behavior has occurred very rapidly. Although reported teen pregnancy rates in Japan are very low, and even declining (as opposed to the tripling of the rate in the United States over the past thirty years), sexual activity has gone up. When the Japanese edition of this book was being prepared in 1993, the Japanese editors were concerned about the section on sexuality and asked if some of the data might be relegated to footnotes instead of displayed in the text. They doubted that young teenagers had any sexual experience at all, but after some informal checking, they kept the text intact.

There are, however, new constraints as well as new freedoms

in sexual expression. In spite of the rhetoric that has allowed the Japanese to continue thinking, for many decades, that they live in a remote and narrow island nation, Japan is becoming "globalized." The critical mass of people with experience in other countries, through study and travel abroad, has had an impact. The importance of global interdependence was emphasized by the "oil shokku" (energy crisis) of the 1970s, the trade concerns of the 1980s, and the Gulf War of the early 1990s. International contact has also produced a new and more deadly effect, that of the appearance of AIDS in Japan. Until the beginning of the 1990s most Japanese thought of AIDS (if they thought of it at all) as a foreign disease, and some young people even thought that it was physically impossible for Japanese to contract it.

Now, however, AIDS has come to Japan, though the number of reported cases is still small, under two thousand, and the news stories emphasize that many of these are foreigners. Yet sex education in schools often does not address AIDS at all; if it does, it is only in connection with condom use, without detailing AIDS's consequences. Sex education is more complete and straightforward in the popular teen magazines, and there it does include warnings about AIDS and detailed descriptions of how to use condoms, but the notion that one might be at serious risk is still foreign.

AIDS is a topic of particularly great concern, however, for those worried about the rise in teen prostitution in Japan. High-school and college women have found it profitable (and as one teen said, "fun") to engage in prostitution after school and on weekends. Their customers are usually middle-aged businessmen, who, it is feared, may also be clients of AIDS-infected prostitutes in Southeast Asia, where the businessmen may have travelled on the notorious "sex tours."

While these are risks unforeseen a decade ago, Japanese teens of the current generation do have future advantages not enjoyed by many earlier generations. Today's teens will come into the labor market at a time when projections show a labor shortage, and thus will be seen as "golden eggs" (as were their early postwar predecessors) much in demand by employers. This advantage may allow them to bring about change in the workplace: they may ask for, and get, flextime, longer holidays, less unpaid overtime, and more opportunity for family leave. Women in this group will be especially sought after, and they will demand careers, not jobs, and promotion schemes allowing for time out for childrearing. Many of these young people also say they are not interested in lifetime employment at one organization, but rather see themselves as "freeters," (from "free" and "arbeit," the German word for work), freelance workers or job-hoppers.

Demographic factors like the falling birthrate and increasing number of elderly in the population will definitely bring change to Japan, and today's teenagers are the generation that will see the practical outcomes of these changes. This group will create new definitions of the good life, of work, of family roles and responsibilities, and of membership in society and the world. The forces that influence these young people today will have potent echo effects in the twenty-first century.

Friends in Japan and elsewhere, knowing publication is not the end of the process, continue to supply me with provocative data and ideas. I want particularly to thank Kazu and Mari Yamazaki, Sumio Kondo, Kuniko McVey, and Dave Schmalz, who persuades me to trust stories to tell themselves. While all errors of fact and interpretation remain mine, I am deeply obliged to my family and to these friends.

Merry White
April 1994

Glossary of Japanese Terms

akarui   lively, high-spirited, active
akaruiko   active, positive, lively child
amae   (appropriate) dependency, encouraged in certain relationships at all ages
amekazi   "American" casual style of dress
arubaito   part-time work, usually in student years
asshi-kun   colloquial term among girls for a boyfriend who is a
"legman," who runs errands, etc.
bishonen   cute young person, (usually male)
boifurendo   boyfriend, not necessarily romantic
burabura suru   to hang out
burakumin   member of disadvantaged minority, the former
outcast community
burikko   false innocent, childlike girl
cheenayja   marketing and media term for "teenager"
chuto hanpa   neither one nor the other, in-between age
dasai   nerdy, uncool
enryo   modesty, self-restraint

furio   gangster-style
futsuu   ordinary
gambaru   persevere
garufurendo   girlfriend, not necessarily romantic
genpuku   coming-of-age ceremony for boys in ancient court
hankokki   adolescent rebellion
hansei   self-examination, critical self-reflection
hensachi   statistical "grade" used in secondary schools for
     advising on future college expectations, etc.
honne   reality
ichigozoku   "strawberry gang," market jargon for fifteen
     year olds
ijime   bullying
info-maniakku   information fanatic
johoshakai   information society
juku   after-school private enrichment or cram classes
kami-age   traditional coming-of-age ceremony for girls
kawaikochan   "cute kid"
keigo   polite form, in language
kodomo   child
koibito   lover
kokkan nikki   exchange diary: a semiprivate journal that is
     shared between close friends
kohai   "junior" (see sempai-kohai relationship)
kyoiku mama   education-focussed mother
kuchikomi   word of mouth
kurai   dark-spirited (also, *nekura:* opp. *akarui*)
machikomi   "word of town," meaning how young people learn
     what's in through window-shopping, observing on the
     streets, etc.
manga   comic books
manuaru shokugun   manual syndrome: the overdependence of
     young people on "manuals" for learning about behavior and
     performance in many aspects of life
ningen kankei   human relationships
omiai   meeting with a prospective spouse
omoiyari   sensitivity to others
otakuzoku   "distance gang," solitary youth obsessed with
     comics or soft pornography
raabaa   lover

ronin non-matriculated student preparing for college entrance exam

ryukogo slang

seinen youth

sempai/kohai relationship between senior and junior, especially in school activity groups

shakaijin adult, "member of society"

shibu-kaji "Shibuya" (a district of Tokyo) style

shinjinrui "new breed," media jargon for affluent youth in the 1980s

shinyu best friend

shonen youth

tatemae principle, official or ideal form

tomodachi friend

tokokyohi school rejection or avoidance

utoi ignores trends

yakuza gangster

yobiko full-time cram schools, usually attended between high school and college

yutaka (na) affluent

yutori leisure

zurui sneaky, hypocritical

Introduction

I was a teenager in the 1950s, when the American idea of the teen itself came of age. Our house was on the line dividing two towns: one self-consciously liberal and academic, the other working class and industrial. Some official arbiter had determined that our house was taxable in the first town, and so my parents could claim the more prestigious mailing address. But they constantly reminded us how close we were to "the gangs," and how dangerous the other town was. And how vulnerable WE were, as innocent overeducated, nubile, and weaponless teens ourselves, to the barbarous, violent influences of the raging hordes just over the line behind the house. When a beer can ended up in our yard, or when, on a hot summer night the air carried the sound of firecrackers or a revved-up jalopy, our parents would lock the doors and windows muttering, "It's the JDs"—that particularly potent epithet for juvenile delinquent. We were all paralyzed with fear— of teenagers.

Since the 1970s, I have worked with teens as teacher and researcher in the United States and Japan. In the United States, I

1

now live—again—near the turf of those gangs of the 1950s. In Japan, I recently lived in an industrial wasteland on the edge of a provincial town. Almost every night, *bōsōzoku*, motorcycle gangs, circled there under my apartment windows, and I was often snapped awake by the frightening roar of their engines. Today, my Japanese neighbors worry about these working-class youth much as my parents did in the early 1950s.

Elite Japanese today worry about their children as well, though their children are very like those of the "right" side of the American tracks in the 1950s, childlike, innocent, and sometimes studious, rarely a concern to society. However, the growing Japanese media and consumer focus on youth as a market has now created an alternative concept of the *cheenayja*—a more diverse and less predictable image, one of some concern to their society.

The Material Child is an attempt to show how images and realities converge and diverge, how within Japan there is a diversity invisible to most visitors and how among both American and Japanese teens, the mirroring of diversity helps to clarify our view. "Material" may be taken literally or figuratively: our children are all trend slaves to some degree living in "a material world." It is not, however, things alone they crave, but the relationships and identity that are part of their new profile, encouraged by the market that has in part created them. But youth are also "material" to our survival as societies; they cannot be ignored or contained as transitory phenomena or fearful threats—they are our future.

To me, the boys on their motorbikes in my Japanese neighborhood are not a concern, only a nuisance; they seem to present no real risk. I know that even rebellious adolescents in Japan have self-imposed limits and goals for the future, and that drugs and lethal weapons are very scarce. There is no equivalent to "wilding" in Japan. Having been present at the formation of the contemporary American concept of the teen, and having been trained in the images and realities of young people in both societies, I was drawn to a comparative study of the nature of adolescence.

Comparisons, to be true to the differences, must not be drawn in strict parallel: a category that counts in Japan, such as entrance exams to high school, may have no clear counterpart in the United States. I have chosen to emphasize Japanese youth and to use American experiences and evidence as a mirror, I hope both reflecting and illuminating.

I began the study in June of 1988. I had been visiting Japan since 1963, and had conducted research on children's lives there since 1975. I expected no surprises in learning about these older children, but rather, continuity with my prior research on younger children, because to some degree I had bought the notion that the American brand of teen doesn't exist in Japan, and because Japanese themselves did not project a view of an indigenous but recognizable model—at least, not at first.

I started slowly, soaking up atmosphere in Tokyo teen territories. What *was* evident at first was that teens were in the marketplace, so, looking for crowds of them, I strolled the youth consumer hubs. Here is an excerpt from my notes from my first Sunday afternoon, prime teen shopping time:

> I took with me the section from *An-An* (a girls' magazine) on Shibuya, and followed its recommended course with illustrated maps to trendy places for teens to hang out. I started at Hachiko (the statue of a faithful dog in front of the station, a well-known meeting point), and followed the young crowds to Seibu, Loft, Wave, Seed, and Parco (trendy department stores and specialty shops catering to young people). Wow. These young kids are spending $150 for a shirt, $200 for a jumpsuit, and more for French imports, without blinking. The "look" now seems to be gamine, perky and black, but not quite punk. The favorite hat is a small, round, brimmed, black felt, perched back on the head, worn by boys and girls. They look easy, relaxed, happy, "self-expressive." But even all the self-expression doesn't lead to jaywalking or rowdy behavior. They all wait, well-socialized, for the lights to change even with no cars in sight—even the androgynous kid in ominous black lipstick, oval shades, one long earring, and black leather.
>
> I went on to Yoyogi and the rock dancers. Something has changed from two years ago, when I last saw them. They are not all the gentle highschoolers I remember. Some are clearly professional, full-time performers. Some are counterculture druggies. Many are clearly dropouts and working youths, since they have high-spiked punk hairstyles and permanent hair dye, not the temporary stuff they used to apply to their school-appropriate school haircuts and wash out before going home. I wonder if the pros, well-organized and disciplined, have taken over this site, and if the sweet part-time deviants are elsewhere now? I'm impressed, nonetheless, with these performers. I'm impressed with the affluence of these "delinquents," if that is what they are. Their costumes must be expensive. They could, I calculate, cost them up to $10,000 a year for gear and clothes. Affluence affects even the margins.

The weeks after these diary entries were filled with more focused interviewing and data collection, and meetings with marketing researchers, trend-spotting social commentators, as well as psychologists, teachers, and sociologists. I spent the next three years alternating between Japan and the United States, visiting and revisiting the same teenagers and the same observers in both countries.

What I learned was surprising. Rebellion, for example, does not dominate the experience of teenagers in either society. What does command attention is the combination of conformity and diversity dictated by adolescent development and the seeking of an identity, and by the demands of peer influence. These universal elements are differently experienced in Japan and the United States, but in both societies, they are promoted and amplified as the age group becomes targeted by consumer industries: marketing and the media tell them how to be a teenager.

What teens say reveals similarity and diversity, but overall, Japanese and American teens echo each other: Who am I, and do you like me? We're cool, but they aren't. I like her but I can't tell her that. Mom, I can't wear that, it's nerdy. If I do the dishes, maybe my mother will stop bugging me. I don't have any money so I can't go out with my friends.

And what adults say in both countries sounds similar as well: These kids are sending our country down the drain. They are nothing but children, and we have to protect them. They won't listen to us. When I was your age. . . .

American parents remember their own teen years, and those of us raised in the 1940s and 1950s remember an especially complicated environment—our parents feared *for* us, feared on our behalf, feared the influences that might assail us in blackboard jungles, and, later perhaps, feared our being drafted and sent to the jungles of southeast Asia.

There was a big gap in experience between our parents and us—they knew the Depression and World War II and the mobilization for survival demanded by both. They did not understand the possibilities for rebellion of the 1960s, or any reason for it.

Japanese parents since that war have been concerned about the educational imperative, the engine driving the examination experience, and its effect on children's lives. Americans, however, now both fear *for* our children, and we also fear our children *themselves*, even though in material and historical terms, we have more in common with them. Parents of current teens were raised in times of greater peace and prosperity, though we may have fought, or fought against, the war in Vietnam and many of us recently have known hard times.

It is easy to understand what we fear *for* them: we fear physical violence—even in their schools—we fear drugs, rape, unplanned pregnancy, sexually transmitted diseases, crime, and psychological pathologies. We fear that our children will be disaffected and lose their self-esteem and ambition. We fear they will run away and end up pictured on a milk carton. We also fear *them:* we fear that they will not love us, that they will reject us, not trust us, and that they will not accept our love, knowledge and authority.[1]

Some of what we fear our parents feared for us. Although we of the 1950s, with the rosy lens of nostalgia, may remember a comfortable middle-class childhood and yet do not think ourselves soulless or amoral, we imagine that our "material children" have no moral core. Our parents too felt that our interest in *things* was of a lower order. Our media also sold *us* sexual images and "dangerous" lifestyles (drinking, smoking, and fast driving), and yet we worry that our children whose music similarly tells them to take risks will go to the dogs much faster—and much more permanently—than we did.

But some of our teens' experiences may be new. There have been changes in our children's environment, and in them. Children are now at an early age, at least superficially, far more sexually knowledgeable, learning from friends, the media, and from adult warnings about sexual disease and violence. Information is not the same as experience, however, and we can assume that many young teens are only talking a good game.

Children are, however, truly tougher and quicker on the streets—at least urban kids are—because for many, being streetwise means survival. Their music is no longer only about romance and seduction (Come on, let's do it, baby) but also tough and self-protective (something like "Go fuck yourself, you louse"). It is not just *our* fears, from a more protected past, but those of the children themselves that shape their environment and behavior.

Our media and marketers have similarly become streetwise and savvy. Both in the United States and Japan, advertisers know their audiences, and more than in the 1950s, have helped to amplify the separateness of a "youth culture" in their societies. With more disposable income from parents or part-time employment, middle-class American and Japanese young people can support habits of consumption beyond those of even their baby-boomer parents, and what is purchased is often not teen versions of adult goods, but footgear (pump sneakers), music (rap), and clothing (neon stripes on leather) created for and dedicated to the youth market. In America, younger children and even adults might imitate teens, but teens rarely imitate the clothing of another age group. In fact, you are more likely to see a tee shirt on an adult saying "Middle-Aged Mutant Ninja Father," than a teen in suit and tie.

Changes in school experience have also been notable. In America, there have been palpable losses in mood and learning. Our teens are testing no better in math and science than their counterparts twenty years ago, in spite of Sputnik, and the German and Japanese postwar miracles. In these subjects, American teens test thirteenth of fourteen countries in a recent survey.[2] Literacy has fallen as well. Half of our young people cannot use a map, read, and understand simple documents such as job applications, or balance a checkbook. The test scores of Japanese children in academic subjects are so good as to provide grist for the trade war mill: a protectionist American reaction might be that Japanese children are being disciplined and programmed as instruments of Japanese economic supremacy. The Japanese literacy rate is 99 percent to our 80 percent, and all high-school seniors have studied calculus, earth sciences, physics, chemistry, and biology. All children have studied two musical instruments and several artistic media, including calligraphy—well-known tools of economic imperialism. Meanwhile, American SAT scores, results of the test given only to college-bound high school seniors, have fallen continually during the past fifteen years. Ninety-five percent of Japanese highschoolers test at a level achieved only by our top five percent.

However different the test scores are, and however different the atmosphere of the streets, both American and Japanese parents are concerned about their teenagers. International supremacy in math and science doesn't make Japanese parents complacent about their schools: they are highly critical. We both are concerned about the effects of changing family structure on children, of absent fathers and working mothers, or stress caused by economic hardship, of the effects of modern affluence on the moral condition. Japanese parents are worried, too, about a perceived decline in the mental and physical health of their children; but unlike American parents whose health cares focus on drugs, sex, and AIDS, Japanese parents consider a fast-food diet and habits of late-night study to pose dire problems for the future.

Japanese teenagers, like their American counterparts, are a relatively recent discovery and invention. American teens emerged or were identified in the postwar years as "teenagers," feared by parents and sought by marketers in a newly affluent "youth society." Japanese teens have appeared and been identified only more recently, as the economic boom of the late 1970s and 1980s targeted and reached a new "youth market." In both societies, the conjunction of adolescent development and new affluence produced generations both intrinsically conformist, ready to buy as a cohort what the market defined them as wanting, and intrinsically diverse, needing distinctions for a newly identified sense of self. Teens want both the safety of numbers and the safety of solitude. Both needs are amplified by media and marketing in both countries.

This book deals with commonalities among and differences between Japanese and American teenagers' lives. We will examine the social and economic forces influencing their experiences, their aspirations, and their search for identity. The voices of approximately 100 teenagers interviewed in both countries between 1988 and 1991 are used to illustrate these themes in young people's lives. With my research assistants, I interviewed adolescents in several parts of Japan, in Tokyo, Yokohama, Gumma Prefecture, Osaka, Saitama Prefecture, Hiroshima, and Chiba Prefecture. Teens also prepared diaries, time budgets, and essays on their school life, friendships, and hopes for the future. Also heard are family, parents, teachers, psychologists, marketing specialists, and music promoters as they describe the lives of adolescents and their influence on and expectations for these young people. Family, school, friendship, sexuality, and the consumer market are treated as focal topics in the consideration of adolescents' lives.

Above all, teens in both countries are the product of our cultures and the product, to some degree, of our abundance. They are marked by the "stage" they are in—by the hormonal surges and the social marginality of adolescence. In both Japan and America, they are also torn almost schizophrenically between the *busshitsu-teki*, "material" side of their lives, on the one hand and

the outward-looking idealism characterizing their new awareness of a larger world and bigger obligations on the other. While
Americans might find this contradiction between materialism
and idealism puzzling, Japanese young people comfortably em-
body both, for the same children who are spending large amounts
of money on expensive clothing and "trend goods" are also talking of spending years of service in volunteer corps activities in
Africa or Southeast Asia, working to improve the environment at
home, or are already working in their communities in homes for
the elderly or in day-care centers. All our children seem to want to
help; all want to live in a more peaceful world.

Looking at modern society through the eyes of its teens illuminates two kinds of transition: the personal passage from childhood to adulthood, and the historical development of new models
for youth in a postindustrial age. The study also forces a startling
revision of several commonly held notions about culture and society; looking at Japanese teens in the comparative reflecting
glass of the lives of American teens allows us to see commonalities in lives and life courses and distinctions caused by historical,
economic, and cultural factors. Commonalities and distinction
should equally give us pause, for the teens of both our countries
are the future for us all, and perhaps, given the disproportionate
influence of the two nations, for a much wider world as well.

1
Rethinking the Life Course

Mixed Messages and Complementary Contradictions in the Creation of Adolescence

How do we know that we are young, or middle-aged, or old? How we understand our chronological age is determined by class and history, as well as by culture and commerce. In Egypt, a ten-year-old may be called a domestic servant; in Des Moines, a fifth-grader. A fifty-year-old may be in the prime of life in the salons of Paris, or exceeding the local life expectancy in the streets of Harlem or the villages of Bangladesh. How age defines our experiences and how societies create and manipulate these definitions are more than semantic puzzles or demographic problems. Legal and social definitions of childhood and adulthood may send one child home to his parents while his partner, only a month older, goes to jail for twenty years. In less dramatic contexts, the relationships, responsibilities, and the futures of our children are still strongly influenced by these cultural and economic calculations.

This book will treat the stage of life we call adolescence, both as an experience and as the product of such manipulations, and will compare young people's lives in two of the world's most youth-

and consumer-oriented societies, those of Japan and the United States.

Our societies are seen as modern and democratic, and both are active members of the "international market." Our teens belong to the "youth" segment of the global consumer audience, yet what we sell to them, and how we sell it, reflect our different values and perspectives on youth.

In America, the concept of "the teen" emerged during this century as a dangerous limbo period in which adolescents are at risk to themselves and others—but through which all must pass as a natural stage of development. Running the gauntlet of temptations is seen as the task of the stage, at the same time that the child's future is determined by educational and occupational choices made during the storm and stress. The mixed messages are many: Just Do It, and Just Say No; Get a Job, and Stay in School. Parents and teachers take the brunt of the confusion; adolescence becomes pathology needing control.

In Japan, adolescence is not a limbo period but the most critical, most fully mobilized time of life. Adults and young people both agree that one's teens are key to one's future prospects. Free of the suspicions of American adults—which become self-fulfilling prophecies—Japanese adults have high expectations for their young people, who are less inclined to disagree with their elders than are their American counterparts.

School in America is then an uneasy setting for concerns about diversity and relevance, a social-class-based battleground, and relationships between teens become trials of rebellion and conformity, innocence and sophistication, competition and possessiveness. School in Japan is an unadorned, serious training ground where equality means similarity of goals and potential, and relationships are where you learn social realities applicable to adult life. Learning is relatively nonconfrontational in Japan, whereas in America, there appears to be more ambivalence over the role and value of organized academic activity.

In the generational dialectic, American parents are in competition with their children—for control, for freedoms and choices, and for youthfulness itself. Parents are constrained by their resources and by the opportunities society offers for their children, and yet are also told that the success or failure of their children is their responsibility. In Japan, the cultures of youth and adulthood are more congruent—and today one can see the parents of young teens merging in interests and perspectives with their progeny.

The teen has emerged at different historical moments and has a different cultural profile in the United States and Japan. The meanings reflect divergent, rather than convergent, patterns of relationships between generations, life course trajectories, and ideas of the good life. The teen becomes a focusing lens for our ideologies and cultural values. For example, in the United States, use of the word "teenager" refers not only to a specific term of life, but also, popularly, to a certain kind of behavior to be expected in those years. Above all, it seems to mean problems and conflict between generations.

The Japanese, on the other hand, have borrowed the word—it is pronounced "cheenayja"—but, as in many Japanese linguistic borrowings, they have not adopted the image and expectations we have associated with it. There, teenagers are relatively unmarked as occupying a special stage of life. The words *shonen*, *seinen*, and others refer to periods within and overlapping the teens, and most generally mean "youth."

But "cheenayja" isn't common parlance. Nor is there consensus on what it means. When asked, "What is a teenager?", Japanese informants groped for meaning over a wide age range: some said nine to fifteen; some, ten to eighteen; some, fifteen to twenty-one; and some, most inclusive of all, ten to thirty. Most people chose not to cite age at all, but to stay with safer institutional identities: a teen is a middle-school or high-school student. With more than a third of the population under twenty-four years of age, and the second baby boom now peaking at fifteen to eighteen years of age, there is a large unnamed segment of "youth."[1]

This period of life comes with few and imprecise expectations of behavior peculiar to it. While the American parent modifies, lowers, or perhaps suspends expectations of the teenage child almost as a matter of course, the Japanese parent does not. A high-schooler might still be safely called *kodomo*, "child," in Japan,[2] receiving parental and institutional attention as a student—or might be a worker, treated as a responsible adult. A child in premodern Japan was in childhood until he or she entered adulthood, defined by leaving school to take up a job or leaving home to get married. In modern Japan, too, such institutional definitions have more weight than social and psychological identities. The social bracketing of the years between twelve and twenty as a marginal and deviant age is for the most part absent in Japan. Why we have such different expectations is a question to be answered through a look, in Chapter 2, at our recent social histories.

The factors that distinguish us make it clear that our paths are not converging, that a modern economy does not simply trickle common effects down to ordinary lives. Japanese teens are not "catching up" to their American counterparts, evolving and overcoming the oppression of "feudal" or "Confucian" age hierarchies. They do, of course, share common features with American teens, from hormonal changes to tastes in music.

What they share, too, is the range of access to the goods of modern life. Class and opportunity have also influenced the definitions of youth, in both the United States and Japan. This effect may be more strikingly seen in a country where development has been more notably uneven. The Egyptian child who entered domestic service at ten is still a servant at fourteen, and no more a "teenager" now than she was a "child" at ten. She may also be—at fourteen—a mother. Other Egyptian young people, privileged by parental wealth and status, can be schoolchildren and even, in Western terms, "teenagers" enjoying a modern material culture, while the fourteen-year-old servant cleans their kitchen.

Nor is opportunity evenly distributed in Japan and the United States. An American high school dropout at sixteen may be a garage worker, for example, servicing a car driven by a seventeen-year-old prep school student. In Japan, too, a seventeen-year-old may be preparing for the university, protected and nurtured by her parents or may be working all day on an assembly line in a factory. And in both Japan and the United States, the distinctions between rural and urban areas also create different experiences for teens, as 44 percent of our population and 13 percent of theirs live in the countryside, with somewhat less access to the gear, goods, and risks of urban teens' lives. The rural teen in Japan is, however, well-connected by media and marketing to Tokyo, the center of teen culture, while the rural American youth (if lacking cable television and a shopping mall) finds urban teen culture fairly foreign.[3]

Discrepancies are not very surprising. But we might at least expect our *middle-class* children to be similar to each other. Don't they listen to the same music, wear the same clothes, engage in the same search for identity, and work to achieve the same academic credentials as their counterparts elsewhere in advanced societies? Indeed, middle-class children in Japan, like middle-class children in America, haunt department stores, enjoy Nintendo games, are embarrassed by their parents, and don headsets to listen to rock music and create a private space. They try to enter good universities by studying hard in high school. And working- class children in both countries aim at stable jobs and marriage and try to improve their family's conditions. But Japanese adolescents look like teens in Des Moines, wearing similar trendy clothes (haut Euro-punk in Japan) and listening to Madonna in their earphones, but they are not just Japanese versions of Americans and are not even heading in that direction. What makes the difference more profound than the difference between Shakey's Pizza (with pepperoni) in Los Angeles, and Shakey's Pizza (with sweet corn and squid) in Tokyo? The answer lies in the meanings they attach to growing up, to family, school, sexuality, friendship, and the wider world, and in the expectations adults have for them in all these arenas of life.

Families construct lives for their members and provide unconditional support, solace, and relief from the constricting forces of ~~Wrong~~ school and society. In Chapter 3, we will examine the experiences of home and family relationships as our cultural codes and economic realities shape them. Schools, too, have their codes and construct models for identity and performance for adolescents. In Chapter 4, the role of the school in shaping teen experience— the agenda and curriculum for adolescence—is examined.

Consumerism, Money, and Morality

It is undeniable that in both societies, young people with the resources to be so are "material children." And they cross consumer paths frequently, our teens buying Japanese audio equipment and their teens buying Levis and Ben and Jerry's ice cream. But the cassette player doesn't make your fifteen-year-old Japanese, and the chocolate-chip cookie-dough ice cream doesn't produce a culture-change operation on a Japanese child. The similarities of our material worlds only throw into relief the different meanings attached to consumerism and popular culture, as well as the relationship of these with our goals for teenagers.

Consumer marketing amplifies aspects of teen life, such as fashions created by rock or rap stars, food and drink teens might share in a social setting, and cutting-edge music and entertainment. Both creating trends and reflecting interests, these industries also exacerbate the factors that distinguish teens from each other in less comfortable ways—either, as in the United States, by delineating market segments by class, ethnically, urban, and rural designations, or as in the more mass-marketed Japan, by forcing teens to recognize distinctions by ability to pay.

Young teens in Japan are *infomaniakku*, "infomaniacs." When they get together, it is to share the latest on their favorite pop-music stars, news on where to buy that great shirt, or what CD rental shop has a special offer this week. The young teen is intensely focused on being appropriate, and she negotiates the path by testing on friends what's learned in the media—discovering who she is by what her friends like—to wear, to hear, to buy.[4] American "mallies" are little different—though perhaps with less ready cash. The chief difference is in how they obtain and transfer such information. The magazine industry in Japan has captured the youth market. Japanese children tend to read far more than U.S. teens and to rely on information from such publications as the means for communicating with friends. From dispensing information about pop stars, the *kawaiikochan* (cute kids), to cataloguing current fashion trends, the publishing industry flourishes with the help of the teens it helped to create.

Becoming a shopper, a consumer, is in both societies, part of growing up. In the United States, a child's allowance is supposed to provide an important life lesson, either in spending or in saving wisely. American teens, even middle-class children, work in part-time and summers jobs as soon as they are old enough, and learn quickly to say, "It's my money and I can do what I want with it." Our brand of consumerism focuses on ownership, while Japanese teen consumerism focuses on keeping up in the rapid turnover of trends.

Japanese parents, too, pass on consumer lessons to their children, but these are more about quality and brand names than about the relationship between money and "character." Americans tend to use the context of money, like sex, as an opportunity to maintain moral control, as points of expected moral divergence between the generations, and "just say no" is part of the generation-gap discourse in both arenas of self-expression.

Japanese parents usually do not concern themselves much with moral lessons to youth about money *or* sex, and instead focus on education and preparation for adult occupations as proper contexts for building moral character. What children are doing in school, then, appears to be a much more important signifier of character and morality than their sexual activity or how they spend their money. In Chapter 5, we will examine teen consumerism as it relates to peer culture and to adult goals for their children.

Distinction or Deviance?

So we find significant distinctions, even amid our similarities. For example, Japanese young people do not exhibit the qualities we attach to adolescence, attributes we insist must be attached to those universally raging hormones. They do not seek separation from their parents—at least, not as American youth are said to—and they do not often act out frustrated biological urges in violence, self-indulgence, self-destruction, or delinquency. The Western negative image of the teen is hard to find embodied in Japanese youth. Why we might have chosen the negative images we often wrongly use about our own teens and why the Japanese are overall more positive about youth will be discussed later in this book.

We have provided lessons confusing at best and experiences chaotic and damaging for many teens. Japanese messages are not, however, uncomplicated either. Along with the illusion of uniformity and consensus, there are confusion and damage for the teen increasingly conscious of diversity and conflict. However, rather than "mixed," in the sense of oppositional, Japanese contradictions might rather be called "complementary."

Here we will look at the origins of our constructions of the teen, as they have evolved with American "mixed messages" and Japanese "complementary contradictions." In the United States, we need to look at adolescence in the agrarian past and the postindustrial present, in the context of our ideologies of individualism and diversity, and in coming to terms with our social realities and the unmelted pot of differences; in Japan, in the complex social reality of inequalities and scarcity in the midst of affluence, and of generational differences in relationships and diverse personal trajectories in the midst of an official "consensus."

In spite of stereotypical images of obedient youth in Japan, there *are* of course young people who have gone beyond sniffing paint thinner (a recent drug of choice). Alcohol and tobacco are readily available to the young. There are *many* teenagers who are sexually active. Certainly, the strict legal control of drugs contributes to low narcotics use in Japan, as does the extension of school regulations and teacher supervision to include after-school time and vacations. The media attention given to what seem to Americans very minor offenses and statistically miniscule levels of crime helps to patrol deviance and maintain rather close-in limits of permissible behavior. And the U.S. media like to emphasize that even Japanese adolescent "rebels" who dance to high-decible rock music in the park during the permitted Sunday afternoon hours, in well-choreographed and rehearsed "abandon," will then wash the colored gel out of their hair when they are through and put on their school uniforms before returning home in the early evening. Some do, but many do not.

While much has been made of this public bacchanalia there are striking differences that bear a second look: the punks do not terrorize neighborhoods and are rarely seen beyond these short city blocks on Sundays. The older ones, the school dropouts from the provinces, are, in fact, at least semi-professional musicians building a following in these performances. Delinquency is not necessarily part of the act. Walking through the Harajuku teen flea market on a Sunday afternoon, I saw contrasts between performance and reality. The stall keepers were bedecked in metal-studded leather, and the males had earrings and long hair, sometimes in dreadlocks. Girls of junior-high-school age in "innocent" clothing, were the customers. To me it all seemed innocent play-acting, and the stall keepers were careful, polite, and far from abusive or rude in their dealings with customers, wrapping tee-shirts neatly and efficiently and delivering exact change with a brisk flourish, just like shop keepers in any neighborhood in Japan. But they could also be seen as threatening, representing a marginal life-style that might seduce young people into more than compartmentalized Sunday-afternoon countercultural activities. It is all, however, *costume*, at least in this setting.

Deviance has its own social history in Japan and the United States, and the emergence of the "juvenile delinquent" as a piece of American culture has had its parallel in the *bōsōzoku*, motorcycle thrill-riders, or young punks, in Japan. Teenagers who dance in the streets are not "delinquent": they are *playing*.[5] But they stand for other kinds of differentness that highlight the contrast with the safe "mainstream."

While popular culture provides similar entertainment and menace in both societies, media representations in Japan and the United States prefer to emphasize the exotic differences between us. Yet the voices of teens themselves show us how similar we are in the basic facts of social and psychological experience. We especially see commonalties in young people's perceptions of the place of friendships, sexual development, and the youth market as forces shaping teens today.

The Curriculum of Friendship: Peer Pressure or Social Training?

Friendships are critical in both societies, and are powerful influences. While American parents cringe at the effects of "peer pressure" on their children, Japanese children and parents see friendship as a training ground for adulthood, as appropriate socialization rather than dangerous "peer-ing." And yet, to Americans, Japanese teens appear to lose their individualism in group identity, much as Americans to Japanese appear lonely and isolated in their quest for individual autonomy.

What are friends for? A refuge from the shared pressures of the educational system, and private, noninstitutionalized togetherness are part of what friendship offers in Japan. Friendship is thus also training for adult relationships and for learning how to negotiate the hierarchical necessities of society. Such training takes place even in the playground and ice-cream parlor. In the context of adult views in both societies, chapter 6 treats friendships as "peer pressure" in American, as social training in Japan.

Sex: Some Surprising Facts of Life in the United States and Japan

Information on sex is popular in the communication of young teens in both Japan and the United States, but high interest among middle-class junior high school children does not necessarily mean notable levels of experience. While surveys show that American teenagers' number-one preoccupation is sex, Japanese teenagers place sex at the bottom, and study and their futures near the top. We might be led to the conclusion that if they aren't thinking about it, they must not be doing it. The young teen in Japan may not be flaunting her physical attributes in revealing lycra stretch clothing, but that doesn't make her a less sexually active young person. Japanese children do have other things than their bodies on their minds but they are undeniably sexually active.

It's possible that just as the hair color is washed out at the end of the day, and the rock dancer becomes a high schooler again, so the young girl gets out of bed in the Japanese love hotel and goes home to do her homework. Chapter 7 explores the meaning and experience of sexuality among teens in both societies.

Comparisons: What Can We Learn?

Comparisons teach a most important lesson about categories of similarity and difference. It is a complicated question of cultural choices and priorities. East-West comparisons usually stress exotic differences, but we should also be permitted the investigation of commonalities, and not only to suggest that Japan may be headed in our direction. In the case of the study of adolescence, our position here is that our teens in Japan and the United States are broadly similar not only in biological development and rock music, but also in the effects of market forces—the emphasis on youth as a market. What makes these apparently similar forces different are the ways in which music, clothing, and other gear are locally interpreted and given meaning. The genre of rock music, for example, is only a neutral template for local interpretation; sexuality in adolescence, too, is open to local construction—in America, it is commonly seen as part of a moral curriculum, but in Japan, it is much less part of the intergenerational discourse. There are high schools for children roughly fifteen to eighteen years of age in both Japan and the United States, but there the similarity ends, for curriculum, pedagogy, school, and personal goals are very different. Comparing our understanding of teens will reveal, for example, why in the United States, when teenagers are mentioned, psychology and the law are the contexts most invoked, while in Japan they are education and the family. We see the teen years as rife with psychological risks or social destructiveness; the Japanese see the teens as the critical time for mobilizing maximum effort to earn a successful life, wholeheartedly supported by the family.

How we see the changing adolescent is closely related to our views of what drives social change in general. Western psychocultural views see adolescence both as a stage in which young people are trained to conform to the needs of their environment, and as a partial moratorium in which teens have (limited) permission to rebel. Psychologists focus on the process of creating a mature self, and, influenced by European and American ideas of individualism, give priority to separation and autonomy as prerequisites. Leaving home and breaking away thus become not only expected but even required. The phylogenetic evolution of American society itself then may be seen as the product of ontogenetic development in individual acts of creative iconoclasm—the Fords and Einsteins; whereas in Japan, societal cohesion and cooperation—the team players—have typically been seen as the basis of national progress.

Japanese attempts to tie the experience of learning to the status and tasks of adulthood have succeeded in providing a higher-level base for all, even for those with only a high school education. The elite levels of the system, however, have recently tended to reproduce themselves through the combination of wealth and social network reinforcement, getting their children into schools feeding elite occupations through academic networks. The self-made man, the entrepreneurial innovator has also appeared and has provided an alternative model of success.

Contradictions and Complements:
The Messages of Our Theories of Adolescence

As we will see in Chapter 2, the social histories of America and Japan have led us in different directions regarding the messages we give teens. American models of personal development are diverse and contradictory: we offer teens mixed messages at all levels—personal, familial, and institutional—and in all areas of experience and relationships. We give confusing messages about sexuality, we teach children to obey and to rebel, and we say that learning and work are necessary evils. In turn, they learn that they must be consistent in thought and deed. As a result, the hypocrisy of adult life is the source of great confusion and anger to American teenagers. The Japanese also offer their teens some lessons that to us do not seem completely straightforward. These Japanese lessons, however, I choose to call complementary contradictions instead of mixed messages, as they have at their heart an understanding that the gap between the ideal and real provides an acceptable area of freedom. Japanese teens learn that they will have more responsibilities as they grow up but that remaining in dependent relationships will provide support and solace; they learn that their bodies are available for sexual pleasures but that public, social recognition of sexual relationships is taboo. They learn that as long as they perform their roles well, their private activities and dreams can safely deviate.

These two ways of characterizing adult perceptions and lessons to teens are the products of our differing psychosocial environments and themselves characterize the institutions and experiences in which our teenagers grope for personal and social identity. In America, a "teen problematic," a sense that adolescence is above all a problem for both adults and teens, has emerged as a result of such mixed messages; in Japan, complementary contradictions have to date buffered both teens and adult society from pathological situations. How have these different outcomes occurred?

The answer lies in the social history of adolescence, in our contemporary cultural contexts, and particularly, in the *meanings* our societies attach to adolescence. *I Was a Teenage Werewolf, Blackboard Jungle,* and *Rebel Without a Cause,* are movies in the American tradition of mistrust and fear, in which social confrontations, intergenerational opposition, and introspective personal struggle are understood to be facts of adolescent life. In Japan, within a tolerated range of differences, teens can more safely test options and their emerging identities under more benign adult surveillance. In Japan, B-grade movies are more apt to have teens as victims than as monsters. American ambivalence is based on the contradiction between Calvinist notions of inherent wickedness and Rousseauian images of the natural goodness of children. Japanese perceptions, on the other hand, are based on the idea that children, born good, want to do what is right and acceptable.

Contradiction itself is differently perceived. Inconsistency, in spite of Emerson's encouragement to the contrary, is still a "hobgoblin" in American ethics and the moralistic label "hypocrite" is deeply wounding. We are taught that to have a single, integrated personality is the goal of personal development and consistent behavior is the outward evidence of good character. Being two-faced, behaving differently in different situations, is a pathology. An American negative stereotype of Japanese personality structure holds that Japanese behavior is *situational,* that linguistic and social etiquette in Japan demand that a person be different things to different people, and we find this distinctly unhealthy. We cannot imagine that a person who can successfully negotiate a variety of performances, living socially embedded in a group that makes such demands on an individual, can have a coherent self.

Rather than seen as a logical or moral contradiction, however, this lesson teaches complementarity, the valued and functional fit between apparent opposites in Japan. In Japan, growing up does indeed mean taking responsibility for the correct performance of a range of behaviors appropriate to the situations and relationships involved. Nor is this seen as hypocritical in adult society nor as dangerous to psychological health. Moreover, even within the rigidity implied by "correct performance" and the notion that there is *one* right way of doing things, there is also the idea that there are permitted gaps and loopholes—an institutionalized area of freedom—allowing for different, even deviant, behavior to coexist for the most part quietly with the more public "correct" expectations. For the Japanese teen, this is a lesson to be learned through the social relationship with peers, whereas American social morality is often taught in a more hierarchical relationship by adults to children. Learning, for example, to use correct language to superiors is not taught by adults in Japan, but by those only a year or two older than the child, within the context of peer-run clubs or friendship groups, while the American child learns across a greater divide what is expected by adult society. American teens travel in a relatively undifferentiated pack and the lesson, as we used to say in the 1960s, is "Don't trust anyone over 30."

With this background, we may better understand the differences and similarities in our treatment of teenagers. These contrastive notions may be summarized under the umbrella idea of mixed messages versus complementary contradictions.

Being a teen in America today, according to popular belief,

means being at risk: in Japan it means, most people imagine, being at promise: A recent New York Times editorial captured our mood in its subtitle: "The Nation's Future Is Also our Shame."[6] However high the test-score rankings of Japanese teens, adults there too decry what they perennially see as materialistic hedonism and lack of seriousness in the young.

The critical and interesting question in these images is how closely they correspond to reality. It is quickly evident that there are contradictions in America at every level and that there are enormous gaps between the perceptions of generations and among social and cultural environments in which teens live. These gaps allow for mixed messages: both of the do-what-I-say-not-what-I-do and the I-say-no-but-mean-yes varieties. The gaps also create fear and loathing—the teen as four-letter word—as well as (unwonted) optimism about our schools and society. As we will see, a recent Gallup poll noted that American teens feel that their schools are preparing them well for their future, while Japanese teens are highly critical of their educational system and less optimistic about their own careers than are Americans.

Japanese leaders conventionally base social policy on the notion that all Japanese are the same, that a consensus exists on important matters in a homogeneous population. And indeed, on many issues in many contexts that affect teens—on education, health, and public and consumer behavior, there is indeed a more generalizable viewpoint and population than exists in the United States. Where there are generational and other gaps, they appear in matters such as sexual behavior, future occupation and family aspirations, and world view. The teen population in Japan, like that of the United States, is also diverse, but along different dimensions, perhaps. We see teens, although somewhat uncomfortably, emphasizing distinctions among their number that their parents have trouble recognizing, for example, differences of class and ability.

The American teen lives in a climate of mixed weather and the forecast has mixed messages as well; while the Japanese teen, in a somewhat more uniformly safe and predictable environment, sees change on her barometer as well.

Allowing for some overstatement, then:

1. Americans believe in *fixed traits*, at the same time believing that you can at any time remake yourself; Japanese believe in

fluid possibilities, at least within the range provided by one's ability to commit effort.

2. Americans believe that coming of age means acquiring legally encoded rights and yet we fear the consequences of those licenses to drink, drive, and spend. Japanese believe that young people will meet the moral obligations contained in the responsibilities that are the signal of maturity.

3. American folk psychology is based on institutionalized *ideologies*, such as the principle of individualism, and yet we are confused by the diversity that ensues; Japanese folk psychology is based on *pragmatic idealism*, such as the ideal of the triumph of effort over obstacles, and Japanese generally get high performances.

4. Americans believe that adolescence is the most problematic stage of life and that getting youth through this stage safely is the adult's job; Japanese believe that youth are society's future and that providing motivation to achieve will serve both the child and society, whose fates are inextricably tied.

5. Americans believe that a child must both love and leave his or her parents in order to grow up; Japanese feel that the family is the source of ongoing support and that breaking away or leaving home is not a necessary step in maturation.

6. Americans believe that learning is an individual activity and that "cooperative learning" may be another word for cheating; Japanese believe that learning is an interdependent activity and that autonomy means loneliness, while cooperation enhances the self, even though the moment that determines the future for a middle-class child is the individuated, isolated experience of the examination into college.

7. Americans encourage young people to participate in consumer culture and the media, but also warn of the sin of materialism; postwar Japanese tend to be less conflicted about acquiring material goods, less puritanical about money, even if their grandparents extol thrift and minimalism.

8. Americans support the idea that teenagers should be socially popular, but fear the effects of peer pressure. Japanese support teen friendships and peer associations as a source of social and even hierarchical training for adult life, and only in rare cases, are they concerned with the negative effects of the pressure to conform to teen standards.

9. Americans teach children both that growing up means be-

coming sexually active AND that becoming sexually active is dangerous, if not immoral. Japanese believe that sexual activity is not inherently a problem and sometimes now even encourage healthy, although *private*, sexual expression among teens both through popular media and professional clinical support. There is, however, what we would call a contradiction between the private expression of sexuality and the public appearance of "innocence" in adolescence.

10. Americans teach children that they are a part of a larger community, a larger world, a global society; to respect differences between people and to seek an international role for themselves and their country. "Internationalism" is still a recent conscious construction among Japanese who, in practice, emphasize the intimate community of face-to-face relationships and the similarities rather than the differences between people in their "island community."

These contrasts provide us with a useful, if somewhat overdrawn, template of the messages we give our young, a contextual model that we will tune more finely in analyzing the actual experiences of teens in America and Japan. The sequence of the above statements roughly establishes the order of the argument in the chapters that follow.

It would be wrong to say that there is no sense of a problem in teen behavior in Japan, just as it is wrong to say that only problems dominate in the United States. The Japanese teenager does indeed engage in sexual exploration, in socially inappropriate behavior, even in criminal activity, and the appearance of low delinquency rates and high academic test scores should not lead the Western observer to think the teen as we know him does not exist in Japan. Nor should we assume our children are all creating blackboard jungles and physical and social risk for themselves and others.

Social commentators, teachers, parents, and marketers in Japan do not, in any case, see their adolescents as uniformly obedient, disciplined, equally endowed young people: we are alike in fearing that the next generation may let us down. Statistically, however, images are confounded by reality, since in the United States more children conform to middle-class behavioral standards, and in Japan more children do not, than in either society we are led to believe. Conformity is stronger in America and diversity is stronger in Japan than the images of either would maintain. Idealists and dreamers, good citizens and altruists, adventurers and risk-takers, cynics and pragmatists, materialists and hedonists, oppressors and oppressed, and just plain nice kids—we both have them all in the populations we have reduced to the cartoon image called the teenager. The complexity of their lives is a much better story.

2
Youth in Time

Culture, History, and the Idea of the Teen

I wish there were no age between ten and three-and-twenty, or that youth would sleep out the rest; for there is nothing in the between but getting wenches with child, wronging the ancientry, stealing and fighting.
—William Shakespeare, *A Winter's Tale*, Act III, scene 3, lines 58–62.

I was so much older then; I'm younger than that now
—Bob Dylan

Some Questions of Relativity and Culture

We all think we know what a teenager is—the phrases "biological maturation," "identification with peers," "sexual experimentation," "separation and rebellion" seem obvious and universal. Such characteristics have not always been assumed, and are even now not evident everywhere. Why does such a conceptual model exist in some places, and at some times, and not everywhere and not throughout history?

Obviously, there are some universals: the physical maturation of a young person at puberty can be observed everywhere. Behavior and attitudes, however, vary considerably; and yet a Western observer in Japan or Samoa, for example, can find evidence that behavior there is not so different from that of our own teens. However, the degree, style of behavior, and the meaning attached to it may diverge considerably from what we would find normal.

Generational differences in judging what is normal or good (often a different matter) are themselves normal everywhere in

27

the modern world. Young people in both societies are sure to be noted by their elders as different from what they themselves had been as youth. Fashion, for example, is always a marker of the modern generation gap, and teen costumes often seem calculated to shock or at least to create distinctions. In traditional societies, young people wore clothing that marked their status and role as youths; costume then was evidence more of life stage than of creative rebellion. Clothing as symbol of age stage is no longer a requirement set by adult society but by youth themselves, producing a kind of competitive solidarity among the young. The engine of the fashion industry has set the speed of change in clothing trends for youth, and whether it is flower-child bell-bottoms or military boots, the requirements for keeping up with the gear of the moment are stringent.

Since the 1960s in America and Japan, some of the "different" behavior young people exhibit has not represented mere stage-appropriate iconoclasm, but rather, new directions for society, trends that began as rebellion but end in larger change in the wider culture. In the United States, the mobilization of youth in civil-rights and anti-war movements has created a significant watershed in American political behavior, as did the resistance created by young people and farmers in Japan to the building of Narita Airport in the 1970s, and to the United States–Japan Security Treaty negotiations in 1960. In Japan, young people today are creating smaller-scale campaigns for changes in behavior and customs that may well endure beyond adolescence. In Japan, the contemporary teen does things her parents never did, such as eating on the street or on subway trains (ice cream, hamburgers, crepes, slices of pizza, soft drinks), neglecting culturally encoded distinctions in language by status and gender. Today's girls talk like boys and most teens, ignoring the politeness levels built into correct Japanese, use the latest slang. Some even neck and pet in public. These teens neither behave as their elders did at their age, nor as their elders do now. When they themselves become the elders, many adult behavioral norms will change with them.

Today's teens in both societies have more than their elders had: more space and (often) more money. More than in the past also, because of these luxuries, they are defined by media and marketing, and the dedication of specific music, goods, clothing, technologies, and behavior to their age as a targeted peer group defines and distinguishes them more than any previous generation.

They are, however, not all the same—even within their own market segment.

It is also misleading to assume that the export model of the teen is a Western monopoly. Those who see Japan as converging on Western models, as the country's social modernization catches up with its economic modernization, will most likely expect the American model of the teen to appear soon in Japan. I would argue that *to a point* all modern societies are influenced by global markets and media. The differences that exist are in part due to the cultural spin we give them, so that what we emphasize or just quietly assimilate from this supermarket of trends depends on basic sociocultural factors in our societies—it is this strong power of culture to choose and mark that makes the difference.

The psychology of the family is a good example of cultural selection and amplification. Americans have emphasized intergenerational conflict and Oedipal rifts, while Japanese have emphasized nurturance, dependency, and what American psychologists might call "merging," between parents and children. Takeo Doi, a Japanese psychoanalyst, noted that a word for positively valued and actively sought dependency exists in Japanese but not in English: this *amae*, he notes, is a psychological reality shared by both cultures, but is marked and given significance only in the Japanese language.[1] Similarly, it might be said that while Japanese are well aware that there are teenagers in their society, the word "teenager," with American connotations, has no firm footing in Japan. We both *have* them, but Americans have culturally designated them, while Japanese have not.

I am not sure I agree

Before Teenagers: American Precursors and Premonitions

Until the twentieth century, in most parts of the world, young people were either defined as children in family and school or as adults in fields, workshops, or in domestic or industrial service. Either as dependents (learning and obeying) or as productive laborers (earning and obeying) they were safely occupied. They were not in limbo, for as soon as they could work, they were adults—as farmers, soldiers, craftsmen, and mothers—or, in the more privileged classes, preparing for elite roles. Duty and responsibility characterized these adult roles.

Universal schooling, however, changed this task-oriented definition of maturity. As school became the measure of the child, and the institutional identity of "school child" persisted past puberty, for many children a new, disconcertingly undefined category emerged. This was a time of physical maturity without adult economic or social function. However, before industrialization and the extension of secondary schooling to most children, this lack of definition did not produce social dysfunction or psychological confusion for most. It was not until the midtwentieth century that adolescence began to develop the profile in America that it has today, and not until about twenty years ago that its Japanese counterpart emerged.

The question becomes, why in the West, and particularly in America, did the phenomenon of the adolescent emerge and why did the teen become threatening to adult society? Why did the images of warring gangs in *West Side Story* become emblematic of the condition of youth in America, even as middle-class teens moved to the safety of the suburbs? How did the teen become a four-letter word?

Any society's choices change with time. For example, what Americans once viewed benignly we may now disparage: the individualism encouraging youth to innovate may now to some seem like dangerous deviation and rebellion from their elders; the pluralism espoused in our society's founding ideology may now to some look like anarchy.

Disapproval of youth is not new in Western history. Attempts at damage control were evident in ancient Greece and Renaissance Italy, and of course in Victorian England, in admonitions to young people to be filial and obey elders. Youth were sent to apprenticeships not only to be taught trades and crafts but to build character and control rebelliousness. To protect the purity of the family escutcheon from the effects of wild oats, English parents who could afford to send young gentlemen of the eighteenth and nineteenth centuries overseas for a "continental tour" in hopes that their adventurousness might be spent abroad and that they would return, matured and reconciled, responsive to the needs of the family.

Nineteenth-century German romanticism characterized youth as a time of wild emotional extremes and lofty ideals, capable of furious creativity. The "sturm and drang" (storm and stress) view of youth underlay the fervor and idealism of the *Wandervogel* movement (an episode in which youth were encouraged to learn about themselves and the world through unfocused rambling), modern American echoes of which were seen in the exaltation of Jack Kerouac and the fantasies of flower children on pilgrimage to Haight-Ashbury.

This view influenced European and American psychologists whose theories of the stages of development echoed the imperatives of sturm and drang and the *wanderjahre;* (the year of "wandering" before settling into an occupation). The storminess of youth and the need to sow one's wild oats became formulaic in popular consciousness, and institutionalized and even "required," aspects of normal development, as seen by academic and clinical psychologists.

While earlier European ideas about adolescence did influence schools and philosophies in America, there was no popular recognition of adolescence until psychology and economic development created it anew as a scientific and material stage of life. G. Stanley Hall, in his two-volume treatise on adolescence, published in 1904,[2] has been called "the father of American adolescence", but he merely distilled and codified the concept. His ideas, like those of Charlotte Bühler before him in Vienna,[3] were influenced by those of the German romantics, and combined William James's notion of separate arenas for the development of the self with the idea of evolutionary stages in development.

If Hall put adolescence on Americans' psychological map, other influences and forces were converging in the early twentieth century to create adolescence as a social and marketing category as well.

At the turn of the twentieth century, American adolescents were given, as John Demos notes, "a measure of codification and confinement."[4] Young people were organized and attended to differently because of several factors: First, as more children attended school, schools were increasingly age-graded, and school curriculum and experiences were standardized by age across the country. This created, as both cause and side effect, more attention to differences in age, and a greater sense of identity among children with their peers. Second, with smaller families, there was an increase in parental attention and resources given to each child. At home, then, adult-child relationships became more crucial and with fewer siblings, a child was less focused on peers. Further, particularly in middle-class families, there was prolonged financial dependency on parents as longer schooling became a prerequisite for elite occupations. Third, new institutions such as the Boy Scouts and YWCA promoted among young people more conscious identification by gender and by age, of course under adult direction.

American teenagers' philosophies may to some seem like a twisted and trivialized version of qualities and values we traditionally held dear—individualism, independence, and even anti-establishment rebellion. Breaking with traditional oppression and constraint as embodied in the seventeenth-century pilgrims, the eighteenth-century revolutionaries, and the nineteenth-century frontiersmen, who left the established settlements of the East to push America beyond domesticated lands[5] becomes today "This is a free country, Mom," or "You can't tell me I can't go out tonight."

In the nineteenth century, the untamed frontier or at least rural areas were seen as a proper testing ground for youth, purer and more character-building, than the overcultivated, decadent, and polluted townlife of the East,[6] and to be young meant at least to *want* to go West. This became a test of manhood and leaving home became an American metaphor for becoming adult, even as the "hometown" was still the locus of sentiment and attachment. The cowboy-frontiersman fantasies became manifestations of the imperative to grow up by going away. Going away in order NOT to grow up, as in "running away to join the circus," or later, "riding the rails" and "going on the road" were the flip side of the independence coin. There are similar sentiments expressed now, by young people, and sometimes by middle-class parents too, who fear that staying home waiting for a good career or for inspiration may mean unhealthy dependency. Today, our younger teenagers may stay home, at least through high school, while their counterparts one hundred years ago had probably left home by the age of fifteen.[7] In any case, today's young teen practices daily escapes in body and spirit.

The experience of having our founding ideologies thrown back in our faces by youth does not, however, clarify the problem of our complex inheritance of mixed messages for youth. There remains a cultural contradiction in our society between the idea of youth in training for adulthood and youth as the last period of natural freedom and spontaneity. Twentieth-century views characterize the contrast as youth needing society's limit-setting structures versus youth looking for resistance-points, for confrontation with adults.

Another such contradiction remains in debates over the sources of creativity in youth. On the one hand, we believe that young people should as individuals break from traditional forms and content in order to create new ideas and things as part of our idea of social progress, but, on the other, such iconoclasm puts adult authority and the social order at risk.

Creativity has recently become a topic of debate in schooling. Whether or not in our turbulent classrooms individually spontaneous creativity can be taught or experienced, we look to schools to make our children creators. A contrast between freedom and structure is only one of the paradoxical juxtapositions of ideologies affecting youth in education. On the one hand, modern ideas about adolescence include both the notion of time of release from authority and the importance of a framing adult moral order. Education in the nineteenth century was to be a builder of character but was also seen as a source of opportunities unknown to earlier generations. At the same time, a new iconoclastic, entrepreneurial ideology taught that there are many paths to success, not just through educational credentialling. Thus there were chances and even a special glory for the self-made, untaught, person whose success and creativity were gained through experience rather than learned in school. A diploma from the School of Hard Knocks was a valid entrée to opportunity, and even had a kind of romantic toughness transcending—in our morality—the scholastic atmosphere of the cloistered academy.

This contradiction between the founding principles of universal education in the United States and the cultural dispositions of the historical moment at which access to education became widespread may indeed account for later ambivalence about, and indeed alienation from, education's function as creator of a homogeneous cohort of well-socialized children. Schooling and the peculiar brand of individualism that historically has emerged in the United States are perhaps at odds.

America as a Mixed-Message Society

The history of what can only be termed confusion over adolescence in America is a long one. The values placed on individualism, free choice, and independence were not always and evenly put into practice in the sense they are invoked by teenagers today. And they were generally seen as rights for adults, not children, and not all adults might experience these liberties. Women of the eighteenth and nineteenth centuries, for example, might not have characterized their lives in terms of these ideas. And rarely was the idea of freedom of choice invoked in individual terms, for anyone, because originally communal choices were emphasized.

Some confusions are caused by a historical lag involving the persistence of an ideal under new social conditions. The idea of individualism was easier for communities to come to terms with when they were relatively homogeneous. The current value placed on diversity is an adjustment to more heterogeneous conditions, for our contemporary pluralism would have been as suspect in a nineteenth-century New England village as it would be in a twentieth-century Japanese mainstream workplace. It is one thing to be seen as harmlessly different in a society that is relatively homogeneous and relatively static, with social supports available for known and predictable members of the community. While it was marginally acceptable to be counted "eccentric" in a small village, it has paradoxically become increasingly difficult to be "different" in the more bureaucratically managed institutions of modern life.

Individual identity for young people, like diversity, has had a history in America. There were perhaps three distinct periods in the creation of an individualistic youth culture in the United States as seen from the perspective of family ties and getting ahead.

The first emphasized individual achievement, but in service to the goals of one's group, notably the prosperity of one's family. One's future in any case depended almost completely on where and to whom one was born, and the occupation of a son was usually that of the father. In the late nineteenth century and early twentieth century, this static notion of heritage yielded to a new idea of potential: among new immigrants, the possibility of moving beyond the family's oppressed and impoverished past in the old country to new opportunities and comfort in the new one provided potent motivation. This was no less "communal," for the unit moving up was seen to be the family, not the individual. One aspect of moving beyond the family's past status was acculturation as families invested heavily in children's education to help their children speedily assimilate and become successful in American terms.

The next model of individualism encouraged young people to

break more completely from family-based incentives in order to succeed and to develop their own goals separate from those of the family. During and after the Depression of the 1930s and World War II, self-advancement of this kind began to take priority over a more communal incentive for most youth. Supported by post-war affluence, a boom in consumer industries, and the nuclear-ization of the family, the isolation and suburbanization of youth culture began at this time, as well.

In the third model, becoming adult depended paradoxically on releasing oneself completely from the influence of adults. As a re-sult, after the late 1960s and early 1970s, the goals of young peo-ple rarely had reference to their natal families. In the phenomena popularly called SINKS and DINKS (single income, no kids, and double income, no kids), career trajectories sometimes even seemed to preclude marriage or children. Adolescence seems prolonged: "In fantasy, Americans remain perpetual adolescents, while adult commitments represent the defeat rather than the ful-fillment of the quest for identity. People are 'trapped' into mar-riage; work is a loss of freedom, a shameful 'settling down.'"[8] Of course the nature of the career, in its actual work routinized and conformist, belies the individualistic identity supposedly fueling the drive for success and the path seems just as predictable as those some criticize in Japan as "groupist."

These culturally accepted methods of "doing it my way" are part of a well-disseminated value system. There is a mixed mes-sage in career success today: the young are encouraged to find self-fulfilling work as individuals, to develop a unique résumé, but also to seek networks and mentoring, a community of a sort to sponsor their progress.

Hypocrisy and Realism:
The Mixed Messages of Home and School

Our ambivalent attitude towards differentness is, however, obvi-ous: we are quick to make the odd into the mainstream and to domesticate all manner of weirdness. In children's lives, this is especially apparent, as our tolerance for "independence" in the American classroom is slight, and as children themselves favor what their peers favor. The current stress on "classroom manage-ment" in teacher training—the fear of losing control of the class-room or of children who exhibit "inappropriate behavior" (meaning disruptive)—is one indicator of how difficult it is to encourage independence and individualism in an increasingly bureaucratized institutional environment. Individualism, like creativity, may be extolled as an abstract ideal, but in practice it is difficult to promote and maintain. Further, American adults tend to be ambivalent about the institutional extension of rights to teens.

It is hard to permit such freedoms in an age group we have come to fear. For several reasons to be explored here, Americans have created a mythical teen beast—sometimes not only mythical—and adult society, to teens, appears hypocritical. They are frustrated by the distinction between our ideals and our realities. They can storm against their parents, illuminating the contradictions between our beliefs and practices. A teen of my acquaintance upbraided his mother for suggesting changes in an essay he was to submit with his application to an independent high school, saying that she was restricting his creative expression, (creativity she had earlier encouraged), in service to institutional expectations. The educational ideologies he had encountered in school and popular media, and in his mother herself, were at odds with the idea of accommodating an admissions committee, and such young people can indeed claim that we are inconsistent.

But such inconsistency exists, yet is hard to accommodate within a universalistic base of law, religion, and ideology, constructed to allow space to the diverse elements it contains. We do not and cannot have laws and customs assuming a homogeneous culture and population, however untroubled such a situation might appear to some uneasy American communities.

American adults have conveyed their unease about teens directly as well as indirectly. Teens themselves are taught that their biological development is a dirty secret, however expected (and even celebrated, sometimes) and necessary. A young American can now excuse himself by saying in effect "I behave like this because I am a teenager," and even a nine-year-old child can say, "After I get through puberty, and my voice changes, I'll calm down and learn to play the guitar." Adults, too, assume this biological developmental imperative will color the teen's behavior: a teacher in Winnipeg, Canada, reports that he is always on the alert for the time "when the testicles begin to drop. . . ." And my own seventh-grade teacher viewed puberty with such distaste that she began every class day with a compulsory deodorizing spray, up and down the aisles of presumably reeking adolescents.

In America, one aspect of our distaste is related to the assumption of sexual rebelliousness. In the creation of our particular brand of adolescence, we may construct an imperative for sexual rebellion through our mixed messages. Even five-year-old girls are dressed in halter tops and tight pants, and their preteen sisters affect elaborate makeup as well. And yet we fear that they are preoccupied with sex, and in a strangely self-fulfilling prophecy, we both market sex and refrain from providing thorough sex education programs. However, according to a recent junior high school study, adults greatly overestimated the extent of their charges' sexual preoccupations. The teachers assumed that 82 percent of the children were obsessed with sex, whereas among the children themselves only 50 percent reported that they thought about sex a lot.[9] It is most interesting to note that while Japanese high schoolers are often sexually active, they put sex on the bottom of the list of things they think about, while American high schoolers place it at the top.[10]

Rebellion is more feared than evident. Children in both Japan and the United States do not show a strong drive to rebel or to be iconoclastic, nonconformist individuals. Rather, most are worried that they are not normal. Peer expectations and standards are more powerful than the urge to break with societal expectations, though of course some teen groups' raison d'être is resistance to adult standards. Most children do not go through a dramatically turbulent puberty, but show very continuous development.[11] The facts of adolescent life are much less threatening, much tamer than the anxieties of parents, teachers, and institutions would indicate.

Friendship is for most teens a source of safety, not risk, and yet is seen as a problem by adults. Peer pressure in America is popularly seen as a negative force, rather than, as in Japan, a source of support and socialization for adult roles. Groups of friends may be given negatively tinged names such as cliques and gangs, seen as encouraging teens to destructive behavior. Even without incidences of "wilding," the sight of teens together is threatening to adults: in one American shopping mall, a popular hang-out for young teens, shops defended against them by playing "boring" orchestral music, rather than teen favorites, and claimed that by means of this reverse Pied Piper technique, they rid the area of adolescent pests.

Far from the animalistic or selfishly hedonistic image our teens are burdened with, they are idealistic and even committed to the improvement of society, and show a high degree of admiration and respect for their elders. A recent Gallup poll shows both American and Japanese adolescents citing parents as their role models and seeking advice from adults.[12] In the same study, American teens especially appear to have very positive views of society, their schools, and their futures. It may perhaps be that teens do not themselves see a generation gap and that angst and rebellion— the James Dean view of life—are features of the land-scape of adult perceptions and not aspects of life as teens know it. To some, these teens may even be disappointingly unadventurous.

Official and Practical Cultures of Youth: Institutions and Values at Odds

Our founding ideologies, even with their contradictions, have led to the creation of what might be called an *official culture* of youth. This represents a model of ideal environments for development. One aspect of this official culture of learning is an ambivalence over adult direction; an understanding that while it is important, it may stifle valuable creativity and spontaneous learning experiences. This perspective was particularly apparent in the progressive education movement of the 1920s, and continues as an aspect of the debates about creativity in more constrained times. Individualism and freedom seem, as Thomas Rohlen has said,[13] sometimes to be at odds with the existence of any structure in our society, and the emphasis on rights over responsibilities among young people often pushes the limits of predictability and order. In contrast, and also within what might be called our "official culture" is the idea that adolescence is a dangerous time and that children need protection from environmental risks and from themselves. Control, management, "tough love," structure—these are said to give teens what they need and want in the way of limits and boundaries set on their naturally wild or testing behavior. These contradictions are the product of elemental aspects of America's moral goals and creation myths.[14]

We also have a "practical culture"—one of operational, grounded realities, especially in the institutions of family and school, in which concrete conditions dictate how children are treated by adults. This culture is no more immune to mixed mes-

sages than the "official" ideological culture. The contrast just described between official and practical culture has some relationship in Japan to the contrast between the concepts of *tatemae* and
honne, or "official" form and true reality, which—as Takeo Doi
describes—form a conceptual whole.[15] *Tatemae* and *honne* as Doi
describes them are essential, balancing elements that together
contribute to harmony in Japanese relationships. In this view,
they form a culturally and institutionally stable concept in Japan.
In the American context, however, appearance and reality are not
a matched pair, but a contrasting set, representing not a balance
but a flawed contradiction, a gap arising through social and historical change, a gap revealing instability and demanding adjustment. In this sense, understanding that the reality doesn't fit our
ideals makes us uncomfortable and our practical culture consists
of a makeshift response to change, often ill-fitting the established,
institutionalized ideologies and practices. It is the awkwardness
of this adjustment that leads to the mixed messages young people
in America are asked to respond to today.

Our laws and ideological vows, our contracted options, tie us
together, rather than trust or the unspoken understanding of
long-term relationships and deeply interwoven shared communal histories. Our adolescents must find themselves within this
less than directive and supportive context.

What seems to have created an image of a problematic stage of
life in America are our mixed messages, not a materialistic culture or a decline in "family values." While adults fret over bad behavior (whether the child is labeled as naughty or as suffering
from attention-deficit disorder), they often actually reinforce and
in some sense approve the naughtiness and independence exhibited by recalcitrant children. This lack of concrete expectations as
well a lack of coordination between family and school socialization permit children to thumb their noses at both "establishments" as contradictory or hypocritical. On the other hand, but
strongly related, we overattend to signs of active rebellion, because we *expect* it. We fear the bad behavior we consider basic to
children's nature—whether it is shown in impertinence to the
teacher, in taking apart a perfectly good radio just to see how it is
constructed, or in sexual promiscuity. We are suspicious, while
Japanese adults are not. They do not expect children to want to
behave badly,[16] and are, in consequence, rather laissez-faire in
their attitudes towards their charges. Noise and what would seem

to us disorder in the Japanese classroom are often seen by teachers as a sign of appropriate engagement in activity. Nor is this response seen only in those Japanese "free schools" guided by American progressive educational philosophies.

Adolescence in Japan:
Rapid Change in Concept and Experience

In some form, most industrialized societies have teenagers: the years of adolescence are marked today by the consumption of a global material culture and by a shift from learning only from adults to the discovery of self-in-context with peers. Material goods—clothing, gear, and music carry culture of course, but what is exported from America with jeans and Coca-Cola is not an immutably American view of the teenager. The media may be similar but the messages have different local meaning. A teen in Tokyo lipsynching to Madonna with her friends is no less Japanese for doing so.

Japanese society has modernized rapidly but with far less dislocation and discontinuity than has been seen in the United States, producing a smaller gap between the goals and rationales of adult society on the one hand and the culture and realities of adolescence. The result is a less oppositional relationship, both in ideology and in fact.

This does not mean that Japanese ideas of adolescence have been lacking or static over time. The contemporary notion of the *cheenayja* is a recent invention, and does imply a greater gap with elders than was noted in previous generations, and to some a problematic one. In premodern Japan, the passage from childhood to adulthood was, as in the rest of the agrarian world, noted by a rite, a moment in time. A separate age spanning the years between childhood and adulthood, was only recognized in certain crafts and arts where a period of apprenticeship was provided for the *chuto hanpa*, not-child–not-adult. In such apprenticeships, a child (usually a boy) was often sent to another household where, it was understood, he would not be coddled by the indulgence of his own home, and where he would learn in a systematic way. However, being an apprentice did not necessarily mean being a teen, for this training could be contracted at a wide variety of ages, and "development" meant the stages in which prescribed tasks and skills were learned, rather than predictable, age-related stages of "natural" physical and emotional growth.

For elites, there were different indicators of the transition. In the Heian court, (794–1185) boys came of age at some point between the ages of eleven and sixteen, depending on their court rank.[17] The *genpuku* ceremony, a rite of passage, marked their formal admission to the court. Over hundreds of years, ceremonies and practices of the aristocracy trickled down as upwardly aspiring merchant-class families emulated elite culture. As lower samurai and even low-class merchant families became wealthier in the extended peace and stability of the Tokugawa era (1603–1868), they adopted the custom of a coming-of-age ceremony as one sign of their upward mobility.

The corresponding ceremony for girls was the *kami-age* or the putting up of the hair. At puberty, girls of higher classes were kept at home for domestic training, and restricted in their association with other children not in the family. For girls, actual adulthood came with marriage, and for boys, with full adult work. For both boys and girls, such passages meant *less* freedom rather than more, and more responsibilities and duties.

Samurai boys in some villages had fraternities (*goju*) and these were organized in an age hierarchy: in Kagoshima, *kochigo* were boys six to ten years old, *osechigo* were eleven to fourteen, and *nise* were fifteen to twenty-five. One became a full member of society at twenty-six. Each younger cohort had as mentors those in the group one stage older. Disputes and rule infractions by juniors were handled by older boys. The *goju* also provided instruction and the eldest were teachers.[18] There were initiation rites and a final rite of passage through a test of a boy's bravery. From the age of six, these boys spent very little time with their families.[19]

As in the premodern West, Japanese young people knew who they'd be and what they'd be doing as adults, and there was no drive to experiment or rebel. Indeed, the course of maturation involved an increase in social embeddedness rather than a decrease. Following a family trade in the natural course of things also meant learning from the adults closest to the child, rather than breaking from them. Obedience and diligence from the child, and instruction and nurturance from the parent, were the building blocks not just of an appropriate hierarchical relationship between parent and child, but of the child's future success in life. Insofar as there was an idea of the good life for the individual, it was dependent on his or her meeting the needs and expectations of the family and community. The training agenda of youth, then, included preparation for more involvement with others, more responsibility for relationships, and more commitment to the group.

In any case, there was little incentive for a young person to linger in youth. Adulthood, with Confucian benefits and rewards for seniority, was far more attractive. The parent-child ties, at least ideally, were strong, and by the Meiji Period (1868–1912), Confucian ideology also supported filiality as a *national* virtue. In the family, parents counted on children—especially sons—to take care of them in their old age, and sons counted on parents to provide them with support, a trade, and a place in the community. There was little one could do without family support and almost no chance of mobility, either geographical or economic, without the support and community network of a family.

Modernization and New Opportunities

The Meiji Period (1868–1912) brought great social change in Japan, with the official elimination of the traditional feudal social order and with the redistribution of land and resources. Though there was no violent revolution, there were increased mobility and opportunity as old class barriers were at least officially removed. But as in America during the earlier half of the nineteenth century, mobility in Japan after 1868 tended to mean change for a whole household rather than for an individual. The young person with aspirations did not break away, and the call to rise up and improve oneself, *risshin shusse*, did not mean turning one's back on family and community. Any good fortune, whether through effort or luck, was to be shared, and the significant unit was the family, not the individual. When a young person did well in school, for example, or won a good position, it was the household head who was congratulated for the family as a whole.

But there was novelty, vitality, and indeed there were new opportunities. The opening of Japan to Western contact meant for some young people an exposure to new ideas and "Western Learning" represented the future. Fukuzawa Yukichi, a famous educator and modernizer, revealed in his autobiography the passion of well-educated young men of the time for modern (then synonymous with Western) ideas. Eager but indiscriminate, they learned whatever foreign language (in the nineteenth century, usually Dutch) they needed to read whatever materials came to hand—medical texts, books on armaments, religious writings. They found their classical Confucian education opposed to the more practical new learning, and their futures were determined more by the content of the first Western text they found than by the ethical precepts supporting a fixed Confucian social order. The new learning emphasized technical training and practical detail and demanded concrete mathematical and mechanical skills that had heretofore been explicitly *not* part of the training of a gentleman. In fact, as Fukuzawa recounts, his own childhood education was governed by the samurai code defining what could be learned in his class, and when his father discovered him learning secretly to compute, he forbade him, saying "numbers are the tools of merchants."[20]

The writers of the turn of the century in Japan revealed another aspect of the new vision of youth: along with a sense of vitality and opportunity, the novels and essays of young men of this period showed a new sense of self. The I-novel (*shishosetsu*) established new conventions of introspection, which often look painfully intense. The fresh air of the Meiji Period produced for some outward-looking souls opportunities for change but for others produced an inward-looking, nearly paralyzing, self-absorption. This self-absorption is also evident today in some adolescents, as we will see in Chapter 8. Some Meiji intellectuals, such as Natsume Soseki, wrote of the search for self in his protagonist's adolescence in terms that G. Stanley Hall could have recognized:

> As the caterpillar must pass through the amorphous pupa stage in order to become a butterfly, a child too must experience the unsettled period call adolescence to become an adult.[21]

Literary angst, pangs of weltschmerz, and depression among fictional youth contrasted strongly with the markedly unalienated sense of a new world experienced by most young people.

Education for Personal and National Development

The Meiji Period also brought a new focus on youth as a stage of development with the advent of "bureaucratic" universal education. To catch up with the West whose accomplishments seemed both wonderful and threatening, Japanese planners and officials created an education system and national educational goals. A national curriculum was established and a system of tracking, which led from compulsory primary school to secondary and higher learning or to technical and normal schools, was created. The explicit use of education as the means to national development combined with the traditional responsibility of young people to do well for their families extended now to the larger and more abstract unit of the state. Such an abstraction did not operate as a motivating goal for most young people who became identified as individual achievers, measured, ranked, and rewarded by the universal system of educational advancement.

An important outcome of this system was a kind of egalitarianism made possible by an emphasis on educational achievement. One of the crucial functions of education in the modernizing Meiji era was to select talent for a new technological elite, rather abruptly replacing aristocrats with technocrats. Many, of course, gained their new learning and status through elder elite connections. However, allowing achievement rather than ascription to create this elite anew in each generation meant that at least opportunity, if not outcome, appeared to be egalitarian. A meritocracy, at least in its ideal form, is a social order in which elites cannot directly reproduce themselves in the next generation, providing, again in theory, a sense of potential for youth of all backgrounds.

But this new, relatively open, system also introduced uncertainty along with opportunity. What a young person needed to get ahead was no longer given in the bloodline but was the product of his own effort, and was thus less predictable. The support of family in the struggle provided both solace and pressure, for he was to work hard for more than himself. Of course, families with influence could (and still can) add to their children's "potential," or buffer failure with a backup, back-door entry to an acceptable occupation. And families with fewer resources often could not even provide a child with enough time for study to improve his chances. The existence of universal schooling and the academic achievement track leading to good jobs did not guarantee every child's access. About 80 percent of the population was involved in farming, and the intensity of labor and the inexorable schedule demanded children's participation. Fewer girls than boys attended and graduated from elementary or secondary schools.

Girls in the Meiji Period were rarely encouraged to complete the full track, and almost never succeeded to occupations available to boys. But even for many boys, agricultural imperatives, or sheer poverty, often barred them from the chance to compete.

Youth and Modern Material Culture

Until the middle of the twentieth century, there was a great unevenness in the distribution of the goods of development across the population. "Modern" institutions, goods and experiences spread first in urban areas, and there, first among wealthier and more cosmopolitan people. Yet in any neighborhood, urban or rural, you could (and still can) find older people living in relatively traditional ways, while young people in the same household might have much more modern tastes and occupations. Moreover, even the young person who wore a Western-style school uniform and enjoyed going to the movies on Sundays was likely at other times to be more traditionally "Japanese" in clothing and pastimes.

This "mixed culture" produced the curse of interesting times for some young people who, during the early decades of this century, seemed to suffer from confusion and alienation. During the Taisho Period (1912–1926), university students and young workers away from home participated in movements—sometimes more like fads than organized movements—with slogans prescribing a nihilistic "nothing matters" attitude in which one was to dedicate one's life to the notion of meaningless existence. As in Europe at the time, the romantic search for ultimate experiences and meaning had given way to a more decadent live-for-the-moment credo as a requirement for the limbo years of youth. Like the limbo of the European wandering romantic however, this Japanese version of existentialism was a luxury available only to a few. Those with resources for a four-year university moratorium could indulge in this more than could young workers, but even the latter found time to sit in the newly popular coffee houses reading the latest essays and arguing loudly. For most youth in the 1920s and 1930s, however, middle school represented their terminal educational credential. Only one in thirteen entered high school and one in twenty-five went on to higher education.[22]

By the 1920s, other influences on youth arrived in Japan. From

Europe and America came the Jazz Age, and the new hedonism gave at least a momentary purpose to life. The Japanese versions of the lounge lizard and the flapper were the *mobo* and *moga* (*mo*dern *bo*y and *mo*dern *garu* [girl]), and a popular youth culture emerged to support (or to create) the new lifestyle.

Requiring rich and cosmopolitan (or absent) parents, the modern girl and boy of the 1920s—even with limited leisure—could indulge in experiments in sex, drink, and other forms of decadence, or at least try to look as though they could. Sports, screen (movies), and sex formed what were called the "Three S's" of the new life- style. While there were a small percentage who engaged as full-time participants in this culture, most were part-timers, able to assume the role when other responsibilities were not too demanding. While elders patently disapproved and claimed that society in the hands of the young would go to the dogs, the general optimism of the Taisho Period created a relatively benign view even of this youthful decadence. And youth weren't alone in creating change at this time: the labor union movement was strong and women had participated actively in suffrage and birth-control movements. Marxism and Western democratic ideas created diversity in Japanese political thinking as well.

By the early 1930s, the emergence of a new national mood had affected young people practically and ideologically. Although the confrontation between prewar mobilization and the decadence of the 1920s sent some young people into the artistic and counter-cultural underground, many young Japanese men in the 1930s were drawn into the nationalistic fervor of the times and, depending on their age, were drawn into active military service as well. The movie *Twenty-Four Eyes*[23] emphasizes the effect war had on children, portraying one elementary school class in the countryside as the students grow up in wartime, some suffering at home and some going off to die in war.

Some elite high schools maintained a liberal curriculum, but many adolescents were conscripted or worked in war-related factory production, and some rural children were kept out of school to farm or engage in home production with the women of the household, as the men went off to war. While adolescents in the 1920s had searched for the meaning of life in European philosophies and literature, some wartime youth embraced what Erikson calls the "totalistic" solution[24] of nationalistic militarism, *kokutai* ideology, as the answer to the quest for a meaningful self.

Youth brigades and campaigns focused on children gave young people a role in national mobilization and helped identify them as a peer-focused generation.

Postwar Generations

The war represents a watershed for generational identity labels in Japan. Prewar, wartime, and postwar generations have very clear-cut meanings in Japan, as does each successive generational identity. Those who experienced deprivation and loss in the war are said to be tougher and more resilient than those born without experience of danger and scarcity.[25] Those who were young children during the war especially are seen as victims rather than perpetrators, emblematic of a common perspective on the war either as the foreign destruction of innocent Japanese lives or the result of Japanese imperialist ambitions.

Teens in Japan are now identified by two influences: education and the market. There are several postwar generations now to consider, distinguished by features first of economic reconstruction and then several stages in postwar economic booms. Most contemporary research on young peoples' lives now emerges from marketing and advertising researchers, who are thorough investigators of all aspects of young peoples' lives. In Chapter 5, we will consider these recent "consumer generations."

Other changes have also had considerable impact on children's lives in the fifty years since the beginning of the war. Postwar educational reforms introduced coeducational classrooms and the universalization of secondary schooling as middle schools became part of compulsory education. The postwar boom in higher education also produced a rush to enter a newly expanded roster of colleges and universities, but it was quickly evident that places were more limited than the applicants, and the resulting competition produced the phenomenon known as "examination hell," which has affected the lives of many children, whether or not they are headed to higher education.

As in the United States, Japanese children who stay in school longer also remain dependent on their parents longer, and without any other status, have their identities chiefly designated by their place in the school ladder, either as middle schoolers or as high schoolers.

Why was Japanese adolescence as a stage of life only very recently marked? The answer may be in part related to the relatively recent extension of mass schooling through the secondary years. Higher secondary schooling has only recently become a nearly universal experience, and only since the 1960s have most children completed high school, staying out of the labor market until at least the age of eighteen. Being through with school means work or marriage for most children—adult activities. Furthermore, the idea of adolescence as portrayed in Western development psychology was not evident in Japanese indigenous psychologies, and although Western-trained Japanese academic psychologists do indeed invoke adolescence in Japan, it has only recently been disseminated into popular psychology. Most important, Japanese define teenagers now as a category because they are a *market*. Young people over the past twenty years have been increasingly able to purchase, and it is consumer industries, the media, and marketers, who have given them an image and named them *cheenayja*.

Media and marketing focus alone do not empower teenagers or confer on them conflicting images of hope and destruction. What seems to have created an image of a problematic stage of life in America are our mixed messages, not a materialist culture or a decline in "family values." What so far has protected Japanese society from a negative perception of youth is the persistence of strong historical tendencies towards centripetal rather than centrifugal social forces and a cultural preference for the idea of continuity rather than contradiction between generations. Without a prophecy to be fulfilled—not expecting young people to be a problem, not marking the teen in this way—even the flamboyant pink-haired rock dancer in the streets doesn't represent serious individual rebellion or social decline.

However, late or not, the teenager has arrived in Japan, and as we will see, has created and been created by an economic boom and a youth-oriented popular culture. In both societies, the current manifestation and understanding of the teen does not always signify problems. Teenagers need not be seen as portents of civilization's moral decline. Nor are they only manifestations of cyclically recurring episodes in a society—a cohort of age-mates reproducing the stage-appropriate rebellion of their elders, acceptable in its place in the life course. These generations of teens in both the United States and Japan are the products of historical, cultural, and economic forces. They point backward to our histories and forward to our futures. How institutions such as families and schools, themselves acting as creators and receivers of these young people, define and treat teenagers, and how teen material culture reflects and creates its audience will be discussed in the following pages from the perspectives of the primary actors and their observers—the adults who attempt to understand and shape them, and the teens themselves who of course, in the future, will have the final word.

3
Family Time and Space

I only do the dishes to keep my mother from nagging me.
—High school student, Osaka, Japan

My mother is my best friend: I can tell her anything.
—Junior high school student, Lawrence, New Jersey

Are Japanese parents indeed doing better with their teens than we are? Are they doing it with discipline, tough love, or indulgence? Or do they not need to exert themselves at all—are their children genetically predisposed to docility and cooperation?

Families in both societies are both first movers and last resorts, the environments where children learn what the wider world expects of them. At the intersection between societal goals and ideologies, and the practical needs of nurturance and learning, families are where the mixed messages are most strikingly confronted by teenagers. And, as we will see, the home itself may be sometimes a contradictory and confusing place for parents and teens alike.

Teens in Japan and America seek both separation from their families and intimacy within them. While in both the United States and Japan commentators have mourned the demise of family influence on youth, the truth is that families and parents, whatever their configuration, have still the most powerful impact on their adolescent children. In any case, contrary to popular and

51

expert opinion in the West, the recipe for mature development does not always include separation and autonomy, and the realities of adolescent life in both countries reveal more interdependence than individuation, more ties to family than rejection of the home. And yet, parents in both countries are often concerned about or frustrated by their children, who both flaunt their independence and search for support within the family.

The family has become something of a scapegoat in both countries, as policymakers look for the roots of individual and social problems of youth. Debate over the "crisis" in the family has produced two positions: one, that social disorder and personal alienation—leading to delinquency and self-destructive acts—can be traced ultimately to weak families that provide insufficient direction and support to their young; the other, that our societies do not support families, leading to or exacerbating poor conditions for the development of young people. A lively debate also exists in Japan, spurred by youth problems that, however, would seem slight in comparison to the problems of American schools and streets. In Japan, problems such as bullying, school avoidance, dropouts, and school violence, are seen as symptoms of a critical decline in Japan's youth and thus in Japan's future. There, too, the question is both social and political: as in America, those on the right deflect criticism of social institutions and place the blame on the family (particularly on working mothers), and those on the left criticize social and educational policies and practices—as well as the economic system, for disempowering individuals and their families.

In America, where there has been a decline in investment in family support, crisis prevention, and intervention, adolescents have been defined more as a social menace than as a resource to be developed, and programs that do exist are remedial or punitive rather than preventive. Teens who lack the components of the normative—mythical—American family are said to be especially at risk. If they lack a parent, if family income is below poverty level (the condition of one in four children today), or if they live in high-risk communities where drugs and delinquency provide tempting alternatives to the bleakness of home life or, in some particularly conservative minds, if they have working mothers, then "family conditions" are seen as the first cause for any problems that may develop.

Japanese family conditions are also seen as root of teen evil.

The Japanese working mother is much more likely than her American counterpart to be directly and persuasively criticized even *before* a problem emerges with her child. The "absent father syndrome," family pathologies attributed to the father's long absences from home, looms in clinical and popular consciousness.

Further contributing to the problems of the young, according to commentators, is the fact that families now have on average only 1.53 children. The Ministry for Home Affairs has attributed this low population growth to "the increasing role of women in the work place and the high cost of educating children."[1] Japanese leaders worrying about population decline and labor force shortages tell parents that "only children" are sure to suffer. More than half of all children of elementary school age are "only children," as opposed to only 10 percent of today's adults, and commentators predict that adolescents soon will be even more isolated and unsocialized than they are today.[2] However, for most, the family in Japan does not tend to be the arena for acting out issues in children's lives or the place where we look for the display of tensions created in social institutions outside the home.

Psychologists are concerned that children in small families will be indulged and not properly trained at home, and that without siblings they will not learn to cooperate and compete well. They also see parents becoming less "parental," more concerned with developing friendly relationships with their children. The traditional parent-child relationship, characterized on the one hand by benevolence and clear direction, and on the other by obedience and filiality, has, it is said, been replaced by a *tomodachi no yoo na* (like friends) relationship. Family as training arena has been replaced to some degree by family as rest and recreation.

Pressures and Paradoxes

Underlying the debate in America is the idea that adolescence is a problem—for the individual, the family, and society. Having been redefined by social institutions as not-children, not-adults, teens do not experience the benevolence that adults bestow on younger children, nor the responsibilities and choices of adulthood. Undefined, they live in a world of contradictions, mixed messages, and paradoxes.

Many Japanese teens are under academic pressure; many American teens are under great social and economic pressure.

The complex environments they inhabit do not give them many sources of relief and support. American teens, told they are intrinsically a problem, that their behavior and motivation are automatically suspect, and yet that they must be independent to be mature, have nowhere to go but to their own insecurity and to their peers. Japanese teens, told they must struggle harder, that solitary effort is all, and yet kept infantilized and dependent at school and at home, are sometimes incapable of satisfaction in work or relaxation in friendships. American teens, especially the 56 percent who live in urban environments, combat or are guarded from violence and insecurity in public places. And yet, neither teen is in as much trouble emotionally or socially as the media and popular opinion would have them.

Parents in both countries regret the pressures on their teens but are themselves subject to the same pressures. American parents are often strapped by economic need and Japanese parents also feel the stress of the narrow, hierarchical, and "credential"-based society, where academic success is the only reliable route to a successful middle-class life. Moreover, families' capacity to help their children in both societies is often diminished and such roles are taken by outside agencies—the function of education has been relegated to schools, the function of recreation to friendships, and the function of discipline to law enforcement agencies.

However, the family is not reduced only to residual activities. In interviews with teens in both countries, the figures of parents, siblings, and grandparents still dominate the landscape. Children talk with their parents, and rely on them for support and advice. There is only one exception: the exchange of information about sex, for in spite of great and rapid change in the younger generation, there still exists an intergenerational taboo on parent-child discussions of sex. This taboo is apparently stronger among American families than in Japan, where young women say that their mothers know they are sexually active, even if nothing is said, but, according to the daughters, do not worry about them as long as they do not become pregnant. One Japanese mother in the sample arranged for her fifteen-year-old daughter, now involved with a college student, to have birth control pills prescribed "to control acne," even though they are very difficult to obtain in Japan.[3]

Children in both countries say they suffer from over-involved mothers: the stereotypical *kyoiku mama* (education-obsessed mother) in Japan and the nagging mom in America. The media in Japan, especially during the late winter "exam season," play up cases of exaggerated involvement of mothers in their children's academic success. The 1991 case of an American mother plotting to have the mother of her daughter's cheerleading-squad rival killed to take the rival out of the competition is matched in the Japanese media by similarly extreme cases, such as the mother who killed a neighbor's toddler whose noisy play was keeping her teen from studying. In fact, however, most Japanese mothers say the pressure on them is great and unwanted; they would prefer their children to have more free time and would like to be less responsible for their children's studies.

Home Alone? Time and Space in the Household

Japanese teens are intimate with their kin, even if time for extended contact on a daily basis is limited. There is great variation in all factors of family life that affect teens but two constants among all Japanese families are: lack of space and lack of time. Most teens live in small apartments and houses, and many share a room with a sibling. Walls are thin, so that devices such as earphones for music and even television listening are ubiquitous. Other techniques include the management of time and space to achieve privacy. Teens adjust their home-time schedules to avoid friction when the walls and family appear to be closing in on them.

Teens in both countries described their strategies to accommodate both their responsibilities to the household and their need for privacy and freedom. Some Japanese teens—especially boys—manage to create the illusion of private space by using night as day and vice versa. Arriving home at about six, after club activities or cram classes, a high schooler may bathe and go right to his room to sleep, after having a quick snack. He sets his alarm for one or two in the morning, and then awakens to eat a dinner set out by his mother before she has retired. He dons his stereo headset to listen to music in his room (thus achieving what one teacher called a "personal womb") while studying until four or five, when he'll doze off until his mother awakens him to give him breakfast as he prepares to run for the bus or train to school. The teen explains that he's exhausted after a long school day and needs to sleep immediately, but mothers interpret this behavior as in part a strategy to be alone in cramped quarters.

American teens too, even with more space available, still find the need to be alone hard to accommodate, as the effort may arouse negative reactions from their parents.

> I really need to be in my own room, sit on my bed, and listen to my radio or CDs. That really just lets me think everything out and get my head straight. The one thing that gets on my nerves is my parents! They worry too much about me. I guess that's part of their job as parents, but it really bugs me. If I've had a bad day at school and I just go to my room to calm down, they tell me I'm spending too much time there. . . ."
>
> —Fourteen-year-old girl, New Jersey

Avoidance can be managed in many ways. A Japanese high-school graduate, in her first year as an assistant in a clothing design company, describes her days:

> I usually have supper out, with friends, on the way home, and arrive rather late. I chat with my mother and go to bed. . . . She works too, and we have different days off. On my day off, I clean the whole house . . . and then, in the evening when my family comes home, I clear out.

The Japanese high school student quoted at the beginning of this chapter goes on to say

> . . . If I don't anticipate what she is going to ask me to do and do it, she'll begin to bug me. I avoid having a lot to do with her by just getting the work done. It doesn't mean I'm a helpful person.

An older Japanese teen, now in college near his home, rarely visits. When he does, he brings his friends and his dirty laundry, and asks for a meal before they all go out again. His mother says she would like it if he needed more from her, but she understands that he has little time and a very different schedule from that of the household. She says teens now express their closeness to their families by asking for things, rather than by spending time with them.

Other Japanese teens, usually of junior high school age, indicate that they are more involved with their families, for better or for worse. On the plus side, a 14-year-old girl says,

We are all such good friends in my family—we talk all the time. The only not-so-good thing is that when I have to study for an exam, I'm distracted. . . . Someone keeps dropping into my room to say something.

Another says "My friends sometimes don't want to go home; I'm never like that—I'm lucky, I can really relax at home and I feel most comfortable there." On the negative side, one young teen said that he fights with his brother all the time, and his mother intervenes on the brother's side, "so being at home makes me angry and frustrated."

Family time together is not always something to be avoided. Many Japanese teens are actually at home for most of their non-study time, and whether or not they are tuned into the personal womb of their audio systems, there is communication and intimacy. One teen says, "We spend at least three hours per day together, watching television and eating and talking." Television is a nearly omnipresent companion in family gatherings: in one prefectural study, 64 percent of families (and 80 percent of senior-high-school students) watch TV while eating meals.[4] What is notable here is that over 60 percent of the parents polled in the study said that there was no special concern about this practice, even though 40 percent of children of junior high school age watch at least three hours of television per day. Television also forms a general background in the household, often being left on all day and evening, even if often not actively watched by anyone.

Emotional Alignments: Intimacy, Friendship, and Role Models in the Family

Family is more than the proximity and tasks defined by the physical household environment and the sum of the time schedules of its members. Teens are deeply engaged in relationships with parents, siblings, and the extended kin in the sphere of their daily life. While American teens and parents appear to be less at home together than Japanese families, American youngsters are keyed in to their parents' emotional lives. Japanese teens are even more involved, since casual hanging out with a cluster of neighborhood teens is now reduced, as are accidental meetings with friends in the neighborhood. Neighborhood pals used to provide casual social training and an alternative to the intensity of the family.

Space and time considerations here, too, affect relationships, as more anonymous high-rise apartment complexes and a shortage of time available to teens have, over the past twenty years, produced this condition of isolation. Children are thus more focused now on relationships with parents and more individuated by the need, as above, to find separate time and space within the household.

Separation now also means keeping parents away from friends. The new intimacy with parents cuts two ways. The contradiction between the isolation of the home alone teenager and the close relationship with parents when they are together, seems to produce a need to merge with peers more, and to keep home and friendship as discrete contexts. However friendly the relationship, parents and friends are not the same. A high school boy says,

> My parents are like *shinyu* (best friends); I've lived with them so long they can really understand me. But I keep them separate from my friends. When my friends call, I don't let my parents know who they are.

American teens attempt the same separation, usually noting the potential for conflict or embarrassment that would exist if the twain should meet.

The need for separation does not mean a denial of the power of parents as role models. In a recent Gallup Poll, conducted in the United States and Japan, Japanese teens cited their parents as the people they most looked up to,[5] while American teens tended to refer to parents and such public figures as presidents and rock stars. One junior-high-school student from Lawrence New Jersey said "My role models are the New Kids on the Block. They are like real people and are sincere and try to help other people." (Never mind that some members of this rock group have had repeated brushes with the law.)

Cautionary lessons, negative examples, are also provided by parents in Japan. Several boys described their fathers' work life and said they wouldn't like that life: one boy, the son of a particularly harassed and busy office worker, said he'd rather just run a small shop, "maybe a coffee shop or a convenience store," where he could relax and have control over his life.

One Yokohama high-school senior has learned what she doesn't want, from her working mother's example:

I think housekeeping is such a pain. I never want to be a housewife busy only with housekeeping and bringing up babies. . . . As my mother works outside, I believe housework is *not* the only thing women should do. . . . But I don't think I can manage both a job and a family, so I will work and *not* have a family. I don't want to be like my mother; being alone is best because I can be free.

Attitudes toward fathers in Japan seem to have changed much more than attitudes to mothers. Since children rarely see their fathers at work, and see them only on "off time," exhausted and relaxing, they know very little of what they do. Indeed, a Japanese teen sometimes knows only the name of his father's company, not what he does there. Thus there is some distance, and a sense of unreality with regard to fathers, while mother's work at home is at least visible, whether or not she also works outside the home. The father-child relationship in Japan used to be "terrible, like earthquake and thunder," but the discipline and role-model functions have atrophied along with his presence and energy at home. Mothers, over all, even working mothers, have more influence.[6]

In an international comparison of attitudes about the ideal mother and father, most Japanese respondents (between the ages of eighteen and twenty-four feel that a good father is more like a friend (56.4 percent) than distant and strict (31.3 percent). Seventy percent of American youth want a friend-father, and only 15 percent want a disciplinarian. However, only 58.4 percent of Japanese respondents say that a good father considers his family above his job, compared to 81.4 percent of American youth, and only the Chinese fall below the Japanese in this regard (29.9 percent). In this study, Sweden tops the list in preferences for friend-father and fathers who put family before work.[7]

There is more agreement about the ideal mother. In the same study, responses show that she is one who puts her family above her work (86.1 percent in Japan; 85.3 percent in the United States, and who is a friend (78.5 percent in Japan; 76.2 percent in the United States).[8]

Homework Versus Housework: American and Japanese Choices

Housework and homework often conflict in the Japanese family, but the latter always takes precedence. Most Japanese teens do help in the house, girls more than boys, and overall, 78 percent of children living at home say they do twenty minutes or more housework each day. As they get older, children do less rather than more at home and mothers say they ask for less, knowing that the child is burdened with study. Most girls help with meals, and both boys and girls reported in their time budgets that they cleaned their rooms on Sundays.

Some mothers and children don't negotiate housework sharing so easily. One Japanese girl reports:

> My mother gets angry when she doesn't get help. . . . When she is doing the dishes and I'm just standing beside her, she gets mad and she makes more and more noise doing the dishes. So I finally start drying the dishes, really reluctantly, and she gets angry and says "You don't have to do it if you don't want to." . . . She doesn't ask directly, since she'd rather I offered to do it spontaneously. When I hear her making noise doing something, I feel obliged to help.

This scenario would be familiar to some American teens whose mothers may not be straightforward in their demands for assistance. Most American teens interviewed, however, had clear assignments of tasks required of them and less ambiguity about their responsibilities. American parents tend to feel such tasks are more "character building" than actually necessary for the household's maintenance, and middle-class American children pick up on the fact that their labor is not actually *needed*. Such "symbolic" work then becomes an object of manipulation on both sides, and heroic battles may be fought over taking out the trash, battles that are actually about the clarification of another mixed message.

The working mother in Japan—like the working mother in America—actually *could* use her children's help at home, but usually does not overtly ask much of them. Contrary to the stereotypical image of the aproned mother perpetually available to her children, many Japanese mothers in the study work outside the home and many children arrive home before their mothers do. Most urban middle-and working-class women return to work when their children enter school or when they enter daycare or nursery school.[8] Coordination of home, work, and children is difficult and the standards of the community for all three are very high. A working mother in Japan, away from the house most of the day, is still expected to perform housework and prepare meals for the family.

A teenage daughter is a valuable asset for such a woman. Some girls *do* have regular chores, though their brothers rarely do. One high school girl reports that she and her mother have established coordinated routines. Far from resenting the extra tasks she has because her mother works, she recounts their system with highly motivated enthusiasm:

> We really are a team, but we don't work together. I get home first, so I do things like last-minute shopping (my mother leaves a list), drawing the bath, measuring rice and water into the rice maker and cleaning vegetables. When my mother arrives home, she does the final cooking and after dinner we clean up together. After my brother, we take our baths, and sometimes do a load of laundry.

This girl, it should be noted, is not headed to college; a child studying for exams would probably not be encouraged to participate to this degree, and her mother might even temporarily quit work during the months of examination hell preceding the exams. Mothers of boys are much more likely to do this than mothers of girls, for mothers tend to promote their sons' educational futures more than those of their daughters, even though the number of girls entering college is about equal to that of boys.

Quitting work during a son's exam period represents a need to be at least symbolically available to the child at a stressful time, and to fulfill community expectations—so that no one can later blame her for inattention or selfishness if he does not perform at high levels. Quitting is of course, not possible for women at the two extremities of the class ladder of working women: neither those whose families rely on her income, nor those professional career women whose track precludes interruptions can afford to stop, and their triple load at this time puts a very great strain on them.

Mothers who don't work find new freedom as their daughters are more available to help. A high-school girl says:

> I like watching my mother *"asobu"* (play) now. She seems to be enjoying her freedom, going out in the evening, going to the theater. She doesn't tell us where she's going. . . . Sometimes we can't find her, even when we need her.

The Filial Child: Parents as a Future Responsibility

Even those Japanese youth with a strong independent streak say they will take care of their parents in their old age. Unsolicited statements were offered such as "I will take care of my parents when they get old, and take them to hot springs and such." In the past, caring for parents fell to the eldest son and his family, but now there are open negotiations as to which sibling will provide the care. One family has already established the caretaking pattern for the future:

> My parents only have my sister and me, and she left to get married. . . . My parents want me to take care of them when they get older. . . . While I am young they want me to be anywhere I want, but when my parents get really old and can't move any more, they'll spend the rest of their lives with me, and enter the same grave. . . . We talked about which of us daughters would continue the family, by getting a husband who would take my family name, and it will be I who will do this.[9]

The son of a gas-station owner has always known he will take care of his family and inherit the station. He shows a low-key resignation: "I'm in high school now and I already know what the rest of my life will be like: nothing is left to debate and my future is determined. It will be ordinary, an average life, but that is OK."

Experts on adolescent development describe the lack of clear models in the family in Japan and the West as potentially damaging to children. The classical explanation is that this problematic condition, added to the storm and stress supposedly normal in adolescence, produces role conflict, both as intergenerational strife and as outcome of competing models of adulthood presented to young people. This explanation, however, perpetuated by clinicians and sociologists, does not account for the empirical fact that for most teens in both Japan and America conflict and confusion do not escalate to crisis proportions and that there is more harmony than discord in parent-child relations.[10] There are, however, distinctions between boys and girls in their family position and relationships, more striking in Japan than in the United States—perhaps.

Boys and Girls in the Family: Gender and Relationships

Daughters and sons share the same parents but there are different expectations for them, in both the United States and Japan. As is clear from the above discussion of tasks, girls tend to have more duties at home, boys to be more protected from chores, particularly (in Japan) if they are studying for entrance examinations. The child-rearing practices emphasizing the different paths to be taken by boys and girls persist even in households with working mothers and even in the context of greater opportunities for girls in school and workforce.

As one fifteen-year-old Japanese girl noted, boys are indeed treated differently:

> The eldest son is disgustingly spoiled and pampered. They get everything done for them. . . . They are treated like the king of the household . . . I watched such a boy, my cousin, come to dinner as he pleased, when everyone else was midway through. He created a hubbub as everyone rushed to serve him. Even his grandmother, who was further from the kitchen than he was, got up to serve him. My younger brother too, an only son, is spoiled by my mother and yet she complains that he is hopeless. When I ask her why she spoils him so, she tells me that once he is a grown man, he will have a great many responsibilities to shoulder, so now is the time to spoil him. In my opinion, I don't see how sheltering and pampering prepares him in any way to go out into the world to shoulder responsibilities!

The eldest son is king, and sisters are handmaidens. But age is as important as gender in the sibling hierarchy. The pecking order is established, both of responsibility and indulgence. Older siblings have precedence over their juniors. As everywhere, Japanese children are sensitive to such conditions, but most frequently accept them.

When parents are not sensitive to issues between siblings and when parents appear to favor one child over another, deviating from the usual order of things, there may be very hard feelings. In one family, the summer vacation dates for the short annual seaside holiday were suddenly changed, apparently to accommodate the younger of the two daughters. The elder, a high-school student, had taken on a part-time job to fill out the summer, which conflicted with the new vacation plan. She is deeply resentful that she cannot go and writes in her diary: "I feel like crying in my vexation. Why should I give up this once-a-year event because of my sister's selfish demand. . . . I will have my father buy me a dress to make up for it. But I still cannot forgive my sister".

Many girls see their roles and treatment in the family as clearly related to their gender:

We're just like girls together. It makes her happy when I spend time shopping with her.

I'm the daughter, so I have to be responsible for my younger brother.

I'm a Daddy's girl, but I don't like all the attention I get: he waits up for me late at night, and I feel he is always watching and over-protecting me.

American teens, recently conditioned to issues of sex discrimi-nation, have brought these issues home, and are often quick to correct any gender bias they see in their parents. Girls, particu-larly, are outraged if they are told they can't be out after dark when their brothers can be, and if they are asked to help in the kitchen more than the boys. Both boys and girls in middle-class families are exempted from housework at least until their home-work is done, but it appears that enforcement of the performance of assigned chores varies, depending not on gender but on family style.

American highschoolers are much more likely than their Jap-anese counterparts to have part-time jobs, and this may also ex-empt them from some household chores. Sibling order rarely gives precedence in the American family, for the idea of democ-racy in the family militates against such a principle. But there may be a gap between principle and practice, for sometimes elder children do have perquisites, such as staying up later or having larger allowances, that younger siblings resent. Occasionally, there is even a reversal of privilege when an eldest child will com-plain when a younger one is allowed more freedom than he or she had had at the same age, resenting the benefits the junior sibling has accrued from more experienced and relaxed parents.

Needs, Wants, and Family Battle Zones

Assumptions that what teens want and what they need are differ-ent, make the American family especially a battleground between parents (who assume they know what teens *need*) and teens (as-sumed to have wants contradictory to those needs). Family cul-ture determines how these are played out: the family's social and economic background, its religion, family history and experi-ences (including sometimes mythical references to the values of grandparents and ancestors), and input from the vast range of ac-ademic and popular counseling available in the media. Wants are defined by peers, by what one American teen calls "the underground teenagers' school," and by marketing and media.

The outcomes in overt confrontations differ by family and cultural style but, overall, American parents and teens appear to play into the contradiction as part of their relationship more than their Japanese counterparts. In their diaries and in interviews, Japanese children more often state that they respect their parents' views of what is good for them, and more often say that parents pay attention to what they want: "I don't fight with my family. We talk about school at dinner. My parents understand me and listen to me." Another boy, a freshman in high school, said, "I am a dependent person who likes to have his parents decide about things, like schools and *juku*. I'd rather have someone else decide. I am grateful to them." Never would you hear an American child say this. Moreover, vocal or physical confrontation in the Japanese family is very rare. Subtler communication of displeasure usually works.

Negative communication in Japan is often accomplished through silence. Having to say no represents to some parents that their silence has failed to communicate. Children too retreat rather than attack, but they may be more visibly unhappy. Teenage tantrums, as in the case of an American girl who threw all the potted plants in her living room onto the carpet, are as rare as a family shouting match in Japan, yet both are not altogether unknown.

This is not to say that there are no issues and conflict, and where conflict exists, it ranges between the rages known in some American households and quieter "acting in," Suzanne Vogel's phrase for the inward turn of unhappiness, acting as a signal of trouble in Japanese adolescents.[11]

A boy in Osaka says:

> My mother gets very emotional. . . . When she gets angry, she goes on and on, telling me all the other complaints she has had. . . . Sometimes I feel it's not fair that she gets to change the subject like this, and once she gets angry . . . the whole family starts getting angry. . . . Fighting in my family is contagious.

A boy in semi-rural Gumma prefecture, in a family with a quieter style, said:

> My mother considers me more or less an adult. . . . I once told her not to interfere with me too much, and she looked really sad and

seemed to say, "Oh, I see." I didn't mean it to be very important, but for my mother it seemed as if it was a very significant moment.

Japanese and American teens, however close and noncombative they may be with their parents, all express the need for conscious strategies in dealing with them. Japanese mothers describe the process of "psyching out" their children so as to be better able to get them to agree with them (*wakaraseru*). This is a long-term process begun in the child's infancy, in which mothers learn to understand in great depth what motivates their child in order better to get the child to understand and accede to their parental goals.[12] Japanese young people similarly develop long-term methods for manipulating their parents using their intimate knowledge of *them*. This is the strategy Americans call "using psychology" on someone, to manipulate a relationship: a mother of an angry teen said, "If you were smart, you'd use psychology on your father to get what you want instead of blowing up."

One Japanese high-school boy gives a lesson in the Japanese version of using "psychology" in revealing to your mother something important and potentially controversial:

> I'd tell her as if it were nothing important. . . . I would start talking, wandering into the kitchen in a casual way, maybe taking a snack while she is cooking in the kitchen. Maybe I'd *amaeru* (seek her indulgence, a trait mothers like to see in their sons) by asking sweetly for a cold drink. I'd perch somewhere in the kitchen, and sneak the topic into the talk, just really casually, first putting it into a matter of a general question, an abstract idea I share with her.

Mothers are clearly key figures in scenarios for getting what one wants in both societies. Fathers may be manipulated, especially by girls, but are seen especially by most Japanese teens as remote, marginal figures, carrying little weight in household management.[13] Some teens see their fathers as nuisances, especially girls who help their mothers serve the father who arrives home late and strews his clothes about, before a late supper they prepare. Such a girl sees her mother as self-sacrificing, her father as a bother.[14] One girl's father lives on a job assignment in another city, and she wrote indignantly in her diary that far from reducing her mother's work load, the new arrangement forces her mother every week "to go to that city to clean his room and do his laundry." Boys seem to notice such things less.

What has become known as the "absent father syndrome" in Japan is more than a media-amplified social trend; it has indeed caused problems for children, particularly as mothers find it hard to manage alone. When fathers of school-age children are transferred to another post, families rarely move with them, and this presents problems for children and mothers. Even fathers who do live with their families may be "absent," however, as work and compulsory socializing keep them out of the house most of their children's waking hours.

One result may be that mothers over-attend to children, and some have associated the rising (but still very small) incidence of mother-son incest with the fact that fathers are often posted elsewhere,[15] or sometimes suffer from what is called "a fear of returning home," keeping them at offices late or forcing them to stay overnight in hotels near their offices. Other pathological situations, such as homes where children beat their mothers ("battered parent syndrome"), are traced to the isolation of the mother-child relationship.

But even in families with available fathers, there are problems. A high school senior discusses her alienation from her father, and what that has done to her:

> When I was young, I was my father's favorite child. I tried always to be a good girl. But my father was hard to get along with. He is always tired and in a bad mood on weekends. And he is not dependable. A fortune teller told me I have a complex about my father. I detached myself from him early and since then I have been looking for someone who is dependable, and who really loves me. . . . I don't like my father as a person or as a father, I just can't accept him, and I don't trust anyone in my family. But I feel lonely, and that's why my boy friend is so important for me. . . . I see the ideal image of a father in my boy friend.

Boys and girls both see their mothers as key, friends and nurturers, and as the responsible adult decision-maker. Getting permission to buy a motorcycle from his mother seemed impossible to one boy who engaged his mostly absent and far softer father to help him keep the purchase a secret, further enlisting his paternal grandmother, who lives in the mountains, to keep the vehicle stored secretly at her house safe from the school rules against such bikes and from his mother.

Grandparents do play a key role, when they are available to

teens. The best arrangement according to teens is apparently when a grandparent lives close by, but not with the family, for then the grandparents can provide respite space and support without creating possibilities for disloyalty and dissension in the household. Especially where parents are seen to nag and interfere, grandparents are welcome visitors and Japanese teens seek them out. This working teen delays going home, instead stopping at her grandmother's house:

> My mother asks too many questions. . . . She worries about what other people would think when I get home late. . . . So I go to my grandmother's house whenever I can, and I sometimes even call home to say I'm staying overnight there. She empties her refrigerator to cook wonderful meals for me. I am her favorite. And when I leave, she loads me down with fruit and food and sweets."

Another teen actively cares for a disabled grandmother, who lives with her family.

> I give her a massage every afternoon after school. I like to do it, because she tells me stories about living in Nagano in the old days, and she really listens to me, and helps me with my problems. I hate to think about her dying.

Conclusion

The quotations strung through this chapter will have evoked responsive echoes in American and Japanese readers both, whether as people recently emerged from adolescence or parents and relatives of teenagers. The similarities are evident, though the environmental contexts and the cultural values shaping the experience of those contexts may differ. As most Americans would note, overall, Japanese children—even urban youth—grow up in a less physically and socially hostile environment than do their American counterparts. The contradictions between cultural definitions of development—the popular view of growing up—and the realities of family, school, and society are less striking in Japan—and rarely represent major and damaging discontinuities in children's lives. Both Japanese and American teens are in a stage of life inherently confusing for our societies. Being in between childhood and adulthood has intrinsic problems for understanding and management. But in our families, in our relationships at home, American young people must deal with many of the problems given them by the wider society, whereas Japanese children do not. For the most part, Japanese teens understand adults not to be enemies, and families, for the most part, do not take the brunt of social and institutional ambivalence over the treatment of the young.

Insofar as the crisis in the American family is a result of unresolved social responsibility for individual needs and conditions, it is the place where problems resulting from society's lack of care have come home to roost. A lack of support for the family has had circular results, producing strains and tensions that cripple young people's potential as individuals, and weaken their families. Blaming the family for producing dysfunctional young people has not been a useful strategy.

Across the Pacific, Japanese families are seen, at present, as a source of positive development for teens—but social policy to support them has not kept pace with social change, and may not be more enlightened—day-care provision for working mothers, for example, is far from adequate. The consensual supports for family, however, have continued to target the home as prime motivator of successful children. What works through social consensus in Japan, however, may need policy intervention in the United States.

Families in Japan, then, do not generally become the battlegrounds where tensions created by society's ambivalence get played out. As we have seen, parents have a safe, nurturant relationship with their children and there is little of what we would call a generational Oedipal rift apparent between parents and children. Thus, with little expectation of strife, these problems of school and other concerns do not have an available battle stage on which they are played out at home. It is not a simple picture of uniform strength and stability, however.

Families in Japan are very sensitive to changes in outside institutions and in the economy, and in Japan, too, there is an increasing gap between the comfortable and the disadvantaged that has also taken its toll on families and, directly, on young people. There has been a rise in the numbers of teens who do work while attending school but this does not in Japan represent increased independence among youth, but rather, real need in their families for income. But most families, however restricted in their resources, place a high priority on providing what they can for their children. Poorer families give to their children disproportionately large amounts of pocket money, clothing, and other socially desirable accoutrements for their teens. Blue jeans bought at discount in the stalls in side streets near Ueno Station in Tokyo may look the same as those bought in expensive department stores in Shinjuku, but the label makes the difference. Because market forces rule a child's social acceptability, families, like their children, struggle to provide that label.

Education, of course, has a more lasting effect on a child's acceptability, and so, there too, parents try to overcome their own restrictions to provide more support. It has, as we will see in Chapter 4, become a greater struggle as the flaws in the meritocracy become more apparent. American and Japanese families both cope with scarce resources as they attempt to calculate benefit for their children. Schools share families' responsibility for children's future in both countries, but the relationships between family, teen, and school are strikingly different in the United States and Japan.

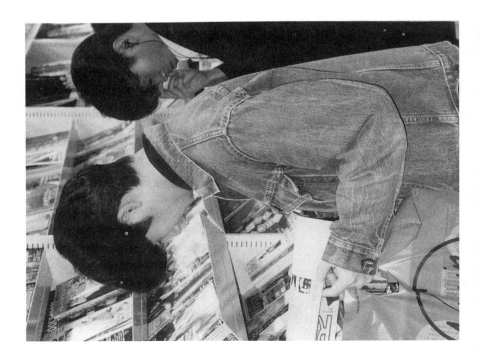

4
School in the Life of the Teen

My mother really keeps after me to get good grades so I can get into a good university—I know she's right, but I sometimes wonder what it's all for.

—High school junior, Boston, Massachusetts.

I really like going to school—my friends and I hang out after school and go shopping to buy tapes and clothes, and as soon as we get home, we call each other on the telephone. School is great.

—High school junior, Tokyo

The power of education to shape young peoples' lives in Japan has increased since World War I. The rapid acceleration of economic prosperity has inflated the power of a college degree and, since the war, a high-school credential has lost its market power. Children stay in school well into what used to be considered adulthood. But along with the prolongation of the period of learning has come an emphasis on a competitive mode of learning at earlier ages as well. The middle-school years particularly have become critical to children's futures, sorting them in and out of the academic status track. In the United States, except for a small minority, middle school children focus on friendship, sports, and especially among girls, the opposite sex. School is the place where,

71

for both Japanese and American teens, everything significant happens—and not always in the classroom.

The character and habits of young teens in both societies are said to presage their future development and recently these young people have shown precocious maturation—both academic and sociosexual. The Japanese educational message to children has been more consistent than ours, however: the more you work, the better life you will have. However single-minded the mission of education in Japan may seem, Japanese schools encourage all children to visualize success. American schools, while more diverse in resources and options, also appear to support an egalitarian vision of children's potential. Our mixed message in schools, learned early by children, is that our schools are not supported by an "educational imperative" for all children, do not in fact provide opportunity. As a result, most children labor in the confusion between the rhetoric and the reality. A sixth-grader, hearing that the library in his school was to be open only one day a week, said "They aren't very serious about us, are they?"

Two Young Teens

Okuda Kenichi is a fourteen-year-old middle school student, in his second year in a Chiba public school. He is the eldest child of an employee of a local car rental service in Chiba. The business is secure (a franchise operation with a good reputation) but small in scale, renting small vans and trucks and an occasional sedan to a salesman from out of town. Because Mr. Okuda, a high-school graduate, is manager for his company's smallest location in the area, he does all the work, occasionally helped by a part-time employee who washes the cars with him and helps on busy holidays and weekends. Mr. Okuda is lucky to have a job even marginally managerial, and he has no ambition to move to another job, though it is hard for him to summon much loyalty and commitment to such a small and unremunerative post.

Kenichi has a younger sister and a baby brother, the latter something of a surprise to the parents who hadn't thought they'd have more than two children, and who worry now about the cost of raising three children. Kenichi's sister is in the fifth grade of elementary school and she helps her mother with the baby after school. Kenichi's mother is also a high school graduate, whose family wanted her to go on to junior college, but she rebelled and, after graduating, went right to work for a real-estate company, answering the telephone and making arrangements between clients and salesmen. She liked this work, since she also accompanied salesmen to survey properties and take notes, and she felt that it broadened her experience to do such work. She was, however, ready to leave work when her boss introduced her to her future husband, his nephew. But her commitment to doing a job well remains intact and she has, in Suzanne Vogel's term, indeed "professionalized" her role as housewife,[1] making her career her children's entrance into college. She is not worried about Yumi, her daughter, but she is worried about her own ability, without college experience herself, to help Kenichi, who is definitely falling behind in math. She regrets the pressure on him, and remembers her own more relaxed high school days as continuous with the happy days of elementary school.

Kenichi resisted when his mother and teacher arranged for a home tutor in math. He did not want to go home after school to find another teacher there. He was used to delaying his homework until late in the day and doing it while watching television, as a member of what are popularly called the *nagarazoku*, or tribe of "whilers"—children who do several things at once, an act seen as deplorable to the older generation, trained to focus on one task at a time. His tutor, a junior at Chiba University, is a relaxed and kind young man, but his commission from Kenichi's parents is to put the pressure on their son.

What Kenichi does care about are friends. He has been in school with virtually the same group of children, with some exceptions, since the first grade. Unlike American school children whose discontinuous relationships reflect the transient nature of the American population, most Japanese children have long-term relationships with schoolmates. When a Japanese worker is transferred to another location, his family is less likely to follow him, with priority given school continuity over family togetherness. Furthermore, Japanese children are rarely put ahead or kept back in school by ability, so that the age group progresses together through the system.

Kenichi attends school primarily to see his friends and he misses them during even the relatively short vacations provided during the Japanese school calendar. Japanese schools are in session 240 days a year, including half-days on Saturday (now suspended one day a month), compared to 180 days in America.

Summer holidays are less than six weeks long, although there are many one-day holidays during the year. Rarely do families go away together for the entire summer holiday, especially in Kenichi's neighborhood, where most students come from poorer shopkeeping or factory worker families. Even during holidays, there are school-related duties and activities. Kenichi is a junior, no longer at the bottom of the three-year middle school pecking order, and he has responsibilities in his track club that he did not have as a freshman: he must prepare the ground for the freshmen, a sort of training in seniority-system life. During the summer break, his club met for a whole week of practice, full-time, and planned another full week of practice just before school began. Also, he is in the nature club, and since the garden they began in April needs tending throughout the summer, Kenichi helped organize weeding and watering shifts. He actually enjoys these tasks and activities, since they provide a regular way of getting together with friends. He is also kept aware of school through summer homework assignments, including a journal and other writing for Japanese language class and a nature observation notebook for science.

Jeff Silver is a ninth grader in Lawrence, New Jersey, in a public junior high school. Jeff is a bright but distractable boy, socially a bit inept (in his own words) but academically keen—when he is paying attention. His father is a computer programmer; his mother, a nurse in a local hospital. They worried when Jeff was younger that he had an attention-deficit disorder, or was hyperactive, but by junior high school, he calmed down and was able to do very well academically in school. He hopes to go to a good university and perhaps to be a writer. Mr. Silver went to a state university and his wife to a nursing school, and they are encouraging their son to go to an ivy-league school. Because Jeff is an only child, with both sets of grandparents living nearby, he gets a lot of (sometimes unwanted) attention. However, because of his parents' work schedules, he sometimes doesn't see them until dinner time, and when he was in elementary school, his parents arranged for him to go home with a neighbor's child until they could pick him up. By the fifth grade, however, he was embarrassed to have this "babysitting" arrangement and protested that it was insulting and undignified. He wanted to be trusted to stay home alone, and he now does, and enjoys the freedom.

Jeff will go on to the local high school and his parents are now talking about getting a math tutor for him, like Kenichi's, from nearby Princeton University. Even he is beginning to think that would be a good idea, as his poor grades in math contrast strikingly with his very good ones in English.

Jeff is a bit of a loner, and is sometimes teased by larger more athletic boys, and by, as he puts it, "a particularly obnoxious group of girls." He assiduously avoids the girls in this class, who see him as a late developer. When his mother rashly suggested that he join his friends on a kind of group date to go to the movies, with girls, he replied "Are you trying to jump-start me into puberty?" He has three close friends, with whom he enjoys playing computer games and Dungeons and Dragons, a role-playing game. He is a self-styled "couch potato," and doesn't have many other hobbies. The close friends get together about three afternoons a week, and on weekends. During a recent summer, Jeff spent a month at a computer camp and two weeks with his parents in a rental beach house on Cape Cod. The remaining month of vacation he spends "vegging out," and hanging around with his friends. Depending on their families' schedules, he may spend much of that month on his own. His school has only a suggested summer reading list as an assignment for the three-month vacation and he has read most of the books on the list.

School is central to the lives of American and Japanese teens, but not in the ways we might think. For both, school is an institutional step towards the responsibilities and rewards of adult life, but school is also a training ground where a child learns to be a friend, a member of an age set, a group, a clique—and where a sense of self is discovered through friendships.

School is where the teen is institutionally identified and the construction of the image of the adolescent as student or member of a school community may complement or contradict the popular conception of the teenager. As a member of a "schooled" cohort, a child is first identified by the school itself, its status and image in the community, the status of the child, and a range of options for his future. In America, a teen's school—if it is a neighborhood school—gives clues to social class background as well as to the child's future opportunities. In Japan, public junior-high schools are heterogeneous, like their neighborhoods, while entrance to high school selects and labels children by ability. High schools are more significant in Japan than they are in the United States as indicators of future life chances, for admission to college—the real marker of occupational opportunities—strongly depends on high-school preparation.

As in America, Japanese schools also have "institutional personalities" beyond their ability to place young people in the employment ladder. These personalities are more pronounced among private schools than public, which show greater internal diversity. A "jock" school, an "artsy" school, or a "brain" school in the United States might have their equivalents in Japan, where, for example, a school with a winning baseball team would actively recruit athletic boys. The most prestigious high schools, though, concentrate on academically high-achieving children with less specialized interests.

Schools are highly visible today in America and Japan, but for very different reasons. High schools in the United States frequently provide media events, as places where students kill each other for sneakers or jackets, where newborn babies may be found in washrooms, or where drugs may be bought and sold. Media attention to schools in Japan also focuses on problems, but they are quite different. School violence of any kind is rare in Japan, but where it does exist, it provides headlines. The Japanese public finds out about dropouts, paint-thinner sniffing, bullying, and "uniform vandalism" (meaning pegging the pants legs, or lengthening the skirt of a school uniform) to a degree equal to that of revelations of much more extreme crimes in the American press.

Schooling defines a child as a future member of society, or at least, that is the intention of modern education in both countries. What happens in school is meant to create opportunities through academic and social learning. The problem in America is the mixed message again: what is learned socially in school, although in theory valued, is also seen as suspect by adult society, while what is learned socially in Japan is viewed not only as benign, but usually as actively important to the development of a good *shakaijin* (member of society). What concerns us here is less what children learn in academic terms than the ways in which going to school creates new identities as students and as classmates, different from those of the elementary school years and different again from those of the workforce or college to come.

The first epigraph for this chapter is from an American child, and the second from a Japanese child—both high school students, and both ostensibly headed on an academic path to college or university. The American child may sound like the stereotypical *Japanese* child laboring under the ambitions of an "education mama," while the Japanese child appears as carefree as the *American* suburban teen, headed for the mall after school. While there is indeed a feeling of greater seriousness in the high school years in Japan, and, relatively, a more casual attitude toward school in the United States, neither of these students is very bizarre in his or her own country. We both have both.

The Shape of Schools and the Shaping of a Teen's Life

When you ask Kenichi, the fourteen-year-old, who he is, he says "I am a second-year middle school student at Higashi Middle School." In spite of whatever inroads have been made by Western-style teen culture, affluence, and Japanese versions of individualism, Ken-kun (the informal mode of addressing Kenichi) sees himself primarily as a member of his school, and in terms of his position there, not—as an American would expect— in terms of less institutional, more personal attributes, such as, "I'm fourteen and I like to play hockey."

The entrance to secondary school is a positive but serious moment in a Japanese teen's life. Graduation from elementary school represents a passage from carefree childhood to greater responsibility for one's achievement. The engaged, open, nurturant atmosphere of elementary school classrooms gives way to an increase in homework; for some, the donning of a school uniform; and, again for some, enrollment in private afterschool *juku*, or cram classes.

Japanese middle schools have curricula continuous with those of elementary school but are separate three-year establishments, the last stage of the compulsory education system, from which progress to the more ability-tracked high school is by examination. Often elementary school classmates will move up to junior high school together, but may well lose touch with each other on entrance to high school, a milestone of far greater seriousness than is entrance to junior high school. As one Japanese child said,

> Middle school was fun; I was with my friends and I could throw myself into sports and I didn't have to study very hard. I couldn't be sure which of my friends would be with me in high school. Now that I am in high school, I know these will be my friends for life— they've been with me through very tough times.

The classroom atmosphere of the middle school provides a transition between the emphasis on harmony and group life in elementary school and the more organized discipline of the high school class.[2] Junior-high-school children are encouraged to consider social morality in concrete incidents and problems. These are analyzed and treated by the class as a whole through *hansei* or self-examination as a group. These sessions are not under the authority of a teacher, but are run by students themselves, as adults recognize that to be authentic, cooperation and sensitivity in children must emerge from children themselves.

In spite of this encouragement to be harmonious and consensual, differences between members of the class are increasingly apparent to these children as they begin to focus on their own development, take a new interest in their peers, and wonder, as do all adolescents, "Am I normal?" Friendship becomes an arena for testing one's own appropriateness, for finding norms for the desired normalcy and, as we will see, for patrolling the peer group for signs of nonconformity in others.

Learning what is cool and what is not in middle school takes place in an atmosphere pressured by the examinations to enter high school. The children are not immune to the influences of parents, media, and each other, as they test not only their present acceptability as classmates and friends but their future life chances by how well they can perform on exams.

Credentials and the Degree Marketplace

Most children (94 percent of the age group) now complete high school in Japan. The extension of schooling for most children to the end of high school is a fairly recent phenomenon in Japan, as it is in the United States. Before World War II, junior high school was the most common terminal level, and ending there, especially for girls, was not considered dropping out. Indeed, middle school graduates, called "golden eggs," were very valuable to employers, as well-trained but low-cost labor in industry and lower-level office work. The rapid change in educational opportunities after World War II quickly shifted terminal education for most people up one rung, to high school.

As more and more young people progressed to senior high school, however, "golden egg" positions had to be filled (at greater cost to the employer) by high school graduates and gradually a high school diploma became all but required for any entry-level work. Whereas 86 percent of those entering the labor force in 1950 were middle school graduates, only 6 percent in 1985 were junior high graduates. Now 52 percent are high-school graduates; 42 percent, college graduates.[3] Currently, more females than males progress to postsecondary education. Degree inflation in higher education and the workplace[4] has continued as the baby-boom population ages.

The relationship between academic credentials and occupational chances has become stronger since the war, and the emphasis on academic performance has affected children in all families. A recent television comedy set in the Tokugawa Period (1603–1868) parodied contemporary study hysteria showing a bookwormy boy of about twelve, with pre-Franklin eyeglasses, studying late into the night as his mother hovers with concern behind the *shoji* paper doorway to his room, making sympathetic and encouraging clucking noises. For a Japanese audience, the joke is in the backward historical projection of a very contemporary phenomenon, rather like Americans watching Fred Flintstone worrying about his taxes.

The experience of middle school varies, of course, and the anxiety of high school entrance tests does not affect all children. Many, especially those outside large urban areas, do not have very difficult tests and rural high schools tend to be more regionally comprehensive, taking in all children in the area, rather than academically homogeneous, taking only those at a testable skill level. For families with the ability to pay, there are private schools that incorporate elementary, junior, and senior high schools, and these are often attached to colleges and universities. This situation means that children beginning at the lower levels can ride up the escalator even into college, without difficult examinations. Of 11,264 junior-high schools in Japan, 608 are private; but at high-school level, there is a dramatic increase in private schools, 1,311 out of 5,511.[5] Public schools in the past were at the top of prestige hierarchies and there were no competing private preparatory schools of the American and British variety. In recent years, however, some private schools have become more popular for those who can afford them, for preparation for college is said now to be better there than in most public schools. Some parents even opt out of the system, sending children to international or overseas schools, planning to have them attend foreign universities where the entrance requirements are not so rigorous.

There still exists a separate status ladder for girls. A good junior college is often sufficient for a girl to be employable and marriageable. Some even feel that a prestigious university education prices a girl out of the market for a good husband.

The new seriousness implied by these future considerations defines the differences between the daily life in a middle school and that in elementary school. In elementary school, the homeroom classroom is truly home, and a single teacher guides learning through most of the day. It is also the class lunchroom, study hall, and general hangout. But in junior high school, students move from room to room for different subjects. Lunch, however, is still served in the home classroom, not in school cafeterias as in many American schools. Lunch is served to classmates by teams of children and includes bread, milk, and a main course such as stew or curry, rather plain food. Children themselves say it helps to build character to eat such meals, and it is hard to complain when the teacher eats the same thing with them.

Each class lasts fifty minutes and there are ten minutes between classes. These ten minutes are crammed with intense activity: runs to the playground for a quick game of volleyball or basketball; to the halls to practice a musical instrument; or to clusters of friends for a quick review of the next class' material. The noise and action between classes is considerable. The day ends after a brief class meeting at 3:00 p.m. and children disperse to afternoon school activities. These are religiously attended, especially the sports clubs. Teachers may be present as coaches and assistants, but the clubs are really run by the middle schoolers. Most children leave school by five in the afternoon, and those who do not go right home or to after-school cram classes gather with friends at this time. In contrast, few American schools have such intensive after-school programs, and those that exist, primarily in sports, are not inclusive of all children.

While academic criteria primarily sort children into their next schools, private high schools and some public ones are somewhat interested in a child's participation in clubs and school leadership.

High school represents more intense study, a greater variety of courses (but not approximating the diverse menu of electives and

Study and Other Activity *(hours per week)*

Activity	U.S.	Japan
In class	26.2	41.5
Homework	3.8	19.5
Sports/play	7.0	.7
Sleep	60.3	53.0

options in a large American high school), and for those aiming at college, more hours of homework. But high school is also a time for club activity after classes, and especially for those not engaged in "examination hell," involvement in sports and arts is high. Homework for a Japanese high schooler on average takes about 20 hours per week, whereas for an American high school student, the average is 3.8 hours per week.

Baseball is, in Japan, the dominant high school sport. The high school baseball world series is held annually in October, and is given national media attention. Those on a school team have year-round obligations to work out, to practice, and to play, and have little time for other activities. The seriousness of high school athletics in Japan matches the most serious of college and professional sports in the United States. However, those who are college-bound tend to participate only in their first and second years, devoting the third to study. American psychologists say that the lack of such intense involvement in sports or other activities in our schools is a problem for many children: the cutbacks in such activities as "extras" have especially hurt children who might, without this involvement, seek violent outlets elsewhere. An urban high school student in Boston said:

> I use football to stay out of trouble. When I'm playing football I leave school after everyone else has left so that I don't have the pressure of everybody hanging around wanting me to participate . . . I have a legitimate excuse to go straight home and rest."[6]

The engagement may serve different functions in Japan—access to peer activity rather than rejection of it.

Japanese high schoolers' use of time in school outside of classes is parceled out between time with friends and study. Club and student government activities (*seitokai*) are in second place, except for athletes. The "serious students" spend less time in these latter two activities, since they "don't count" for college entrance.

Continuity and commitment are the bywords of Japanese school participation, and family plans yield to school requirements, schedules, and less formal school-based club activities. It is not just workplace demands on working parents that constrain family vacation plans: school has a central place in the calendar that middle-class American parents would find unnecessary or oppressive. There have been some attempts to cut back the school week and to increase summer holidays in Japan, but they have not been popular—strangely, not even among teachers and parents. The six-week summer holiday comes in the middle of the school year, not between school years as in America, and educators believe that this promotes continuity, rather than learning loss, over the vacation, since there is homework for the summer usually in every subject.

Because teachers are paid on a twelve-month basis, helping to supervise club activities or run review sessions (or later, in high schools, help with job forum or employer interviews) at school is expected summer-duty work. Teachers and parents both prefer children's relationships to be part of a larger institutional framework: hanging out, on the street, may lead to, at best, unpredictable and, at worst, antisocial behavior. Some schools send teachers into the streets and shopping districts to be sure children are not in the proscribed game arcades and coffeeshops. As we will see, the relationships emerging from the classroom and club may be just as emotionally challenging as pressures from street gangs and the lures of delinquency.

Academic programs share a core curriculum: all students take three full years each of Japanese, mathematics, social studies, science, and English. The remainder of time is devoted to such courses as physical education, home economics, health, music, and art. Classes are large in American terms, averaging forty-three to forty-five students to one teacher, whereas classes in the United States average twenty-four to twenty-six per room.

Examinations and the Fallout from Universal Optimism

In 1971, when the protests against the building of Tokyo's new airport, Narita, were at their peak, a high-school student joined the protestors camping out in the farmers' fields in Chiba, bringing his tent, and, since it was a few months before the college entrance exams, his textbooks for study. After a few weeks, he returned with others through the police checkpoints, where they frisked this ragged and dirty fellow as a potential Red Army terrorist. They found his metal tent poles and were about to arrest him for carrying weapons, when a policeman noticed his textbooks. When he said he had just gone to the countryside to isolate himself in the woods for exam preparation, the police immediately let him go. Such is the power of the examination imperative in Japan, that, disguised as a student, you can get away with almost anything.

The examination imperative exists because of the once-and-for-all nature of the selection system.[7] Although some students (a larger percentage of the entering classes of the most prestigious schools) repeat the process if they don't pass the first time, for most the end of high school is the test point that determines their future. American universities and colleges are more open, allowing students to apply or transfer later in their lives and basing admission on broader and more diverse measures of appropriateness. Further, college board and SAT examinations are universal, whereas in Japan aspirants must take exams given by each college to which they apply.

By the third year of middle school in Japan, a student of fourteen or fifteen years usually has a sense of the limits of his or her academic future and occupational opportunities. There is no place for a late bloomer in such a system; second chances are available only under special conditions. Limited second chances are provided by taking a year or more out between high school and college for extra study, often in special full-time cram schools (*yobiko*). (This practice has become so common that the 6-3-3-4 educational system is now called by some, the 6-3-3-X-4 system, the "X" standing for a year or more of cramming at *yobiko* after high school. These, however, command rather steep fees. Further, to enter the best *yobiko*, the "masterless warrior" student-without-a-school (*ronin*) must pass an examination, and the student must cram for that as well.

Counseled by teachers and specialists, students aiming at college begin early to select potential schools, so that at least one is a school likely to admit them. There are various measures used, but most students rely on a standardized test given to a large population of students, which teachers use as a criterion in advising students. The *hensachi*, or cumulative, comprehensive, positioning grade, gives teachers and students a guideline for setting expectations. This is a number calculated from school tests and homework scores, and it is the first reference used in choosing the level of school to which a student should aspire. Of course, each university and college gives its own entrance examination, and all are within a few weeks, so that the exam schedule of an applicant to several schools can become very complicated. Most of such highschoolers' final year is spent preparing to squeeze through the narrow gate of entrance by means of a good score on the examinations.

These examinations are made up of multiple-choice questions and demand a finely tuned and detailed knowledge of subject matter. Educational reformers are pressing for a more open-ended evaluation allowing for essay questions and testing of analytic ability, and for the incorporation of teacher recommendations, personal interviews, and work done in school as part of the application process. Tokyo University recently initiated a special track of admission for students who excel in one area, rather than in all, and allocate 10 percent of the entering class to such off-balance geniuses.

While it is possible to take and retake the entrance examinations to most universities several times, and indeed half of the entering class at Tokyo University, at the top of the university status ladder, is composed of students who have tried more than once before succeeding, this is an expensive option. Entrance figures reveal how common this option is, however. Of the 1,160,000 who took entrance examinations in 1989, 290,000 were *ronin*. Those who fail to pass the exams each year are about 450,000 and many are repeat *ronin*, though many give up after one retake, and enter vocational or specialist schools instead.

Not everyone sees the experience as bad: a first year *ronin* says "Everybody should experience being a ronin. . . . There will probably be no other period of my life that has such clear and definite purpose. . . . I always do my very best, so I'd have nothing to repent of even if I should fail again."[8]

And *yobiko* and *juku* teaching are often cited as more interesting and innovative than that of ordinary schools: they are competitive and can pay good teachers good wages. Yoyogi Seminar, a large chain of *yobiko*, is one of the oldest ai.d most famous, geared to the entrance exams for Tokyo University and the top private universities.[9] Yoyogi is a showcase of talented teachers and high-tech innovations in pedagogy and presents a striking contrast to the drabness of a typical high school. The mood is of a high-school pep rally, the pace rapid, and the teaching very engaging. Such yobiko are of course in the business for the money and their success in placing students creates their reputation. They are, indeed, expensive, as they pay their star teachers moviestar salaries, sometimes as high as $500,000 per year.

The pressure now felt in middle school is resisted by the Teachers Union, the Nikkyoso, whose members do not want middle school classrooms to become academic battlegrounds, in service to the examinations. Parents, on the other hand, are not about to check their ambitions for their children, fed by the media and by unspoken competition between families. Parents rarely compare their children overtly—this is taboo—but people generally know where their own children stand in the school rankings.[10] Parents invariably request that teachers make their children work harder, keep up the pressure, and teachers cannot deny the importance of study. The child is seen as full of potential, and is caught between the stark rigidity of the fixed tracked to academic credentials and the rallying optimism that is embodied in the "effort is all" philosophy. A teacher can only tell parents to protect the health of children while they study, and help them to persist (*gambaru*). It is no use telling them that the battle can wait for high school.

Pressures and Pathologies

The result of these conflicting pressures is sometimes severe: truant children resisting going to school (*tōkōkyohi*) now total about 42,000 per year through middle school.[11] School refusal has become a media headline topic in the past few years, replacing previous news leaders such as bullying and school regulations abuses.

School refusal has been defined as skipping fifty or more days per year, but the Ministry of Education now hopes to lower the level for recognition of this problem to thirty days, to catch cases earlier. Primary schools are also afflicted, and the numbers there are growing rapidly. The ministry says that sudden change in family circumstances is the primary reason for truancy, such as a father's transfer to a distant city, and bullying at school or pressures to succeed follow as reasons. Critics say that the ministry is ignoring another provoking factor: corporal punishment in schools. Many local school boards deny the existence of physical punishment in their schools, but even the ministry itself noted that, in 1991, 331 teachers were disciplined for administering corporal punishment.[12] These are high-profile issues in Japan but data on the United States may put this in comparative perspective: 30 percent of senior high school students in America surveyed by Gallup Polls reported that someone they know is a school refuser, whereas only 10 percent had such an acquaintance in Japan.[13]

School-related health problems among Japanese children are on the increase, according to recent reports from children's hospitals in Japan. There has been a rise in the incidence of stomach ulcers, a rise in allergy disorders among children, including rashes and asthma, and some abnormal cholesterol levels and high blood pressure. Low ability to concentrate and hyperactivity are also reported. Children also report sleeplessness, backaches, and low energy levels.[14] The researchers mentioned greater stress on children as well as ignorance of parents who do not sufficiently recognize the physical and emotional environment of today's schools. And of course, predictably, the researchers correlated the incidence of such problems in children with the incidence of working mothers. According to one researcher on children's allergies. " . . . mothers with jobs might have less time for cleaning their homes and taking care of their children's health."[15] The Health and Welfare Ministry established guidelines in 1989 for the eating habits of children, particularly expressing concern about greasy and salty foods, instant meals, and processed foods, as staples of the diets of students and teenagers.[16]

Masahiko Okuni, a pediatrician at Nippon University Hospital, said that it may be neither pressure nor maternal neglect, but the *over-attention* given to children by parents that makes them more vulnerable to stress. Parents, he says, are overprotective and do not allow children to develop their own mechanisms for coping.

In spite of the extreme pressure placed on children in high school, however, and in spite of the saying "Pass with four, fail with five" (meaning, if you sleep as much as five hours per night, you may not pass the exams) Japanese secondary school students still average 7.45 hours of sleep a night, roughly the same as that of U.S. teens.

Relationships at School: Social Training and Testing

There are three kinds of "schooled" relationships: those with adults, those with friends, and those within student-run activity groups, or sports teams. In both America and Japan, secondary schools provide complexity and variety in exercises in learning the ropes of social interaction.

Even in secondary school, when there is less time for the explicit lessons of group life taught in elementary school, relationships are guided by concerns over appropriate behavior and a commitment to peers that echoes the early guidance of home and school. Even though the older child and the adolescent can everywhere be thoughtlessly or intentionally cruel, Japanese children are conscious of their effect on others, a sensitivity trained in home and school. The realities of a complex and demanding social code at school and consciousness of personality and situational distinctions at school may complicate the principles of universal sensitivities and responsible hierarchies.

Americans teens, too, change in their associations as they progress up the academic ladder. More open and individualized relationships shift to group relationships as similar testing of identity and acceptability become the functions of school-based friendships. Overt teasing and bullying, particularly among boys, and subtler but equally painful exclusion or criticism—organized "cattiness"—among girls make peer groups or cliques anxious environments for sensitive children. Power and dominance are the issues: groups do indeed become more *political* and, occasionally, more dangerous places for teens.

In Japan, it is in secondary school that children lose their naïveté about the fit between abstract personal goals and ideals, and the social realities and necessities. Their training has given them the principle of attention to others, and the support and indulgence of adults has allowed them to grow up optimistic, open, and idealistic. One girl, in the third and last year of junior high school in Kawasaki, near Tokyo, sums it up as follows:

> Things are much more complicated now—I can hardly remember how care-free I was in elementary school. It's not only that I have to study so hard for the high school exams, and that my friends are worried about next year and whether we'll be together or not. People are also less kind and more suspicious of each other, and I even

question my own motivation in being friendly to some people I wasn't close to before, just because they seem to be so confident and powerful.

What happens in the teen years is exposure to a range of approved behaviors, and the necessity to suppress some feelings in service to longer-term and more complex group relationships. What also happens in school in these years is the introduction, in peer group activities, to a hierarchical peer social order, not always benevolent, with its special demands for behavior and self-examination.

Revered Teacher, Police Officer, or Pal

Children in both societies are expected to perform in certain ways with adults in school, meaning for the most part with their teachers. These relationships may be multidimensional ones, depending on the personalities of the child and teacher and on the particular needs of the child. In Japan, middle school teachers try to maintain the friendly, open atmosphere of the elementary school classroom, while high school teachers, in service to the greater seriousness of the endeavor, may seem more distant and formal.

In America, secondary school teachers have a difficult challenge: the centrifugal forces driving American teens away from adult-generated institutions complicate the learning process and the child's social development in terms of relationships with teachers. American teachers, more than their Japanese counterparts, are seen to be figures of both intellectual and administrative authority, on the "opposite side of the fence" from the values and concerns of youth. Middle school children in the United States commonly see teachers as authoritarian, challenging intellectually, socially, and morally, and may find the challenge daunting as the authority of the teacher seems occasionally arbitrary or insulting to the child's growing sense of autonomy. Children in America refer to rules, codes, and punishments, and most know, through shared classroom lore or experience, what crimes receive suspensions from school, time-outs in the principal's office, or just a tongue-lashing from the teacher. And conditions may be escalating: an insult to the teacher was formerly punishable by suspension, whereas suspension now may be reserved for carrying a weapon to school. Students in a largely middle-class junior high school in Massachusetts refer to what they can get away with as acceptable transgressions, things adults don't notice, as opposed to things adults will notice and punish. Students, parents, and teachers in this school all sign a "weapons agreement" at the beginning of the year, forbidding guns, knives, and other weapons at school and stipulating punishments for transgressions, in an attempt to arm teachers and administrators against the paramilitary atmosphere of the school. Confrontation between teachers and students in Japan is less frequent, though teachers in some schools describe their charges in less than flattering terms. Japanese teachers worry more that students are indecisive and vague, rather than assertive or aggressive or resistant to authority.

The authority in an American school tends to be explicitly legalistic and hierarchical; authority in a Japanese secondary school is largely informal, within the peer group. Japanese teachers attempt to guide and teach a teen without confrontation, but American teachers from the start work in the context of opposition. In addition, many American teachers must act as social workers, guidance counselors, and even policemen as they struggle with the needs of children often hard to reach academically and emotionally.

In Japan, schools are not institutions of social welfare as they must sometimes be by the default of other institutions in America. It is rare even to find a school psychologist on full-time duty in a Japanese school and not because of lack of resources. The secondary-school teacher in Japan does take on multiple functions, but most of these are involved with academic issues or school placement, and the teacher is primarily a monitor or guide to alert the students and parents to the options and limitations each child has in progressing to the next level.

American secondary school teachers have a greater range of functions, not all academic, and greater stress in meeting the needs of students, overall, than do Japanese teachers, but they are comparatively poorly rewarded for this work. Teaching is a highly-sought-after career in Japan, and the top quarter of college graduates seek careers in schools, whereas for the poorly rewarded and less prestigious work in America, it is the bottom quarter of graduating college students who apply. Teachers in

Japan by law must be paid 10 percent more than other civil servants at the same seniority level, and other benefits and enhancements such as lifetime employment, good maternity leaves, and inservice training make teaching an attractive career for men (who in Japan still do higher-status work than women, in general).[17]

Most Japanese children said that a good teacher had two important qualities: they keep high standards in school work and they were "like a friend." One said, "the teacher should be like a parent too, taking care of us and not letting us go too far." A child does not want to disappoint such a teacher, and often later gratefully attributes success in school performance to the teacher's attention and care.

Teachers can also be pals: some children find real friendship, as well as role models, in caring teachers. Favoritism towards a "teacher's pet" (yutoosei) may result in teasing by other students, just as in the United States, but since there is much less of a gap in Japan between adults and children, friendship is more normal and approved. A high school graduate recalls, "My teacher was my friend. We were very close and we would joke around a lot." Especially in afterschool clubs or in summer activities and out of class time, teachers and children have benign and even close relations in Japan.

There are problems, however.

One high school freshman reports that her teacher observes regulations very closely and is "so strict that he hits hard those who break the rules, regardless of sex . . . if you don't wear the permitted color of socks, he'll hit you."

One particularly alienated boy says he'd never go to a teacher with personal problems, "because I hate teachers . . . You can't ever trust a damn teacher."

Children cite incidents where teachers have betrayed their trust. Teens in Japan tend to be very concerned with moral uprightness in relationships, and suffer shock when the ideal and real are strongly at odds. This high school student found an ethical problem in the behavior of, of all people, her ethics teacher, who is also the coach of her badminton club. The student writes in her diary:

> The teacher is a heavy smoker and the classroom smells of his smoke . . . I feel so sick, I ask to open the windows. . . . So, on the

exam, in the free comments section, I wrote, "You really smoke a lot. Is it one of your pasttimes?" (We had just read Pascal's *Pensées*, on pasttimes.) My friend said that I should never have written that, because he is particularly hard on members of the badminton club, which he never attends anyway, and will give me a bad grade. If her words are true, it is unacceptable behavior. What club you belong to should never affect grading . . . Teachers must be fair, especially on essay questions since these are most subjectively graded. . . . They should teach their students without favor . . . I got a bad score. Should I talk to him about it?

Newspaper articles report other more flagrant violations of professional behavior such as the incident in July of 1990 when a high school teacher, trying to enforce the schedule, sharply closed the entrance gate at the precise moment of the start of a school day, catching a student's head in the gate and killing her.[18] This case has recently been cited often in Japan as an example of the overreaction by teachers in some schools to the increasing lack of discipline among students and the consequent enforcement of a range of punishing school regulations. Corporal punishment is not unknown, as above, but it is rare, and more common in *juku* and *yobiko*, and in some private schools, than in ordinary public school classrooms.[19]

American and Japanese high schools differ on the matter of enforcement and regulation, though on the face of it, a large, city high school in the United States and an ordinary one in Japan share a need to set limits on behavior. Both have rules, ranging from very explicit to unspoken codes.

Thomas Rohlen recently noted a general difference between American and Japanese school order and discipline: he says that a comparison between the two could be graphed in the form of an "X", with American schools beginning with control and discipline in the early years, and ending in high schools with more freedom and permissiveness, while Japanese schools begin with indulgence and end with extreme controls in high schools.[20]

What we get, then, are high schools where not much is expected. As Ernest Boyer reports, "High school is certainly not too demanding. They know with very little work they can meet the basic requirements and that the prospects of being judged a failure are remote. There is probably not a price to pay if you don't

excel . . . regardless of level of achievement, you can probably negotiate your way into higher education. Most students know
that."[21]

Kosoku: Solutions Without a Problem?

The question of how much control is relevant to the age of adolescence and what responsibilities schools should take in guiding
behavior has recently produced a debate in Japan focused on the
escalation in the number and severity of school rules, *kosoku*.
Such rules are often very specific, for example, the exact length of
hair permitted for boys, and the color of underpants for girls. At
one school, the schoolbag strap is to go over the right shoulder on
the way to school, on the left on the way home (see the Appendix.).
Such rules are created by individual schools themselves, and are
not centrally directed. Kosoku especially proliferate in middle
schools, where administrators and teachers see them as a necessary protection from the lack of discipline and the potential disorder and even violence currently seen among young teens. Teachers say that because parents do not teach correct behavior at
home, such rules are now necessary at school.

In some schools there are up to 200 such refined rules. As one
teacher said, "Students need to know that something is expected
of them: they are healthier if they are disciplined." Explicit regulations of this sort tend to proliferate more at schools with lower
academic levels, and violence, bullying, and vandalism at such
schools only make the list grow longer. Slight adjustments to the
school uniform are well codified among teens whose strategies to
make the uniform their own also conform to teen fashions. One
style is called *gakuran*, with longer jacket, higher collar and more
sleeve buttons than regulation, and with a gaudy patterned lin-
ing, creating a counter-authority fashion statement.[22]

The testing of rules (perming one's bangs, bringing the wrong
kind of book bag to school) tends to label rule-breakers as deviant, rather than as children with a momentary need to be bad or
different. This new tendency, caused by *kosoku*, to label behavior
seems to run counter to the more pervasive cultural permissiveness, or at least to the reluctance to mark children as bad or different.

Children and parents are beginning to resist. When a teacher
called a parent 300 miles away, while the class was on a school

trip to Nara, and told her to bring a pair of pants whose cuffs were regulation width to her son, and when a teacher actually killed a child while punishing him for bringing a hairdryer on a class trip, newspaper headlines lambasted the pressure to conform, and the mindless enforcement of trivial regulations. In 1989, parents and lawyers met to protest these rules and held a symbolic public rally in front of the Imperial palace in Tokyo, but since there is no national policy on *kosoku*, change is difficult to achieve.

It is not clear that children are actually worse behaved than in the past; the statistics are not convincing. But the rules themselves have produced some testing of adult-determined boundaries, as children become creative in breaking them. Students look for areas not covered by the rules, to test adults tolerance; teachers add more rules; and students escalate the battle. When Yutaka Ozaki, a famous rock singer, died in April of 1992, almost 38,000 teenagers went to his funeral, attesting to the popularity of his protest songs against school regulations.[23] Hayashi Takeshi, a young veteran of school rules in his early twenties, has become a youth hero, having written several books on the subject of regulations—popular illustrated books protesting such inhuman and insulting rules. They are instant bestsellers.

In one of his books there is a satirical photo essay: a middle-school girl performs perfectly at school, obeying every rule. Her uniform is spotless, her badge pinned to exactly the measured spot, she greets her teachers in the prescribed manner, raises her hand in class at exactly the right angle from her body, and places her materials on her desk in the manner required. On the way home she daydreams, reviewing what a good day she'd had, and suddenly finds herself in the middle of the road, with a van bearing down on her: quickly she reviews in her head the rule handbook, and discovering that there is no school rule on this situation, does nothing. She reasons, if there is no rule for this, then it must be all right; the school would have a rule if there were some danger. She is killed.

In fact, the issue of correct behavior and discipline is in limbo in Japan. Parents of young teens do behave differently with their children than did their own parents—they are now more like friends than parents—and clinicians have noted a lack of direction and a "softness" among young people. But most do not see them as at risk to themselves or to others, as one author recently put it, they are a "kinder and gentler generation."

Further, since childrearing customs in Japan are based on the idea that going against the child in any way is counterproductive, adults are not intrinsically seen as oppressive authority figures by children. Japanese adolescents generally have very positive relationships with teachers. Training for adult relationships and responsibilities is actually conducted more in the peer relationships of classroom and activity group, and social ethics are learned, as we shall see, in the junior-senior hierarchies institutionalized in such peer groups, rather than from adults.

The surprise for Americans, assuming high discipline and adult control in the Japanese school, is that behavior is trained more by peers than by teachers and the administration. This is not a formal curriculum established by adults, but a constantly renegotiated and student-perpetuated system, built in and reinforced by generations of students passing down the rules to the next group. It is in the senior-junior relationships between children that the culture of hierarchy is reproduced.

Sempai-Kōhai: Learning Hierarchy and Responsibility

When a child chooses a club, he or she initially chooses it because friends are making the same choice or because of an interest in the activity. In some high schools, a child may also follow in the footsteps of older siblings or family connections, who act as "Old Boys" or "Old Girls" in clubs, as alumni bringing in appropriate new recruits, reinforcing the existing structure of obligation and hierarchical responsibility in senior/junior relationships, called *sempai-kōhai* relationships. All activities and duties in the club, whether it is focused on computers, comic books, or volleyball, are played out within this relationship.

The freshmen, the new recruits to a club, experience this most fully: everyone is their *sempai,* and they are senior to no one, *kōhai* to all. Entry into any new group in Japan means beginning as a blank slate, to be filled with the customs and rules that set the group off as a unit. Learning these rules is the *kōhai* obligation: teaching them falls to the *sempai*. This lesson is not an abstract principle of obligation, a kind of ancestor worship of the living, but rather a curriculum of detailed, concrete, minute, procedural aspects of behavior that must be understood to be a successful member. *Sempai* customarily require of their *kōhai* very precisely tuned observance of the niceties: the junior members learn quickly to bow at the right angle, to deliver greetings in polite language (*keigo*) to seniors, even when they meet by accident on the street. And far from seeing these details cynically as strategically necessary to be accepted, children also understand (or try to) that being wholehearted about them is important: it can't "work" unless you mean it sincerely.

A freshman in high school who joined a boys' basketball club as the freshman manager, has a job for the club similar to that of an office lady in a large company office—she anticipates team members' needs, makes tea, and runs errands. She writes in her diary of her conscientious attempts to please, her desire to learn, and her organized approach to her responsibilities:

> A junior, vice-captain of our club, said to me, "You make very good tea. Better than the junior manager's." I'm happy. I will do my best to make good tea again, and also, I was happy that N-sempai, our captain, talked to me for the first time. . . .

> WHAT A MANAGER DOES
> Cleaning the members' room (folding their clothes and sweeping the floor)
> Making tea (5 kettles, 3 tea bags and 3 Tb. of sugar for each kettle)
> Then later fixing lemon or milk tea putting lemon juice which we buy at the supermarket or powdered milk in it
> Go to watch training
> Collect club fees

> I will make every effort to be a model manager.

The next day, concerned that her iced tea wasn't successful, she fished for reactions from a senior and gathered that indeed it wasn't cold enough. She says to her diary, "OK, I will bring more ice tomorrow." And on the train home, she noticed that almost all the passengers in her car were her club *sempai*, and she bowed her head deeply, looking down self-consciously. She examines her motivation for being so "shy and dark" and says, again to the diary, "OK, next time when I see my sempai, I will say goodbye with a smile on my face." She means it.

The girl quoted earlier who suffered at the grading of the badminton coach also reported that there are problems in her club between juniors and seniors. In her club, the second-year students are resisting the authority of the third-year students and so are *not* performing their own duty to be strict and train the first-year students well. Instead, as an act of rebellion, they are spoiling them through indulgence and informality, not expecting formal address, errands, or menial duties from them. This indirect act of resistance was making everyone uncomfortable.

For the student living in a private high school dormitory, the obeisance due to one's seniors is often harsh. What Americans and British call hazing and fagging have also been a tradition in Japanese private boarding schools.[24] One boy in a boarding school emphasizing athletics says that his dorm mates tend to work problems out physically:

> "We often fight, and they often make me cry. . . . Even though I was told I'd only last in the dorm for three months, and others are dropping out, I'm still here—but the sempai are frightening."

In his school, the sempai have a special way of tormenting younger students, making them "do performance." This means mimicking a pop star and singing or dancing, on demand. He says it is not so terrible, and when you sing, the seniors applaud and support you.

Learning Friendship: Defining the Self with Others

In high school, sempai/kōhai relationships vary depending on whether a student belongs to a "hard" or a "soft" club. Athletic groups are likely to be "hard," cultural groups to be "soft", and the degree of formality required and intense supervision by sempai is greater in hard clubs. One senior opted out of a soccer club but was pressured heavily, even by teachers, to stay. He left and joined what he calls a "loser group," made up of "softies" (yawarakai—sissies or wimps) who practiced folk music together. It was the rigorous hierarchical relations of the soccer club that made him uncomfortable.

Such a high school student is not likely to count club sempai or kōhai among his close friends. As one girl said,

> When you are not doing club activities, there is really no relationship with sempai . . . it's almost like it's better not to have anything to do with sempai. First year students would rarely approach the classrooms of second or third year students. If you do run into your sempai, you *have* to smile and say hello nicely . . . and if you don't the sempai might be nasty.

In elementary school, a child may well have played in mixed-age groups in the neighborhood, with no special distinction drawn between children of different ages, but once in junior high school, the older children become the *sempai*, and the younger have to behave like good *kōkai*, avoiding any sign of informality and impoliteness. In fact, friendship is rather closely correlated with similarity of age and experiences, so a same-age classmate is the most likely candidate for close friendship. We will look more closely at friendship in Chapter 6 but it is here important to see that school-based friendships also, like *sempai-kōhai* relationships, make their demands on the teen.

Teens report two kinds of friends, typically: *shinyū* or *mijika na tomodachi*, and *nakama*. *Shinyū* or *mijika na tomodachi* are what an American teen would call "best friends," while *nakama* are "group friends," or a gang, clique, or plural buddies. A best friend (you can have several) is universally defined as someone to whom you can say anything, with whom you can be yourself, while the group friends are where you learn the rules of teamwork—where, in contrast to best-friend freedom, you learn what the group wants you to be like and how to suppress or change to conform to the group and its leadership. Noticing such distinctions and playing them out in "friendship training" alerts teens to the demands of socialization, to the *honne/tatemae* distinction that governs much of Japanese life.

The Japanese teen is, by the end of middle school, acutely aware of the distinction between private propensities and values on the one hand and correct social performance on the other. He or she knows now that behaviors and expectations are situationally determined. Being a good friend to one's best friend is a simple act of love and care; in a larger group or club, it means observing explicit social codes. American teens too are aware of this, but they see more often the distinction as disillusioning: their sensitivity to what they see as hypocritical is conditioned by a cultural norm which favors "being yourself" over an accommodation to others through self-discipline and sensitivity. Adjustment to others then is a problem, and if others are a group, another cultural norm kicks in, which favors the individual, or one-to-one relationships, over a group. (Consider the negative implications of the stereotypical word "groupism" as Americans apply it to Japan.)

American teens see these social codes as embodied in adults and their institutions; Japanese learn them from peers. Both see a difference between "off-duty" behavior and the demands of their societies, but American youth tend to mark the existence of this difference as evidence of hypocrisy (and, indeed, hypocrite is one of the worst epithets an American teen can hurl at adults); while young Japanese tend to accept it as a necessary social construction.

Friendships, both one-to-one and group, play out in the realm of school. Children see each other most in, before, and after school, and the playground gossip, surreptitious note-passing and other slight interactions at school take on much meaning, even though they occur in the interstices of a busy school day, or in the limited time allowed for club activities.

It is not surprising to find that the social lessons of school are learned in interactions with peers and that the lessons of the formal curriculum established by adults are reflected in peer group friendship training, or exposed as only social ideology rather than practice. Japanese young people are acutely aware of what they must do to maintain both an integrated self and a viable place in society. They know—most, for the first time as adolescents—that there is a distinction in context and practice, between public and private, ideal and real, inside and outside, and that they must be careful not to ignore the demands of both, not dismissing these distinctions as the product of adult hypocrisy. Being able to enjoy the unconditional support of a best friend, while enthusiastically falling into line in a consensus-minded friendship group may provide some moments of problematic consciousness for some teens, but most manage them without social or psychic discord.

Teens in Japan as in the United States enjoy the creation of codes and typologies: personality types, life-style types, and even study types are part of the lore of adolescence. Recently, in a teen magazine, a typology of Japanese high school students who won't make it to college were portrayed: the pseudo-gangster, the airhead, the gothic romance girl, the loner, and the fashion plate. Japanese teens, like their American counterparts, have their own pop sociology and tend towards such labels. American teens categories of winners and losers, include a wide range: jocks, brains, (or nerds, depending on how anti-intellectual the school environment is), princesses, kooks, and dropouts or druggies, are terms that characterize many school populations.[25] One difference between Japanese and American high schools is that for the most part, it is not uncool in Japan to be college material—though nerds exist there too, that is, people whose study habits may conflict with social obligations.

Is a College Student a Teenager?

Entering college in Japan means acquiring a status, based on the prestige of the school, that will shape an adult career. It does not mean, usually, four years of disciplined hard work, and for many, these years are, as they are called in Japan, a "moratorium," or "leisureland." The most serious part of college life may indeed be participation in club (or "circle") activities, where *sempai/kōhai* relationships continue to train a young person to the demands of adult life.

In fact, the continuation of a rather childlike (to Americans) style is a positive thing, for in Japanese terms, childlike means open and sincere, while "adult" may have connotations of over-socialized, smoothly political in relationships. Even college students usually enjoy dependent relationships, where their "childish" qualities are valued.

Relationship training within college clubs is very important. If you compare the yearbook of an American university with that of a Japanese university, you will see that the typical "popular" American student will have after his or her name and picture a long list of clubs, athletic teams, and student government positions. His or her Japanese counterpart will have only a few, often only one club or activity. This is not evidence of more time given to studies, or of a less engaged, shyer person. Indeed, it is evidence of the opposite: the much valued ability to engage deeply, to commit oneself to one group, one activity. And it *is* more the group, the human relationships, than the activity itself.

One example is a *manga* group, the Manga Kenkyukai, at a prestigious Tokyo university. Manga are comic books, read by every age group in Japan, but especially loved by college students and college-age workers. This club is called *manken* for short. These *manken* members, comic-book fans, follow the careers of noted cartoonists, and read more *manga* than course textbooks. Their activities focus on the preparation of *manga* for the annual College Festival. The Manken room in the student clubhouse becomes a home away from home for the boys and girls who study, draw, nap, eat, play mahjong, and watch television there every day. Being together isn't always focused on manga. Part of the manken recently went en masse to a driver's education camp in the countryside, to practice driving and to study for the driver's test. Being there in the club room is usually more important than attendance in classes.

The sense of responsibility for one's juniors and seniors is well trained in such a group: the use of respect language for students even a year older, and the nurturant care of students a year younger is taught in the group. A group of sophomore Manken members wanted to take the freshmen on a day trip to the countryside, and they were so conscientious about their responsibility to their juniors, and of course concerned with the need to appear competent and cool, that they took a practice trip by themselves the week before to learn the route, places to eat and stop, and all the costs.[26] This caretaking and attention to detail are lessons for adult life as well.

And yet, in relations with adults, college students may continue to be childlike in their dependency. Once a group of students in a professor's seminar came with him on an overnight trip to an inn to discuss their work. In the middle of the night, two of them rattled their professor's sliding paper door and called out *"Sensei, onaka ga suita"* (Teacher, we're hungry), begging like little birds to be fed. This would be very unlikely in the United States, and might be seen as aggressive mockery or harassment. In Japan, this is *in loco parentis* behavior. Universities no more discourage such behavior than do elementary schools, however inconvenienced an individual faculty member may feel. The answer to the question; "is a college student an adolescent", lies in the fact that such behavior, in a system of relatively benevolent nurturant hierarchies, is encouraged throughout life: there is always someone to whom one can *amaeru*, behave in a dependent fashion, asking to be indulged, and college students are no different from any other stage in life.

The great differences between U.S. and Japanese schools in terms of academic experiences, curriculum, standards, and performance should not blind us to the fact that in both, the adolescent is learning how to be a member of society as well as how to be a sexually active adult, a friend, and a mature member of a family. Children discovering themselves and each other even under the templates created by very different and sometimes internally contradictory cultural norms are going through similar processes. As they learn what is expected of them, the self-consciousness demanded and the high sensitivities aroused at this time form a profile of youth that is recognizable in any modern society.

How these social and psychological processes are guided by the pervasive media and marketing strategies driven by economic forces is another part of the story of our commonalities, though the detail is flavored by culture and history in interestingly different ways. Comic books, sneakers, movies, and CDs figure in the lives of teens in both countries, in complement with the institutions of schools as creators of the stage called teenager. In the next chapter, we will see how popular culture, as created both by the consumer industries and by teens themselves, also contributes to the construction of adolescence in Japan.

5
The Material Child

Buying and Bonding

A girl I see every day on the train was wearing a polo shirt by Ralph Lauren. I'd like to buy one. If anyone asked me, how his or other designers' shirts are really different from those with no brand names, I'd be at a loss to answer, but just to have one makes a difference, and it is important.

—First-year high school girl, Osaka

I *can't* stand Dead Kennedys and I'm getting a reputation for being weird because I actually have a Vivaldi cassette in my Walkman. Sometimes I think it is to show off, but most of the time I think I just like the music.

—Second-year junior high school boy, Cambridge, Massachusetts

I don't have a group of friends because if I get too involved, I'd have to spend a lot of money on clothes and movies and stuff. I can't keep up, and I can't talk to them about it. My best friend understands and we just go home together after school.

—Third-year middle school boy, Chiba

Things and friends are very important to the modern teen. Teens express themselves in their clothing and gear, and commune with or diverge from each other along trend and fashion lines. In Japan, consumer industries and the media are especially aware of this marketing secret and provide the child not just with directions and opportunities to buy, but also directly market teen communication and acceptability. For teens of both countries, at any one moment there are several "standard packages" of goods that help to direct and homogenize tastes. But at the same time, in Japan, there is a new, unintended, and opposite side effect: the amplification of distinctions by ability to pay, created by intense marketing, has forced the recognition of economic heterogeneity.

Teens in the United States and Japan both participate in modern material culture as a recently targeted market. In both societies, the relationship between consumer industries and the media on the one hand and the teen audience on the other is interactive: the teens respond and the market listens. The relationship is based on consumption, of course, but the interaction encourages creativity and quality in the production of goods and communication, and predictability in the audience.

There the similarities end: in Japan, the approach is unifocal— relying on a common peer culture to create a uniform market, manufacturers and media may mass-produce and reach most teens. Teens in Japan, however, are tough customers, interested in quality and innovation and, encouraged by producers, reinforce a rapid turnover of trend goods. The fact that teens in *groups* show and choose their styles in unison is in turn reinforced by the market, which encourages a single style for an age group in a single season.

The tendencies to conformity are encouraged also by the use of media and consumer information as *communication* among teens. Shopping as a group entertainment activity is only the last stage of a process by which teens collect and share information on what's in and proceed to adopt a style.

In the United States, the teen audience is more segmented: diversity in the population is recognized and encouraged rather than ignored or minimized in marketing. Urban styles are different from rural or suburban; regional, racial, and ethnic differences may also be heightened by style distinctions and socioeconomic level is also a factor in fashion and media preferences.

The teen market in Japan, then, reinforces tendencies to conformity on a national scale; while in the United States, the market reinforces differences.

In Japan, however, recent changes in the economy and in the experiences of teens in society are breaking up the monolithic identity and treatment of adolescents. Economic changes have produced more awareness of differences in consumer capacity in the population, and increasing academic pressures have created distinctions between children at younger ages, in terms of selection for adult occupational status—and these, too, are related to ability to pay. The market, however, remains still tied to an image of the age group as homogeneous, and mass trends persist. Diversity is seen in the range of quality of goods sold to different segments, not in a range of types of goods, as in the United States.

Affluence has changed young people's lives in a variety of ways. The *dokushin kizoku*, or "bachelor aristocrats," are young people with money and the desire to buy: before the responsibilities of adulthood set in, these young people spend on themselves at an unprecedented rate. While some commentators, looking at these youth, fear that the "work ethic" that has motivated postwar productivity may decline due to affluence, others point to a growing sense among some young people of deprivation in the midst of plenty, a sense contained in the phrase *kareinaru hinkon*—affluent poverty. Those who have the best CD players, the most expensive electronic audio equipment, the fanciest skis, and the top-of-the-line Nissan have small apartments and no time for leisure activities. Among those who cannot afford these things, there is a new recognition of the distinction between the haves and the have-lesses.

The youth market focuses on the fifteen-year-old, a child at the age when differences are a very sensitive matter. The examination system, itself a consumer industry, has extended its pressure down to junior-high school, and children watch themselves and each other in the climb up the ladder, one which is supposedly meritocratic but one which is strongly influenced by the ability to pay for educational support.[1] Any signs of economic distinction hurts: a child who comes to school in shabby clothes, or with a lunch not made by an at-home mother but bought at a 7 Eleven convenience store, is sometimes teased or scorned. This is, of course, very painful.

In their friendship groups too, ability to pay counts. Extra pocket money is needed for the intensive collective shopping excursions which are a primary source of camaraderie among teens. If a child cannot keep up, then he or she may be excluded or may feel shamed.

The expression, "children have six pockets," is used to mean that they have two parents and four grandparents filling their pockets with cash for competitive consumption. But many families cannot provide so easily, and many middle-class mothers are forced to take part-time jobs at low wages to pay for the luxuries their children "need"—lessons in elegant table manners; resort trips; and large water, electricity, and telephone bills as their children shower profligately, keep their lights burning late, and spend hours on the telephone. Many parents are in debt, making term payments on a piano, computer, or motorcycle, all items creating status for their teens.[2]

Consumer Industries and the Teenager: Consumer Generations in Japan and the United States

Japan's emergence as a modern consumer society began in the 1920s[3] when mass production and urbanization expanded. Within the decade, city populations doubled and improved mass transportation allowed for more mobility, within and between cities. Tokyo's circle rail line was completed in 1925, allowing several suburban stops in Tokyo to become central commercial and entertainment hubs, such as Shinjuku and Shibuya. Commercial production became mechanized and focused on mass markets. Further, in the 1920s, leisure activities became an industry as more people were able to afford such luxuries as baseball games, movies, and radios. Consumption itself became a leisure-time pursuit as department stores became attractive places to meet and stroll, and to learn about new products and trends. Newspapers and magazines supported the consumer boom, and especially directed readers to the attractions of foreign goods and styles.

The social category of youth emerged when urban youth began to spend leisure time as well as school time away from home. However, in Japan, school as a universal experience for teens is a relatively recent phenomenon, as middle school was only made compulsory in 1945. For older teens and young workers, the influence of foreign youth cultures led to Japan's version of "flappers," the *moga* and *mobo* (or modern girl and modern boy). Fads abounded, from ketchup to high-heeled shoes and taxi dance halls[4]. However, in the next decade, the effects of world depression, the mobilization for war, and postwar reconstruction, slowed consumer-oriented production. It did not again flourish until after the economic takeoff of the 1960s.

American consumer marketing for youth has followed similar patterns, but the compartmentalization of goods and fads by age has never been as thorough in the United States as in Japan. Cross-purchasing, buying goods intended for a different age group, and broad spectrum marketing, encouraging people of a wide range of ages to buy, lead to a less narrowly targeted advertising strategy in the United States than in Japan. A strong inclination towards acting and looking young in the United States also makes adults cross age lines more frequently.

Postwar development in Japan quickly led to a proliferation of new and profitable consumer market segments. One of these was aimed at young people, and in the boom years of the late 1960s and 1970s, a youth market emerged and continues to grow, divided into several subsegments, chiefly "low teens," "high teens" (roughly, middle and high schoolers), and the new breed (*shinjinrui*), those in their late teens and early twenties.

By the 1980s, marketing for teenagers had become a specialty in advertising companies. Marketing think tanks had been created specifically focused on teens. Japanese marketing has been known for its anticipatory sensitivity to consumers, attracting people by understanding before they do what it is they will need and want. Consumer industries use information both on teens' psychosocial development and on their disposable resources, and so not only anticipate, but dictate, what they will want.

Market Research and Trendsetting

The chief strategies of such marketers is to get close to teens themselves and they use novel methods. Marketing and advertising in Japan, as relatively new occupations, are among what are called *katakana* professions—trendy, nontraditional work characterized by novelty and international flair (thus the word *katakana*, meaning the syllabary with which borrowed foreign words are written). Among market researchers, those studying the teen market are particularly *katakana*, as they work with the most volatile and novelty-prone population.

NHK, the semi-governmental national broadcasting system, also runs a youth-research unit, studying the attitudes and changing media tastes of adolescents. Such agencies attract distinctly creative, unconservative workers, and encourage nontraditional work and personal styles. Even agencies connected to more established companies, such as the Hakuhodo Institute of Life and Leisure, encourage innovation and hire young and cosmopolitan employees, including a significant number of women.

Some such experts, such as Sumio Kondo, associate director of the Children's Research Institute in Tokyo, are unabashedly devoted to children. Kondo, a Tokyo University–trained educational sociologist, sees them as windows to possibilities for creativity and spontaneity lacking in their parents' generation. He maintains a room in his small apartment in Yokohama, where neighborhood children can find toys and soft drinks and television video games, and where, as he says, "they can do things their parents don't let them do at at home." What children need most, he says, is a chance to relax and be themselves, and when they do, you can learn more about them.

Dynax, another marketing think tank, is devoted to teenagers. Seiji Takekawa, its founder, uses networks of teens throughout Japan to learn about their lives and attitudes and has developed innovative ways of discovering the mood of the market. Extending the idea of a teen panel (used by American department-store fashion buyers) to a more inclusive and open-ended club format, Dynax engages over one thousand teenagers in the JHSCCS, or Japan High School Communications Centers. Dynax establishes, through questionnaires and interviews, a typology of consumers based on "psychographics," rather than relying on traditional denominators such as class and region. They prefer analyzing such things as teens' self-image and other psychological measures and then correlating those with more traditional demographics. Takekawa says he used to call Dynax a "think tank" but now he prefers to call it a "do tank," actively engaging young people even in the design and naming of new products.

Dynax acts also as a conduit for peer counseling by teens, connecting them by means of a telephone network throughout Japan. Children can use Dynax much as they do a teen telephone party line (see page 135) to share problems and issues, usually about parents, school, and friends. A young person calls Dynax and records a question or comment, or presents a problem and asks for help. Others call and listen and then record their own comments. They can listen to previous comments as well. Members also produce their own newsletter-magazines, contributing stories, cartoons, letters and, especially encouraged, consumer reports on new products and fashions. Dynax reports that children in their early teens are more open to each other than at any other age, and thus more influenced by each other in purchasing as well. Takekawa says that if teens feel manufacturers are paying attention to them, and are eager to produce what they want, then they will indeed be happy shoppers.

Change and Consumer Generations

Writing in the mid-1970s, Thomas Rohlen observed that the impact of media and marketing of "youth culture" on teens was low in Japan. He attributed this not to low levels in time and resources among teens, but to high levels of parental control and the demands of schooling, both restricting a child's independence and preventing inroads of an active, youth-oriented material culture.[5] It appears now that affluence has changed children's lives more than could have been predicted only twenty years ago. The impact of material culture has changed greatly over a relatively short period of time, as children's resources, marketing strategies, and perhaps children's independence from parental control have changed. This has produced significant differences between generations, even between the two postwar generations.

The diagram shows that in terms of current youth markets, children A whose parents were born before the mid-1950s have two generations of elders who knew scarcity firsthand, and who have tried to instill in their children and grandchildren ideas of conservation and thrift. However, these young people, sometimes called *shinjinrui* or "the new race" (now in late high school and college years) are also the beneficiaries of at least grandparental indulgence, since people now in their sixties and over still do not want to spend money on themselves, but prefer to provide treats for grandchildren. There is a gap between the parents (called *kyujinrui*, "old race"—sometimes "fossils" or "tombstones") who did not in their own youth experience such lavish donations, and their affluent offspring.

There is no such gap between so-called "recovery parents" B, born in the boom years from the late fifties to the end of the sixties, and *their* children B, the *ichigozoku* or "strawberry gang." (The strawberry (*ichigo*) gang refers to a pun on the numbers 1 and 5, (*ichi-go* or 15, the target age of the teen market). Both generations were raised with a full kit of modern goods—washing

CONSUMER GENERATIONS

1930	1947	1955	1960	1973	1980
Wartime mobilization		Reconstruction	Recovery	Oil crisis	Prosperity
Grandparents A		Parents A *(kyujinrui)*		Children A *(shinjinrui)*	
	Grandparents B		Parents B		Children B *(ichigozoku)*

Based on Kondo Sumio, Children's Research Institute, Tokyo (personal communication).

machines, televisions, and audio systems, for example. They share interests in computer games and comic books. These are merged generations, the baby boomers and the *ichigozoku*, in terms of the experience and expectations of material comforts and luxuries.

The phenomenon of the mass generation is now breaking up, in reality and as an idea, and as Fujioka Wakao says, we may now hear more of the "micromasses" or mini-segmented populations.[6] Fujioka persists, however, in characterizing larger-span generations, and calls those people of about forty years of age, the parents of the strawberry generation, the "ants ... who were taught to value work and to struggle toward a goal."[7] Their immediate followers, those now twenty to twenty-five years old (but not yet parents) he calls the "grasshoppers," the trend-oriented "intuition generation ... who prefer play above all else."[8] Older teens, often with part-time jobs and high levels of disposable income, are now the trendsetters for the younger teens who emulate them.

The forces creating such generations, in addition to the cultural inclination to name them at all, are not peculiar to Japan. Our popular conceptions of the meaning of historical experience among age-mates is a little different, however, as we tend to disparage mass characterizations as much as we are intrigued by them. There are some concrete distinctions: in Japan, both age stage and historical generation work to help guide activities and behavior, which are thus more predictable than those of one's counterparts in the United States. In terms of stages, Japanese at sixteen tend to be in school, at nineteen in the work force, at twenty-seven married, at thirty in midcareer or midparenting roles, at 55 retired and in a second job, or finished with most parenting and in new activities. There is much more conformity to expectation of this sort, much less deviation from the norm than in the United States.[9]

Americans have age-related tendencies, but are also likely to behave in other ways—they may marry at nineteen, divorce at twenty-four, wait to have children until thirty-five or even forty, return to college for a degree at thirty, or change jobs at any time. So "age," per se, means less as a predictor in the United States than it does in Japan. Similarly, generation has diverse meanings: a person of the "Vietnam Era" may have been a promoter or resister of American intervention, and a representative of the

1980s "me generation" may be an aging yuppie or an out-of-work automotive engineer.

Americans tend to want to avoid age characterizations, where Japanese seem more comfortable knowing they are appropriate to age-determined norms. America is said to be an "age-irrelevant" society,[10] where we hope to hear "How young you look," rather than "Act your age."

Marketers in America too, however, attempt to create consciousness, not just cater to it, and so we get conceptualizations that assume more uniformity than we exhibit. For marketing efficiency, we are called babyboomers and yuppies, midlifers and grey power. But living up to an image these categories may represent is another story.

Affluence and Media Consumption

The kind of experiences Japanese children have and the degree to which they actually fit this pattern are influenced by region and social class. The media may to some extent homogenize the age cohort, but there is still diversity, and children are more and more aware of these distinctions. While middle-class children can afford the two to three thousand yen per month they spend on magazines, comics, and other print media, the thousands of yen more spent on telephone party lines, *karaoke* boxes, and CD rentals (let alone money spent on the clothing and gear they are encouraged to buy), such purchases are outside the reach of many.

As a generation, these young Japanese teens are wealthier than previous cohorts, for although their allowances average only about three thousand yen per month (about U.S. $24.00)[11] they receive much larger amounts of gift money for major holidays and birthdays, and ask for and get money from parents as they need it. They have an average of $1000 in savings. Rarely do children perform family chores for money, and rarely do those headed for college do part-time work, except in the summer holidays.

The most popular activity among twelve to nineteen year olds is spending money. When we might go for a jog, or to the movies, or a restaurant, urban Japanese of all ages tend to go out to shop as recreation or entertainment. Middle schoolers spend most on small items, snacks, comics, magazines, music tapes, CDs, and stationery goods, and high schoolers spend more on expensive goods. But the majority of middle schoolers also have larger items, such as a radio cassette player, Walkman, Nintendo, CD player, VCR and TV, and an audio system. Grandparents are usually eager to help with such purchases.

American teens spend about half of their money on clothing or personal items and most save none for future educational or other needs. A very small percentage contribute to their family's resources. Most high-school seniors in America have some kind of outside employment.[12]

The *Info-Maniakku:* Learning How to Be a Teen

Both what Fujioka calls grasshoppers (or the new breed, *shinjinrui*), those in their late teens and early twenties, and our strawberry gang, are avid readers. While Japanese teens watch even more television than do ours, they also manage to read more. American teens average 15.8 hours a week watching television, while Japanese teens average 16.5 hours. Reading for pleasure, however, is also greater among Japanese teens: 1.4 hours per week in the United States, to 3.0 hours per week in Japan.[13] Reading as much as they do for school does not seem to put them off of reading for pleasure, and, in fact, the habit of information gathering acquired in school transfers easily to off-duty trend gathering. Magazines provide a source of news critical to the self-image and relationships teens cultivate. They also act as buying guides for teen consumer culture.

Five factors feed Japanese young people's interest in information. First, of course, they read: the very high levels of literacy (close to 100 percent across the population), an emphasis on constant learning, and the influence of what is called a *johoshakai*, or information society, contribute to the quest for packaged data. Second, they are very busy: the constraints on young people's time and space, make reading, whether on buses and trains or in the created privacy of one's bed or room, a prime escape. Third, they have money: the relative affluence of this group allows these children to buy large amounts of print and other media output. Fourth, they value friends: the importance of relationships needing constant interaction and communication gives all media a key role as providers of the information to be conveyed. And fifth, they are the object of consumer media and marketing: the media themselves actively develop the market and reinforce the idea that youth wants to know, and to pass it on.

What Japanese teen media purvey is information, and teens are eager for information on pop stars, clothes, gear, trendy places, and other ephemeral lore. This data becomes currency in the intense exchanges of a group of friends and teenagers become *info-maniakku*. A *maniakku*, in current teen argot, is someone obsessed with a fad or hobby.[14] The media have secured their market of obsessed young teens by offering them information, the currency of exchange in relationships.

There are two kinds of information especially interesting to the teen: first, the predictable, patterned but gossipy information about pop stars, fashion, music and sports, games and fads, and second, explicit instruction and guidance: on being streetwise in Tokyo (for non-Tokyo teens), on relationships, health, sex, and inevitably, on personality and one's future as divined through astrology, blood types, and other indicators. This course in teen life and lore is supplied by the magazines they read.

Magazines

Magazines provide a wide range of information seen as obligatory for success as a communicating teenager. These *infomaniakku* read at least three different monthly magazines and several weekly *manga* (comic books) and pass among their friends magazines borrowed from older siblings as well. Magazines targeted at a particular age group actually have a much wider age range of readership, and the Japanese version of *Seventeen*, like the American one, is read by eleven- and twelve-yearolds, and is mostly neglected by those seventeen years of age.

Girls' magazines tend to be general, either emphasizing fashion or teen pop music stars, or often some of each, while boys read more special-interest magazines, focused on a hobby such as motorbikes, music, or a sport. There is little crossover reading between boys and girls. More college-age boys now read magazines on male fashions, including general goods and other consumer articles as well. Girls use their reading as a catalyst for sharing personal information and feelings, while boys share the concrete information they've learned from their reading.

Girls' magazines are marketed by publishers to keep their audience for life: a young teen will be "enrolled" as a reader of a magazine for middle-school girls and move the reader up a stepped ladder of age-graded magazines, to the oldest level, a magazine for housewives. Kodansha, for example, publishes such a set: *ViVi* for the youngest, *With* (the most popular), for high schoolers, and *Sophia* for the youngest working woman. Magazine House, the company producing *Hanako*, the leading young "office lady" magazine, has also trickle-down readership among younger groups. *Hanako* and its brother magazine, *Popeye*, purvey information on fashion, relationships, trendy goods and sex, to approximately 500,000 readers each per month.

Both boys and girls read to learn what's new in Tokyo, above all. Tokyo is more than New York, Washington, and Los Angeles wrapped into one—it is the style setter for Japanese youth and their Mecca as well. Magazines spread the rapidly changing taste of Tokyo's haute bourgeoisie. Provincial children are well prepared for their school trips to Tokyo. Boys are informed about where the trendy sports shops are, such as the NFL licensed football gear outlet near the Harajuku Post Office, or the Italian bike clothes shop in Aoyama. Or they go to Wave in Shibuya or Roppongi for CDs and tapes, and Akihabara for discount electric goods, following pull-out sheet maps in their favorite magazines. In similar fashion but down-scale, American children from the suburbs also cruise their urban meccas, in groups, going to second-hand record shops, comic book shops, and other specialities, such as role-playing-game shops or science fiction bookshops, but they are more likely to have learned where to go from word of mouth rather than from the media.

Girls from the provinces are also taught to be street- and shopping-wise in their magazines, which offer them similar guides to fashionable areas. The trippers know before they experience it, that ice cream is best at Hobson's, and that a present for someone at home should have Kiddyland or Loft wrapping paper on it. In the spring of 1990, *Hanako* listed eight pages of restaurants that serve tiramisu, an Italian confection, and after that listing, everyone, even Kentucky Fried Chicken and Baskin Robbins, came out with their versions of this sweet.[15] The young people returning home from Tokyo reinforce the lessons by displaying goods and knowledge to those at home, transmitting what's learned in street and shopping training to the hinterlands. Their magazines even alert them to restaurants and shops overseas, as more young people now can afford and indulge in overseas holidays.

Magazines such as *Duet,* for young girls, use a strategy to incorporate a range of the teens' interests. They particularly emphasize personality testing and stress fortunes and horoscopes, with a special pull-out section, made to fit a girl's wallet. They sell competitively because of this specialty, and because they deliberately undercut the competition, selling at 300 rather than the usual price of 350 yen. Editors say that the difference means a lot to a junior-high-school girl, and they know that the audience reads at least two other magazines per month.[16]

Closest to the audience, mission, and images conveyed by Japanese magazines are *Seventeen* and *Sassy,* in America. The functions of fashion and trend goods promotion, self-help and advice provision, and some degree of reader interaction are served by such magazines for American girls. Advice to teens includes data on beauty and health care, and articles on the changing adolescent body and sexuality. How to manage a "crush" on a teacher and how to deal with a best friend who tries to steal your boyfriend are typical topics. There are also articles on music and film stars, horoscopes and letters to the editors, and, though much less than in Japan, some popular social science, based on readership polls—opinions on AIDS education, the environment, censorship in schools—and even more serious, on what *boys* think. American teen magazines, however, are read by a smaller percentage of the teen population than in Japan, and, further, seem not to be "required reading" as an aspect of an information-based communication among friends.

Maga-trends

Magazines help set trends in material goods as well. There is a wide variety of information about friendship, money, fads and presents (if it is near a gift-giving holiday such as Christmas, Valentine's Day, or White Day) offered. Garfield watches, teddy bears, gold heart necklaces, are all apparently welcomed by girls, while boys like clothes, music, and motorbike accessories. Giving to friends is not a casual act for young teens; they need the safety of knowing they are giving the right gift, much like their parents. In the highly ritualized art of gift-giving, Japanese teens are apprentices.

Valentine's Day, like other modern trends in Japan, is not a direct Western borrowing but a culturally calibrated version. On February 14, girls and young women buy chocolates for all the men in their lives, while men play only a receiver role. The chocolate industry has promoted the idea of *girichoco*, or "obligation chocolate," to be presented to male colleagues and employers. For a special friend, heart neckties, heart socks, heart shorts, and this year, a new CD with love songs underlaid with a subliminal message of passion for the listener's unconscious to absorb, are popular gifts. White Day, the answer-gift day for men to give white chocolates and white lace underthings to women, is a month later.

Other trends are actively encouraged: the recent trend toward obsessive personal cleanliness has pushed sales of soap and shampoo. Most Japanese bathe in the evening, but teens now want a morning shower as well and the consumption of special twice-a-day shampoos has boomed. Teens are the largest private consumers of water and these products, and they cause concern for the National Land Agency and psychologists both. Although it has not been explicitly mentioned in public commentaries on the fad, long hours in the bathroom may provide privacy and insulation for the teen living in cramped familial intimacy.[17]

Magazines encourage reader feedback, on every aspect of their lives. In *Olive*, a popular magazine for high school girls, readers write to the "Olive Club," a readers' forum that acts as a kind of exchange diary. Readers send cartoon drawings of their own, surrounded by messages. Some send short stories or anecdotes, and some essays on "my future," or "let's make the world green." Readers thus simulate the communications of friendship groups and exchange diaries in the pages of magazines whose editors are well aware of the marketability of this "intimacy." American teen magazines tend to have standard letters to the editor, and occasionally publish a reader survey on a single topic, like rock stars, or sex.

How to talk is also important, and *ryukogo*, or new slang, is also offered as information as well as tossed into the text without gloss. Divination of teens' personalities and futures is very popular, through typologies of people of different blood types, people in different places in the sibling order, people with different color preferences. Horoscopes in both boys' and girls' magazines are part of every magazine's format and in girls' magazines, *majinai*, or spells and charms, are also a regular feature. These range from a love charm involving dropping lemon juice on a five-yen coin minted in the birth year of the boy in question, then tying it with a red ribbon to the lower right-hand corner of his framed photo, to spells for increasing your allowance. Such spells are described with obsessive precision, for success depends greatly on doing it exactly the right way, just as in other kinds of learning in Japan. One recent charm for middle-school girls assures her that the seating order at the beginning of the new term in school will place her next to the boy she likes. In sections of big cities popular with teens, fortune-tellers appear at night on the streets to serve the same functions, by the light of flickering lanterns, for groups of girls out on the town.

Articles on fashion, gift-giving, and trendy goods echo and reinforce the goods displayed in advertisements. Magazines for older teens display higher priced items, particularly in boys' magazines where cars, motorbikes, computers, televisions and sound systems are advertised. Boys' magazines feature instructional articles on gifts to give girls. Favored presents are very personal, such as lace underwear, or very expensive, such as a necklace from Tiffany's. Regular features in both boys' and girls' magazines include a section on new products with names and addresses of suppliers. Magazines now appear often more like catalogues of goods than general journals, and children use them as reference works to locate products and the shops where they are sold.

Other regular features are doctors' health columns, beauticians' suggestions, and surveys of teen attitudes complete with pie charts and percentages. These reflect both a reliance on specialists and an interest in what is normative in the population, both features of Japanese adult media as well. Expertise in the guise of a professional sympathetic ear is brought into play in many contexts. Much of the information is designed to help a young person be confident in novel situations, whether it is a school trip, buying a cellular phone, or trying a new sport. The magazine-insert how-to manual or handbook has become a media phenomenon, called *manual shokugun*, or manual syndrome; and Japanese commentators, always ready with critical reflections on the next generation, think it points to a lack of confidence and need for detailed direction among youth today, or what we would call performance anxiety. A young person's worst fear is of being *dasai,* uncool, and magazines play on this fear.

Sex and Other Media Lessons

Performance standards being high among youth in Japan today, it is not surprising to find their magazines catering to their need for information on sexual behavior. Schools have only recently provided sex education, and that only vague and allusive, rather than concrete and informational. Magazines have picked up the slack and provide a straightforward perspective, medical and psychological data, and clear, detailed, instructions.

A large pull-out dating manual appeared in the March 25, 1991 issue of *Hotdog,* a mainstream general magazine read by boys from middle school to college. This manual leaves no course in dating uncharted. Before the how-to section there is social science. A typology of young women and interviews with them highlight the results of surveys of what women want, further emphasized in interviews with their fathers.

Illustrated lessons follow in how to make physical moves, and what to expect as reactions, in a series of captioned photographs of a boy's hand on various parts of a girl's anatomy. Whereas we might see this as the objectification and possession of a woman's body, in Japan this is seen as help to an embarrassed, self-conscious boy, anxious to please and not irritate a girl. How to call a girl on the telephone, and what kind of flowers to give to what type of girl are precursors to this section, of course. A section of interviews about "my most embarrassing moment" allows the most awkward young man to feel someone else has goofed too.

CanCam, a girls' magazine, and *Popeye,* a boys' magazine, read by the same age groups as *Hotdog,* have also recently offered pull-out how-to sections on sex. With the same upbeat, uncoy, very technical approach, a lesson in sexual intercourse is offered, in masturbation, in the use of love hotels, or in varieties of female orgasms, whatever the text of the month, replete with the same battery of survey results and interviews as in the dating manual. The emphasis is rarely on saying no, and seldom on safety, although the use of condoms is illustrated with advice on putting them on in a pleasurable way. It is no surprise that Benetton's recent controversial ad, a double page spread of brightly colored condoms, was readily accepted in teen magazines in Japan, while it was rejected in most American magazines for older readers.[18] An article for boys on "Let's have adult sex" emphasized sensitivity to one's partner, suggesting that sex should not immediately be followed by smoking or watching baseball on TV.

CanCam's recent issue on sex was immediately followed by a special issue on how to conduct a successful *omiai*, the arranged meeting of prospective spouses, so that the social and physical aspects of relationships seem quite separate. The openness about physical aspects of sex should not persuade us that social, public sexuality is condoned. This distinction was echoed in interviews with the director of a sex clinic for teenagers in Kobe, where confident sexuality, rather than protection, safety, or morality is stressed, but where the responsibilities involved in *social* relationships, quite distinct, are also emphasized. A social relationship is one in which people are connected to a wider network of significant relationships to which obligations of a deep and long-term nature are owed. Young people preparing for marriage enter into a relationship that is more than the couple itself, with long-term reciprocal obligations to kin implicated as well, and the social or public aspect of their future status as a couple dominates, rather than the private romance or passion they may share.[19]

Magazines, infotainment and education, communication and gossip, are above all merchandisers. But other, more informal media also guide the budding consumers.

Machikomi and Shopping Communication

The streets themselves form a medium. Becoming streetwise in the terms of Japanese youth involves training in *machikomi*, street observation and hanging out. The Harajuku district in Tokyo is an obvious example of a teen-favored *machi*, a public commercial and entertainment area where young people learn what is *naui* (from "now") or cool, what pop stars are in or on the way out, and many messages about personal style and behavior gained through simple street observation. Harajuku is fashionable among young teens, especially children from provincial areas who flock to the dozens of teen-gear shops of Takeshita Street near the station. They know to eat crepes with jam from street stands, or pizza at Shakey's, and they know to go to the tee-shirt stalls in the open-air flea market for pirated Hard Rock Café shirts and leather gear. Harajuku has a mood—upbeat, an age—young, and a price—expensive. It has become in the Japanese press a symbol of youth materialism and contained decadence, for it is near the street closed off on Sunday afternoons for performances by fledgling rock groups, they too mostly from the provinces. These well-rehearsed deviants dance in what one writer calls amiable ecstasy, only slightly on the edge.[20] Tokyo is central to the youth experience and media and Harajuku is the center of the center.

The first stop at such a teen hub is usually the idol shop, the place where magazines and word of mouth has sent the provincial teen for icons of his or her idol, the teen pop star.

Idol-mania

Magazines focusing on pop idols are particularly important to the middle school girl keen for any idol-*joho*, any information she can get about these stars, created for her and her peers.

Passing bits on about one of the cute boys in the latest hit singing group gains a girl status in her group, and magazines compete to provide grist for the teen communication mill. Promotion companies, such as Johnny's Jr, believe that a girl will attach herself to one boy in a group, and that within a girl's friendship group, it is good to have enough boys in a pop group to go around, so that larger boys' groups are deliberately created to suit the needs of girls' friendship groups.[21] Since the characters of the stars are mostly PR constructs to begin with, revelation of information about them is easily choreographed, for rarely do pop stars cut loose from their handlers enough to create news on their own.

No detail is too trivial to be passed on to the thirteen- to fifteen-year-old. The editors of *Duet* magazine, a typical middle-school girls' idol monthly, with about 500,000 circulation, says constant renewal of the idol industry, with *shinjin* (new faces), is absolutely essential to the survival of the teen magazine industry. You can exhaust the detail about any one person or group very quickly, and fans are hungry for idol-*joho*, star facts, to pass on to their friends. Editors say the Japanese child is "professional" about such information-gathering. While we might call what they receive "infotainment" rather than information, it is taken seriously by young people.

According to *Duet* magazine studies conducted every month through a mail-in questionnaire in the magazine, readers want stars who are like themselves, the girl or boy next door, role models rather than distant or exotic fantasy objects.[22] What readers want is information on what they do to relax (sleep and watch TV), where they go on holiday (skiing, or to Hawaii), how they feel about their parents (my mother is my best friend), and about school (I wish I had more time to study so that I can get into a good high school). The stars' monthly horoscopes and their blood types are always mentioned. Both are popularly considered keys to personalities and moods, and young people often ask each other their blood type much as some Americans ask for astrological signs. Some introduced themselves to me in their diaries and essay by first giving their blood types.

Idols are usually very young rock singers and dancers. They are created by promotion companies, promoted and dropped in a predictable pattern. *Kawaikochan* (cute kids) dominate. At any one time, a typical stable of stars includes a young boys' group, made up of cute and bouncy *bishonen* (cute guys), a single cute girl (*burikko*), full of energy and virginal sweetness, a lonely boy, appealing and wistful, begging to be mothered, a "wild boy", harder-edged but still haunted and romantic, and a tougher greater group, usually in leather but not too risqué. All performances are meticulously choreographed so that magazines can precisely reproduce the hand gestures that inevitably accompany songs, and fans can emulate their heroes. These acts have two or three years of stardom, during which the market is glutted with their music and memorabilia feeding into *machikomi* culture through the idol shops.

Idol shops cluster in popular teen districts and sell everything from pocket mirrors to sweatshirts to *noren*, the traditional doorway curtain, now in neon polyester with the image of a star on it. You can also get your idol on toothpaste or a packet of instant noodles. Addresses are listed in the magazines.

The magazines run fan clubs and convey letters in their pages, including cute home made cartoons by readers. Telephone numbers for recorded idol gossip are provided. One writer is assigned to each star's press club and acts as a surrogate for the readership. Communication back to the idols is important too: it is a two way medium.[23] Idols also "speak" directly to the readers with solidly predictable advice about being loyal in friendships and hardworking at school. And about holding onto that dream about a special someone.

Occasionally, as in *Potato* magazine, there will be a featured interview with a star, with the interviewer (a young girl) acting as a stand-in for the reader, who can vicariously enjoy her proximity to the idol—but the reporter is clearly herself a giggling fan, with no threateningly exclusive intimacy with the star. In the United States, *Sassy* and *Seventeen* use the same device to promote the same feeling when reporting stars' activities. The *Duet* editors said that their only taboo area is the idols' sexual or love relationships, because girl readers might lose interest if a male star were to be involved publicly with someone: the reader must be able to fantasize that the star is free to be with *her*. American magazines like to report on the stars' love life, with some restrictions, of course.

The American pop star industry also, of course, tunes in to the audience, but as in other teen consumer areas, it is not as uniform, nor as rapid in its turnover, as its Japanese counterpart. Also, while certain American groups recently appear to be as "constructed" for teen consumption, as the younger "idols" in Japan, for the most part our pop stars are part of a wider entertainment market, and the appeal is less by age than by style and taste. Movie stars may be more age-graded than are popular music performers, for Keanu Reeves and others appeal to girls of *Sassy* readership age, while, except for Debbie Gibson and New Kids on the Block, most pop music stars span several age groups.

Naui Goods

What teens learn next in Harajuku or like shopping locales is fashion trends—where to get what is "naui" or "now" gear. Metallic gold anklets worn over dark panty hose with corduroy shorts are a recent spring fad, but the black flat-brimmed hat of last season is out. Some girls reported that they do research on trains, and deliberately take one "viewing" trip to the shops before buying. In their diaries they record what people are wearing. One girl's entry: "We just went for fun today, to watch people in

Shibuya and look at the shops." This was accompanied by a series of drawings of fashions seen, with appraisals of which ones were on her list to buy.

Obviously, the next step after observing is buying: and this involves shopping training. Those now in their middle teens learned from their parents to look for name brands, and only the older ones learned from their mothers what quality in clothing means. Teens shop together, for the most part, and learn from each other as well as from the presentation of goods in the shops. This is particularly true of middle-school children who spend more on possessions, while older teens spend more on socializing.

Shopping communication also involves learning about quality. Most teens simply rely on brand name, on known DC or "designer and character" goods. "Brand" is very important, to the extent that a current slang phrase for the most desirable "catch" is a *"burando no otoko,"* or "brand guy." Even teen members of motorcycle gangs, big spenders on hardware to modify their bikes, are conscious of the quality and status of brand names and would not skimp on generic or cheap wheels or other accessories.[24] Teens equate high price with quality, especially Tokyo middle-class youth who may eschew the gaudy stalls of Harajuku side streets for the pricier boutiques of Harajuku, Roppongi, and Aoyama. Shibuya is a fashionable section of town for both goods and entertainment. You have to be dressed right even to go shopping for clothes there. This season, one must be *Shibu-kaji*, "Shibuya-casual", to fit in.

Teens in Shibuya, especially first- and second-year high school students, (before the full pressure of the exams hits) cruise in groups, even spending the entire night outside. In Shibuya these groups are called—in English—"teams," and have names such as Jam Banana, Venus, and Funkies.[25] These are usually single-sex groups, who go to bars and dress alike, some rather like flower children of the 1960s.

Once a fad has caught on, it hits the whole age and gender. A new release in a popular computer game series can create near hysteria among junior-high-school boys, as does a new release of a New Kids on the Block disc among American girls. When new Dragon Quest games (a very popular fantasy series in Japan) are released, boys cut school to be in line at the shops to buy them. Because schools and parents protested, the most recent release was put back to a Sunday, instead of Monday, and a prerelease mail-in lottery for permits to buy the game was established to control mobs and distribution.

The duration of a trend among middle schoolers has become very short—most importantly in the communications media, for tapes and CDs are out of fashion quickly, leading to the popularity of the CD rental shops. Even for a child who has a more durable interest in a particular fad, there is pressure to drop it. One boy, proficient at skateboarding, said he was sad that it was over as a fad: "Only our generation does it now; younger ones don't like it." Kondo of the Children's Research Institute calls this a kind of "trend slavery" in which children are forced to keep up with a fast-paced market.[26]

Novelty "trend goods" are the least durable, and so rapid in their run through the market that the distinction between Tokyo and the hinterlands is exacerbated. A fad may touch high school youth first, and then trickle down to middle- and elementary-school children, but when it has done so in Tokyo, it is just becoming popular among high-school-age youth in the provinces. In 1990, a sunflower motif was so popular it spawned a teen "sunflower culture," but by the time it reached high schoolers in Gumma Prefecture, their peers in Tokyo had scorned it. Whatever was "in" in Tokyo, however, was cool in Gumma. Rapid obsolescence in Tokyo makes it hard for children in the provinces to keep up.

Children are trained young by Japanese department stores. While American department stores reach out to teens with "teen panels" and occasional modeling competitions, Japanese engage children practically from birth in the consumer community. Millie Creighton has described the life-course involvement encouraged by large department stores. She notes that women can enroll their newborn infants in infant shopping clubs, making them eligible for premiums and prizes and shopping credits as they purchase.[27] Another new phenomenon is the children's mini-mall, a coordinated group of boutiques within a department store, selling children's clothing, toys, educational products, sports equipment, and even such services as barber shops and opticians. The most recent, Dr. Kids Town, has appeared in several locations. It is laid out like a small village, with boutiques designed like small houses along a footpath surrounding a "village square" where play activities are available.

What older children buy is also influenced by the department stores, where large displays of novelties attract teens. In 1990, a most ephemeral fad was promoted in such displays—large Mylar bags of helium called sometimes "Duck Voice" and sometimes "He." One boy reported "We went to buy He. You inhale it and speak, which makes your voice sound higher than usual. We burst our laughing. We shared the cost. It is very popular now, though it only lasts a few seconds." Five hundred thousand were sold in the first month, for 500 yen apiece. Other small items, all decorated with theme images and characters of the season, sell fast. There is often an animal motif, such as Snoopy, or Hello Kitty, and inevitably they are *cute*.

Kawaii Culture: Cuteness Is All

Cute is not a concept restricted to children in Japan, though it means childlike and sweet, happy, and upbeat—and vulnerable, something to be taken care of and cuddled. Japanese adults are said to revert happily to such a state, and even macho truck drivers have cute mascots hanging from their mirrors. Childish cuteness soothes and provides a release from adult responsibilities.[28] Teen pop stars are most often *kawaikochan*, cute kids, and a recent top TV show is "Chibi Maruko-chan," a cartoon family situation comedy, whose central character is terminally cute. Her image is on a wide range of products, just as is Bart Simpson's in the United States, but she and Bart are very different. He represents the cynical, rebellious antihero, and she a bumbling but lovable, everykid kind of mediocrity.

The character items that fill the rooms and schoolbags of middle school children tend toward a pastel, sugary sweetness that seems to be outgrown in the United States by the age of eight. In fact, the Sanrio novelty company found in a market survey that their items sold to Japanese girls between the age of five and the time of marriage would be bought in America only by girls from four to seven years old.

The marketing of cuteness has created a seemingly endless flow of products. Every season there are new characters and instant replacement. Renewal and change are of course established principles in Japanese culture, but here we are talking of market opportunities, fed by affluence, competition, and a need to capture the buying power of this age group. Because Sanrio and other novelty companies are aware that the *kawaii* culture spans several age groups, they market widely. However, the fact that a leading fad in Japan tends to saturate the population means that there is less possibility for a variety of items to share the market. A new product has to be marketed aggressively and its cuteness is the leading edge of the campaign. But cuteness is also safe and predictable; it doesn't test the margins of acceptability and provides a teen and industry stamp of approval.

The fact that cuteness sells only to Americans under seven years old is only one clue to our different fads. There is a range of fashion and goods trends in America, less easily characterized by a dominant style or quality like cuteness. The differences range along several dimensions:

1. First, American styles themselves are different: cuteness sells less and toughness or flashiness more.
2. Second, no one style is disseminated across the teen generation: urban/suburban, regional, ethnic, racial, and class distinctions create different styles.
3. Third, a style or fad has a short duration but may hold on longer depending on the tastes of a teen subgroup: thus, the trajectory of a given fad may locally depend on tastes and consensus not subject to the movement of the market. Just as in Japan, however, there may be macro- and micro-trends in teen tastes and marketing.

While American teens too like to shop, and a proclivity for hanging out at malls is characteristic of the suburban teen, they learn how to look and dress from each other rather than from displays in stores or magazines.

Dress follows other distinguishing characteristics of teen subgroups: rappers have a distinctive style, as do punks of various types, "Euro-punk" or "down and dirty," and versions of cowboy and country styles also characterize some teens. As in music, there is no one "total market" for the teen in America.

Dress Code

Most Japanese teens attend school in uniform, and so their fashion sense is expressed after school and on weekends. But there are subtle touches one can give even a nineteenth-century European-style uniform to make it cute or rebellious—if you don't go too far. School regulations in some junior- and senior-high schools forbid changes to the uniform, and penalties are sometimes severe. But in practice, especially in schools with a preponderately non college-aspiring population, styles are more various. On a rural or suburban train in the late afternoon, a sample of safe tailoring and accessorizing may include pegged pants with wide harem-style legs for boys (*henkeizubon*, or *bontan*, "modified pants"), lengthened or shortened skirts for girls, too-tight jackets for boys, permed bangs for girls and 1950s greaser-style pompadours for boys, and shoes (apparently not covered in many codes) with neon-colored laces and broken backs. The more extreme hairdos and uniform adjustments tend to appear among children of lower-income groups. Some particularly *furyo* boys might wear women's mule sandals or wooden clogs (*geta*), along with sideburns and shades, even with a full school uniform.

Macro- and micro-trends in Japan are learned from the street, the magazines, and the shops themselves. The rapid dissemination of style news, on a *national* basis, means that teens everywhere in Japan may choose from the same macro-styles. Macro-styles have a longer term than do the details which may change in a month. One tuned-in girl, living in Hiroshima far from fashion central, bemoaned the fact that a new item might take three weeks to reach her town, almost too late to be fashionable.[29] These styles are basically in two categories: cute and rebellious. Both boys and girls can be either, and there are subset styles for each. The range of styles does not imply individualism, for Japanese children, like Americans, prefer to dress in clothing acceptable to their peers, but the range does offer the peer group a choice.

Each style has an *haute* and a discount version. Even the down-and-dirty looks may be worn by affluent youth spending high on expensive leather or artfully designer-ripped jeans, while their low-cost equivalent will be bought on the cheap with no designer labels, from stalls under the tracks. While brands are still important, a new fad for generic clothing, expensive but label-less, has been growing.

Current trends include styles such as babydoll cute, sporty, preppy, punk, or *furyo* (gangster, Japanese style), and micro-level trends are the details, such as seasonal colors, hairdos and accessories, and makeup, although of course details are also tied to the style of choice.

Hakuhodo Institute of Life and Leisure and INFOPLAN, another marketing research group, identified macro styles which have had some endurance. Cute styles are bright for boys, lacy for girls, and boyishness is accentuated by wearing shirts and pants deliberately too large. Girls laciness is *not* in Japan Madonna-punk lace, but rather First Communion lace—but with a perky falseness, a look sometimes called *burikko*, or false-innocent. A caricature of a burikko girl has a high-pitched voice, giggles helplessly when addressed, and squeals *"kawaiiiiii!"* (cute) or *"iyaa!"* (I hate it) when asked her opinion of a boy, a new soda drink, or a cartoon on TV.

Cute boys in Japan deliberately look goofy and sweet, and make what one American teen calls "Bambi-eyes" at girls, begging for indulgence like puppies, not meaning any harm, evoking nurturant responses rather than sexual ones. Cute boys and girls both may use makeup, but keep to pale tints and natural tones. Schools almost invariably forbid makeup, so even these light cosmetics are relegated to weekend or evening use. Makeup kits for young teens resemble American children's play makeup kits and obvious makeup is rarely seen.

Boys and men are a new and growing market for makeup in Japan. Male teens buy facial packs and may wear foundation makeup for ordinary occasions. One college girl said that she was surprised to come home to find her high-school-age brother listening to tapes as his green facial mask dried on his face. Salons receive many requests for chest, arm, and leg hair removal from young men who believe that girls prefer hairless males. Girls say a boy is an "animal" if he has a lot of body hair. Pop stars are almost always smooth-skinned.

At the other end of the cuteness to nastiness continuum are high punks, rappers, and gangsters, though it should be noted that for the most part these are "baaad" styles (in the American approving sense) rather than evidence of bad *behavior*. Just as the Yoyogi Park Sunday dancers are in costume, so the neighborhood punk fashions are part of a performance as well. Punk ranges from an *haute* punk, expensive Italian leather and stylishly outlandish Madonna and hard metal outfits, to cheaper, home-riveted torn jeans and Korean leather jackets. Both affect unusual colors of hair, but the more conservative youth color with wash-out tints, removable in one rinse in a public bathroom.

Punks of both sexes vie to create artistic to aggressively repellent facial makeup effects with cheek stripes and ghoulish green-grey eye sockets—not at school, of course.

Recently it has been fashionable among teens in Japan to dress "black," meaning in the fashion of black rappers in America. Boys who dress like M. C. Hammer are called, for example, Hammer-O-Kun, and girls are called Bobby-ko-Chan, for Bobby Brown. Most of these fashion followers wear high Reeboks and baseball caps, baggy sweatpants and shiny jackets. They sing along with rap music in concerts and shout "fight the power" with raised fists, but as one commentator noted, "they've no idea that the 'power' is the social system that American blacks are resisting."[30]

The middle ground in the spectrum is given to a variety of what are called "neotraditional" (to an American, preppy) or sporty looks, with some outer fringes given to a toned-down rastafarian style, with yellow, red, and green colors and knit dreadlock caps, or a sixties-American ethnic/hippy look with Indian-bedspread cloth skirts or two-piece Chinese or Thai cotton suits. Some very advanced young men are rediscovering the kimono, which they may wear with an unorthodox dark turtleneck sweater, in a swaggering devil-may-care manner. This is actually more likely to turn heads and offend the older generation, than is the donning of Hare-Krishna-style orange drapery.

The surfer look is seasonal, though it is not confined to those with access to real waves, for styles are images that have little relation to actual activity. Girls' clothing seems recently to be schizophrenic: featured undergarments are romantic and sexy, and outer garments are sporty, boyish, and cute—in the sense of childlike. Baseball caps on backwards, oversized men's shirts with tails flapping, high top sneakers typify one popular "little boy" image. Another is a combination of punk and gypsy, with mixed patterns and colors, and fringes, ribbons, and torn edges on many-layered outfits.

The latest in fashion typologies may be that of 1992's casual styles, though one should assume that the names at least will be superseded as a new marketing season approaches. The styles are relatively stable, however: denim-casual, a funky sort of American casual; *furugi* (old gear), a deliberately down-at-heel style; mods, a leatherish but clean and sharp sort of look; hard *ame-kaji*, or American biker, tough and aggressive looking; club and skater, skateboard and street kid, but not dangerous-looking; and *kire-kaji*, this season's version of neotraditional or preppy.[31]

Fashions do indeed change in Japan, usually, as in the United States, initiated by the industry and encouraged by the media. There is, however, usually a teen leader in a clique or school who acts as the bellwether, leading the pack in getting the new season's gear. Usually in Japan, teen friends shop together, and move on to a new style in a cluster. Innovations that are less market and more individual are initiated by testing them out on your friends first.

In America as well as Japan, urban teens set the pace. The Dr. Martens punk-military boots popular over the past ten years among urban youth have now moved to the suburbs, and urban fashions now include a plaid lumberjacket, black baseball cap on in reverse, and Timberland boots.

Fashion among teens in both Japan and the United States is less a vehicle for the expression of individual taste than it is for the expression of an accepted style. But in Japan, and anywhere, I would suggest, these are not in opposition. The goal is not to establish oneself as an autonomous and idiosyncratic individual, but to learn what's done and do it, or in some cases, to lead the others to a new style. A Japanese teen, who has lived in America said, "While in America people enjoy dressing with individuality, adapting styles to their own tastes, and calling attention to themselves, in Japan it is a bad thing to stand out from the crowd: you just stick out like a sore thumb."[32] Being an individual in this sense in Japan means selfishly making others uncomfortable. She continues: "At first . . . this homogeneity is stuffy, but after a while one finds it pleasant to be among people properly dressed. In effect, fashion in Japan is a group-oriented thing."

In America, too, teen dress is governed by peer, not individual taste and is an expression of the transition from parent to peer orientation. Psychologists advise American parents to allow children to control their own attire, and to guide them only on the possible negative outcomes of too many nose rings and earrings and other long term effects of radical personal style changes. Such fashions change rapidly and one season's criticism may be obsolete in the next.

One fashion that has become perennial in Japan is the reading of a *manga*, and for boys especially a comic book is almost part of the uniform.

Manga

By bulk, *manga* (comic books) are the most read of Japanese print media. The income of Japan's comic-book producers is greater than that of the world's largest steel company. *Manga* are an old phenomenon with roots in the seventeenth century, and earlier, but became mass reading only after World War II. The largest seller, *Shonen Jump*, sells 5.7 million copies per week, to boys and men from elementary school to the work force. Its nearest competitor sells 2.5 million copies per week. *Mimi*, a girls' comic, has sold about 1 million per week. Most manga, however, are sold to particular age groups and there is a large variety of comics. There are weekly comics, serialized comic stories in magazines, collections of serials later produced as separate books. The weekly comics often have about 400 pages, printed on cheap recycled newsprint, with few color sheets. They are everywhere, in bookshops, newstands, department stores and supermarkets, and there are always browsing copies in coffeeshops, banks and any waiting area, such as offices and hospitals. They are read by people in all walks of life, and read anywhere: standing at a book shop or on the train, sitting in a park, even walking on a crowded street.

Teens read *manga* in great numbers. Most read two or three per week. Readers rip through them at an average pace of ten pages per minute. As one teen said, *manga* are like portable television sets, with soap operas, comedies, action, and drama. They give relief from reading for school and exams since *manga* have relatively few words. Teens also read to share with others, just as they read magazines for communicable lore: you need to know what the heroes and villains are up to, and what new twists a serialized plot line has taken. "Owning and reading comic books are (a) means of keeping up the informational dues of peer group membership: if one does not know the latest adventures of salient youth heroes, one has no experience to share with the other members of the peer group."[33]

Girls' and boys' *manga* are very different. Girls' *manga* in all age groups emphasize romantic fantasy, with more realistic school and family situation stories. Human relationships rather than action dominate. There is typically a serialized period romance, often placed in a Cinderella-European setting, fairy tales in which the characters are distinctly Caucasian, usually very large-eyed, blonde figures. Love is the central theme, and star-crossed lovers the most popular, with tragic endings favored.

Mimi, designated for young teens, recently finished a nine-year series based on the *Tale of Genji*, a Heian period novel. This cartoon series is indeed high art, and large portfolios of scenes from it are sold for framing. Its artist was made a star by the series, and Mimi sold one million copies per week for the duration of the tale. There are over three thousand *manga* cartoonists in Japan and they are treated with respect as artists. When mentioning their favorite comic series, children often cite the artist's name.[34] Other themes include problems in relationships at school, problems of friendship and loyalty. One girl said "I like *manga* because they have heroes and heroines I can understand: for example, a club member falls in love with a guy who's really cute."

Boys' *manga* feature drama, action, and violence. Large themes of good against evil are played out in samurai and Western dress, but most have a Japanese setting. Yakuza (gangsters) are key characters, as are sports heroes. Comic episodes are slapstick, and often abusive, the humor turns on one character's making a fool of another. Language is fairly crude and there are many anal references. There seems always to be a character who publicly loses control of his bladder or bowels, and farting and belching appear to be regular forms of communication.

Sexual situations and activity appear in both boys' and girls' comics and many are either violent or slapstick, frequently with anal themes. Young girls in school uniforms are common sexual objects, and in the most pornographic, sadistic violence is typical.[35] Although most readers of such comics are middle-aged men, such adult manga are available in sidewalk vending machines, and teens often read them. Each month, approximately ten million copies of what are called *eromanga*, or erotic manga, are sold per month, and it is thought there are 180 such publications.

Teleteens: Who's Watching What?

The fact that teens in Japan have a lot of homework and read as much as they do does not mean they aren't also watching television. In fact, televisions are on in many homes whenever anyone is at home—which doesn't guarantee that someone is watching, of course. Most parents frown on the practice of doing your homework in front of the television.

Junior-high-school children in Japan are the largest TV youth market, as is true in the United States. The top shows include variety shows and music shows, but pride of place goes to cartoon sitcoms, such as "Chibi Maruko-can" or "Sazae-san," a twenty-four-year hit featuring the misadventures of an ordinary housewife. Action cartoons appeal to boys as do samurai dramas and sports programming. Foreign shows rarely attract wide audiences: "Cosby" and "Teenage Mutant Ninja Turtles" lasted only a very short time in Japan, and "The Simpsons" never appeared.

A new hit genre for older youth, especially the urban young people, is *torendi dorama*, or "trendy drama."[36] In 1991, record ratings were obtained by these light, comic love stories. These are romantic, but have ironic undercurrents and particularly appeal to girls. The stars of these dramas have become heroes and heroines—and are the subjects of fashion features on hairstyle and clothing in magazines.

In the United States, television-watching is the number-one activity among youth at home, and may be to our young teens what magazine-reading is to the Japanese. The teen market is much sought after, and is currently dominated by several shows, such as "Beverly Hills 90210," "The Simpsons," "In Living Color," and "Married with Children."[37] Teens are a small market, but they are good consumers: though they are only 20 million of our 220 million, advertising focuses on the young teen (age twelve to fifteen) as trendsetter, and what is popular with this age group percolates to older teens and to adults.

Because older teens get out of the house more, the fifteen- to seventeen-year-old watches less than the younger ones—either because he or she is working part-time, or engaged in sports or in shopping and "hanging out." Older teens in middle-class families also watch alone more, as they may have their own televisions. Boys watch action adventures; girls watch family sitcoms and romances. Both boys and girls seem to prefer to identify with a character slightly older than they are, giving them a preview of what is coming in their own lives.[38]

Commenting on the leading show on the Fox Network's line-up, "Beverly Hills 90210," Dr. Helen Boehm said that one of their goals is to involve children in thinking about personal and social issues without preaching to them. Presenting them with options for thinking about such matters as sexual activity and drug use, is more useful than dictating behavior. This show is particularly seen as a "public service show," and a recent episode concerning condom distribution in high school was referred to by sex-education experts and politicians as a watershed moment in television education.

Not all the programming watched by U.S. teens is so directly targeted to them, and the range of shows watched includes sports, movies, and for most teens, some MTV—music videos—as a nearly required part of the curriculum. Videos supplement regular television as they do in Japan.

Other media, too, attract teens in Japan.

New Media

Newer, less formal teen media include telephone party lines, the *karaoke* boxes, the continuing practice of exchange diaries, and the institutionalization (by novelty companies) of the old classroom misdemeanor of note-passing.

Talking on the telephone has become a major source of companionship and news for many teens. Their parents note that they themselves rarely used the phone as children, and they are particularly struck with the length of their children's conversations. American middle-class children are the second generation of telephone addicts; in Japan, the telephone was first used only for brief functional exchanges and has only recently become an active source of companionship for both children and adults.

Teen party lines, a new form of *kuchikomi*, of word-of-mouth communication, provide a sufficient removal from—and teasing intimacy with—up to five other young people, usually unknown to the caller, at one's own choice of time and place. A teen joins a conversation often for three or four hours at a time, depending on one's freedom of the telephone and parental permission. Teens whose mothers work are said to be particularly susceptible, as are teens who are not cramming for entrance exams. For teens who otherwise spend leisure time reading *manga* and listening to CDs, this is a chance at least to talk with peers, but the high-tech affluence producing such opportunities carries with it an ironic reinforcement of the solitude and separation characterizing the lives of some young teens.

These party lines are called "Dial QQ," because 0990 is the dialling prefix, and the number 9 is "kyu." There was a sudden expansion in 1990 of the use of this service, from an average of 150,000 calls a month in 1989 to 13,500,000 per month a year later, when the contact area was expanded. Fees are high, ten yen for three seconds.[39]

The amount spent on such calls is particularly stunning. One child said, "Sometimes you do make real friends this way, but should you have to spend over 100,000 yen just to make friends?"[40] One older boy in Osaka was reported to have spent up to $2000 in a month on party lines, but even middle schoolers, using lines mostly in the early afternoon, have spent up to $600 per month. What young teens talk about is similar to what face-to-face friends in groups discuss—stars, fashions, videos, a disco in Hachioji. In any call, you are known only by a nickname you give yourself, and you can change that from call to call. You get freedom from the structures of ordinary relationships, a lack of responsibility, and often the experience of "meeting" teens from other parts of Japan. The calls sometimes become pornographic, either because a line company has hired a young woman to spice up the conversation, or because, especially late at night, older (usually inebriated) men join a line to talk to female teens. There is also a line with sex games in which you can hear the voice of a girl supposedly masturbating and in response to correct answers to a quiz, her voice becomes more intense.

Teens also communicate with each other in "karaoke box" performances. A group of children can rent a small room sometimes a free standing "box" in an empty lot, and sing in turn to the voice-enhancing machine, which makes everyone sound like a professional. The karaoke box provides young teens with a room of their own, and a chance to show their knowledge of the latest hit songs. These tiny rooms appeared around 1984, and were immediately popular as inexpensive entertainment. There are now about 43,000 karaoke boxes in Japan. Recently, however, some karaoke box operators have tried to bar young teens, since there have been incidents of illegal smoking, glue sniffing, and consumption of alcohol, easily obtained from vending machines.

More innocuous media, from an adult standpoint, include exchange diaries, (kokkan nikki), which are a fad at least two generations old. These are most commonly exchanged on a one-to-one basis. There are models for entries published in the teen magazines, and notes on where people can be seen exchanging them (the three-story Mr. Donut in Shinjuku, for example). The *kokkan nikki* is a kind of semi-public diary, almost a letter to a friend, but freer. It has its own conventions. You can write things in your shared diary, however institutionalized, that you might not speak, and thus create a bond of intimacy with your friends. You can also be creative, and most girls like to illustrate them with cartoon figures and detailed drawings of clothing and gear.

Exchange diaries are also didactic, passing on very specific instructions in trends. One girl wrote, with detailed illustrations, "It's popular now to wear this kind of thing on your wrist (picture of narrow multicolored woven tied bracelet). . . . You are supposed to make a wish when you tie it on your wrist and never take it off. It is said that when it comes off, your wish will come true. I saw my friend wear one but it looked strong and on for keeps. She tole me she wore it even in the bath and dried it with a drier to keep it from getting moldy. She really takes good care of it. I saw a boy wear one. That's strange."

The idea of sharing a diary seems like a contradiction to an American teen, who seeks as much autonomous privacy as possible. In Japan, the diary is a medium of communication to increase the intensity of friendship. And the teen novelty industry is on top of this too, with specially manufactured diaries made for exchanges.

Finally, there is the manufacturer-approved custom of illicit note-passing in school. Many students try to relieve tension and boredom with surreptitious communication. This practice is not unknown elsewhere, of course, but what is interesting here is that highly competitive manufacturers do such thorough market research and are so responsive to children's behavior that they create products serving even such ephemeral (and anti-authoritarian) habits as this. Sanrio novelty company, with great market sensitivity, has created a line of special covert notes, decorated with cartoon character designs and even with prewritten messages, for this purpose.

Conclusion

Marketers recognize that teens want to communicate with each other, and that goods and media provide the content for communication. Japanese children are in no way unique in their orientation to peers, and are not unusual either in being the target for consumer advertising and promotion. American teens also seek acceptance from friends and keep up with trends to exhibit solidarity and to communicate with their peers; they, too, are learning from the media and from each other How to Be a Teenager. The Japanese media have a powerful role in cementing friendships but American media would serve the same functions, for better or for worse, for a broader mass of children if our teens had as much money to spend *and* if our educational system predisposed them to reading. We are not surprised to see a cross-over in Japan from academic learning and the absorption of information in school to the leisure pursuits of young people, but the mobilization of the media and marketers to package this information in novel ways provides us with an interesting, almost parodic example of the sensitivity of Japanese industry to needs and custom in its market. The openness of teen media in Japan is also the product of the relatively new loosening of social, cultural, and sexual taboos, along with a wider range for self-expression for teens—especially for girls—than has existed in the past. Whether the teen will be increasingly alone, *hitori de asobu hito*, an isolated member of the "distance tribe," inspiring the developers of party lines, teen home faxes, and other distance communication media, or will continue to find time and space to indulge in more direct and spontaneous relationships with friends, two factors will remain significant, and will be increasingly exploited by the competitive youth industries: the desire to communicate, and the voracious obsessions with goods and information.

Japanese youth are not unique in wanting to be like their peers, but marketing reinforces the uniformity, volume, and pacing of trend consumption. But the market may be ignoring something—that the very qualities it exploits in teens, the intensity of their relationships and the desire to conform, are producing a cohort acutely aware of the economic disparities that increasingly affect some children's ability to measure up to peer consumer standards. While teenagers everywhere are sensitive to differences between themselves and others, as an attribute of adolescent development, the current generation of teens in Japan is noticing distinctions that are socially and historically generated. Without, however, a cultural history of class consciousness, it may be that Japanese youth who are unable to perform as high spenders will, as do youth with other problems retreat into isolation rather than band in solidarity with others who share their problems. However, some groups, such as the *bōsōzoku*, or motorcycle gangs, sometimes appear to express their solidarity in terms of their shared isolation from society. The consumer industries themselves, which have over the past fifteen years focused on youth as their market, may be the driving force behind the rise of such consciousness.

What the economic boom of the 1980s has produced is diversity, and diversity exhibited in and affecting teenagers along several dimensions. The debate over a Japanese identity for the twenty-first century, a *shinnihonjinron*, has produced punditry on the effects of affluence and human resources. A key question in the popular debate is: how can Japan be an affluent (*yutaka na*) society, even a leisure (*yutori*) society, without losing the commitment to work and constant improvement some say can only be learned in the context of scarcity? Scarcity and deprivation certainly exist in Japan, but in the context of a diverse population, scarcity is unevenly distributed and may be threatening rather than motivating to productivity. Teens may force the recognition of the fact that for only one generation, the *kyujinrui*, the hardworking company men, has mobilization around the idea of scarcity been productive, and not all even in that generation have enjoyed the fruits of productivity.

The idea of a universally affluent youth market fueled this drive. It is slightly paradoxical that the age segment targeted by industry should be the one in which children most painfully concerned with the need to be accepted, if not conformist, are still those most conscious of the discrepancies between the *tatemae* and *honne*, the appearance and reality, of homogeneity in Japan. What consciousness there is on the question of the effects of affluence and social class in Japan is created in the testing of similarities and differences in relationships among young people: the outcomes in friendship alliances—or in delinquency—are discussed in the next chapter.

6
Friendship

Best Friends and Group Training

My friend Eriko is a true friend. . . . Without saying a word we can read each others' minds just by looking in each others' eyes. . . . And then there are my group friends: we don't talk about anything deep—we try to avoid problems and just play.

> —First-year student, beauty academy, Osaka, age nineteen

My friends often get me in trouble. There's this one girl who really gets us to do bad stuff to other kids. But they are my friends, and I have to go along.

> —Freshman in high school, Cambridge, Massachusetts

I tell my friend more secrets that I tell my mother. If I tell my mother I have a problem, she will worry, but if I tell a friend, she commiserates with me and tries to solve it. I feel more comfortable telling her.

> —Middle school girl, age fourteen, Gumma-ken

O-kun is one of my best friends. We talk deeply of our views of the world. He is philosophical and looks down on the human race in general. . . . I get irritated at him: how can he deny the meaning of his own existence? My friends who are girls are completely different. They make me feel important and give me good advice.

> —High school boy, age seventeen, Yokohama

There are two sides to me, not contradictory, just by situation. I feel uncomfortable with adults, and I'm a different person with my friends. I know them better, and I'm more like them.

> —Junior high school boy, age fourteen, Boston

Friends are a teen's most important resource, but they provide more than stimulation and solace, in both the United States and Japan. Among American adults, it is thought that teen friendships lead to the dreaded peer pressure (always negatively interpreted to mean the *trouble* adolescents get each other into, simply by being together). Even as teens are encouraged then, by our merchandising to them as an age group and by our sharp delineation of the rights and privileges of age, to think of themselves as separate, their "peer-ing" is seen as dangerous—in another of our mixed messages. For the Japanese adult, teen relationships are not as threatening, for they are seen to provide training in the realities of adult relationships—the constraints of adult hierarchies must be learned young. Friendship, then, complements the lessons of home and school. For teens in both countries, however, friendship and its communications and intimacies are the focus of much of their awareness. Friends influence all sectors of their lives at home, school, and as we have seen, in the consumer market.

In Japan, teens learn about "friendship" in three different kinds of relationships. The *best friend* provides an intimate relationship, a bridge from the unconditional love of the mother to the experiments and responsibilities of friendship among teens. *Group friends* provide standards for peer acceptance, a testing ground for the tensions between a newly emerging sense of self and the demands of a group. The more institutionalized *sempai-kohai* relationships (senior-junior), already discussed in Chapter 4, train teens more explicitly to the structures and duties of group hierarchies.

Friendships among children below secondary-school age in Japan are little different from those of American children. However, Japanese children, even those in the heart of the largest cities, have a kinder and gentler environment and the city can safely be their playground. Japanese children through the grade-school years usually attend school in their neighborhoods, a short walk from home. Even those who voyage further to attend private schools or *juku* outside their area are safe on public transportation at all hours, and still travel, usually, with friends. Students in school uniforms can be seen in pairs and groups on trains and buses any time from the end of the school day until well into the evening, and on weekends, urban children have, visibly, the run of the city. Their counterparts in the United States, more likely to be in suburban areas, would probably not be as experienced in the use of urban transport, and are often not permitted by parents to spend whole weekend days and evenings in the heart of a metropolis. A Japanese child in high school, even junior-high school, may well have taken overnight trips with friends to ski or camp out or visit a tourist spot. High schoolers customarily go with their close friends on such trips, and after they graduate from high school, and as resources permit, may take longer trips overseas, to Guam, Hawaii, or Hong Kong, unchaperoned by adults.

What friends do together in the United States and Japan differs. While American teens have more time to spend together, Japanese teens have more money. Consumer marketing and the pleasures provided by shopping make that, for girls especially, the number one activity done with friends, followed by "talking about the opposite sex," and "hanging out" *(burabura suru)*.[1] Among American teens, the top three activities are "hanging out," "talking about the opposite sex," and going to movies, concerts, and other entertainment. Shopping together ranks lower for Americans, although for many teens in suburban middle-class America, "hanging out" may mean shopping, for at least the locale is often a shopping mall.

In elementary school, in Japan, however, activities with friends are less predictable as children are usually at school or home: children see their friends mostly at school, much less at home or in the neighborhood, unless they happen to live nearby. Elementary schoolmates in public schools tend to go on together to junior-high schools, making for some continuation. Teens value the friends they've had the longest:

> One of my closest friends was with me in elementary school, and in junior high school, but we kept changing classrooms. We're in different high schools, but we are still very close to each other. . . . I don't see her much but we call or write to each other. . . . Even when we don't call, both of us feel that we know each other very well. . . . We don't have to talk, or see each other, to understand each other.
>
> –Senior in high school

As a child enters secondary school, he or she becomes a different kind of social animal because of the structure of school life and the demands of adolescent development. Family life, too, begins to play a different role in the child's life, leaving relational gaps to be filled by friendships. While friends are not direct substitutes for mothers and fathers, who are still by many teens labeled "friends," teens begin to see parents as sometimes problematic, or incapable of providing what the best friend can.

"When I'm with my best friend I feel safe. Talking to her gives me peace. She never gets angry, or tries to get me to change. And she never embarrasses me in public the way my mother does." This statement from a Japanese high schooler could just as well be from an American girl.

However, Japanese children do not always pull away from parents to the extent that American children are said to: an older and wiser college student says, "My friends are my age, so they are just as inexperienced as I am. It's not logical to tell them my problems, so I tell them to my parents instead." Young teens in both countries are in the first stages of a shift from adult direction to peer *(dōryō)* direction. This is more abrupt in the United States, where it may be seen as threatening to adults' control over teens, than in Japan where, in a less oppositional relationship with adults, young teens may have less need to mark the break through an exclusionary shift to peers.

The shape of friendship among Japanese children is that of an hourglass: in elementary school, children cluster in groups of friends; in middle school, groups complement the "best friends," especially for girls; and in high school and college, the tendency is for a wide and shallow friendship group to coexist with very close friends. The activities, emotional tone, and functions of the group friends develop striking differences from those associated with *shinyū* or best friends, as the child gets older. In America, the image describing the friendship "track" looks more like a triangle, with groups in elementary school, smaller groups in middle school, and much more individuated relationships in high school, although, especially for girls, there may be larger cliques also in high school.

Teens like to be popular but Japanese teens are conscious of a tension between popularity as individuals and the responsibility for more socially embedded relationships. The phrase *ningen kankei* (human relationships) figures prominently in Japan. Relationships are both the end and means of a good life and their cultivation is taught young. The earliest lessons of home and school involve sensitivity to others—*omoiyari*—and entering a close relationship involves an emotional tie that carries with it a 100 percent commitment to emotional support and loyalty. It is hard to maintain close friendships under the tyranny of tight schedules and geographical impediments. Friendship must now depend on schedules, class placement, and bus routes:

> I wanted to go home from high school on the bus with my best friend, but I really felt that it was too much to ask to have her wait for such a long time for me. . . . When we were in driving school, she took different lessons so she could get a ride home. . . . We don't talk much now since our schedules have changed completely. I have new friends now. . . . Of course, since I graduated and everyone goes to different colleges, it's hard to see my friends at all.

Shinyū: What Best Friends Are For

While Japanese teen friendships change frequently, best-friend status involves a real sense of responsibility along with the pleasures of intimate sharing. Discussions of friendship among teens center around the term *shinyū*: children make strong distinctions between group friends and best friends and the general word *tomodachi* (friend) covers all of a child's acquaintances. Teens value *shinyū* and often have two or three such best friends. They get together in pairs, rarely as a friendship group, for it is felt that one-to-one is the only way you can be yourself. With a *shinyū*, you are fully your private self, sharing your best and worst, and you do not have to be bright and amusing all the time. You can trust your *shinyū*, and he or she understands you thoroughly. You can talk without thinking in complex terms of how to present your ideas. "Being with my *shinyū* I can have deep discussions without being *kidoru*, putting on airs and worrying about how the other will feel. It is unconditional, like a married couple in the West, able to tell each other everything."

These protestations of deep intimacy and loyalty appear to bely the current concern in Japan that children's relationships have been made attenuated, thinned out and superficial, by the combined pressures of study and material culture.[2]

In a recent study comparing American and Japanese high school friendships, it was noted that American highschoolers spend more time with their best friends than do Japanese.[3] Such studies appear to support what many Japanese believe, that youth in Japan are no longer able to conduct healthy human relationships, the stuff of life in adult society. Our interviews, however, belie the bleakness of the above study, for the intimacy and support cited among friends was notable. Girls tend to rely on the intimacy achieved with a best friend more than do boys. Carol Gilligan has noted that among American teens, girls may be more focused on emotional merging, *talking*, in friendships, boys more on *doing things*, shared hobbies, interests, and activities. She also commented that Japanese girls *and* boys appear in these dimensions much like American *girls*.[4]

And yet, friendship within Japan may vary in its support and warmth, as within the United States. Closeness and the freedom to be yourself are found in a best-friend relationship, but being a popular member of a group involves different and often more trying aspects of Japanese teen friendship. Contradicting the notion that Japanese children and adults *prefer* the camaraderie of the group, relationships in a teen friendship group are often strained, competitive, and difficult, and the solace of a one-to-one relationship with a best friend acts sometimes as a necessary buffer or antidote to the tensions of group interactions.

The Friendship Group: Safety in Numbers?

Especially in middle school where, as we have seen, the pressures of the academic success ladder, the intensity of developing adolescent sensitivities, and the anxieties caused by emerging differentiation within the age cohort combine to make the final year above all a difficult experience for many groups of children, groups of children can cause problems for their members. At their most benign, such groups give teens a training ground for the demands of adult *ningen kankei*. At their most problematic, they exhibit the dark side of two converging forces: those that drive adolescents everywhere to the mutual monitoring that produces the safety of conformity and those that create the mobilized solidarity of a Japanese group.

A friendship group in its simplest form is four to eight girls or boys finding each other to socialize. Some children called the group a "joking friends group," *waraibanashi nado shite iru tomodachi*, or a group of *akaruiko*, "lively kids," whose primary function is to play together and have fun (*asobu*). The object is hedonistic, and, especially in college, unconcerned with having a more specific goal or emotional function. A freshman in college says "My friends are *kibarashi*, something fun, something to change my mood—we play all night in Tokyo and go home in the morning." Younger "fun" groups also play intensely: "In high school, I tried to do everything they did, I even said yes when I couldn't possibly do it. I'd *asobu* (play) until the last train left." Another high schooler says, "High school is so boring and serious; playing with my friends is the only reason I put up with it." There is, however, even pressure to be upbeat. "If you aren't amusing, the others may think you are dull. You have to work at it."

Girls' friendship-group behavior is so intense that there are public rituals of togetherness and separation: one American observer writes,

> High school girls in transit almost always hold hands, and they speak an incomprehensible code language comprised of a single expression—bye-bye. Whenever girl groups converge, each girl in the unit begins a sing-song litany of bye-byes which may last anywhere from 15 seconds to a half-hour, depending on the information that has to be conveyed through the code.[5]

One girl commented in her diary that she had not said the proper greetings to someone in her group that day on the train, and she felt very guilty about it.

Friendship groups also train teens to the variety and pressures of relationships and personalities in later life. As one girl said, "We girls form groups. But being in a group doesn't always mean that you like everyone in the group. To the contrary, being in a group means that you stay very close to each other. And, as a result, you find out both desirable and undesirable things about each other. . . . " She adds, "You learn to form groups with an even number of girls, so that no one gets left out, because people get paired off, and with an odd number, someone will be extra."[6]

Every child revealed something of the strategies they developed to cope with the endless problems of sensitivity and power coalitions within their friendship group. While junior high school students had a sunnier view of their groups, high schoolers said friends in the group (rarely the same as one's *shinyū*) were gossipy, insincere, shallow, and untrustworthy—much of the time. One girl said, "We all gossip . . . but some bad people pass it on back to the victim. That's not right. We all get in trouble, and you shouldn't cause bad feelings."

Boys in Groups

Even within a boys' group supposedly cohering around mutual interests and similarities, differences emerge and may become a problem. One child was careful not to reveal that he has an emotionally disturbed father, for he might have been teased. Another child, taunted for being a little overweight, joined a karate class to get back at his tormentors (but was frustrated by his teacher who instructed him never to use karate at school).[7] Belonging to a group gives a child a place in the larger population of school and a personal identity.

A middle-school boy described the choices of boys' groups in his class: there are two groups of "peaceful guys" (*ottori shita*), a group of bullies (who also steal and shoplift), a group of game players, and a group of card players. The few who are not in the above groups are in what he calls the "kitaku group," who return directly home after school (*kitaku*).[8]

Boys' friendship groups in Japan tend to focus more on a common interest than on generalized or mixed-function relationships, gossip, and shopping, and "social training," though these functions also are served in boys' groups. They congregate, as do girls, in groups by taste as well as interests, so that a "computer-nerd" group will also adopt similar clothing styles. They might be members of a *zoku*, or "tribe," as in *bōsōzoku* (motorcycle gang) which cut across the dimensions of social class, and which change with trends in music and culture.

There is some experimentation and even deviation possible within the variety a class like this provides. But antisocial qualities, as opposed to personal eccentricity, can lead to trouble.

The bullies, and they seem to exist in every school, are the most overt patrollers of conformity, but they may exceed the usual limits of punishing deviants. Ganging up on a weaker person, a person with some physical difference or disability, or a person with any unusual quality has been common in middle schools and this bullying (*ijime*), has become the subject of national concern over the past ten years. Children say that if they are bullied—even physically beaten and injured—teachers and school officials do not intervene. Usually the damage is slight, paint in the hair, glue on one's clothes, slashed bookbags. One kind of *ijime* seems very subtle (and Japanese) indeed: "being annoyed by a kindness imposed upon you" is reported as a frequent kind of harassment, forcing the victim to receive a favor, and the obligation to reciprocate. But it is hard to report such incidents without incurring worse punishment from the perpetrators, and children usually bear their wounds in private pain. Boys' groups based on activity interests are generally kinder, and there are also groups whose reason for being is the fact that their members share the experience of being bullied.

Girls in Groups

Girls' groups are not usually founded on a common activity but are more general in their makeup. Girls do gravitate towards girls similar to themselves in personality and habits. One girl described a first false start at getting into a group:

> I was first friends with a girl who smoked and was a little bit of a delinquent-type, and talked a lot about cars. . . . I joined her group and her friends were like that too. I was a little uncomfortable. But then three other girls asked me to join their group, and I found them much more like myself. . . . they were like me, so I felt very comfortable.

There is always one boy or girl who acts as the leader, explicitly or implicitly. As in adult leadership in Japan, being the boss is not an unmixed pleasure. Leading means being responsible, and if the girl or boy neglects this duty, there may be mutiny. In some girls' groups, the pressure to obey the leader may be intense: "She even makes us go to the bathroom together. We have to stay together all the time and never talk to outsiders, or we will be ostracized just for trying to be friends with others."

Another group, has a mischievous leader:

> We do everything together, from seven in the morning to seven at night, beginning with early jogging since we are all in the track team. We are all lively, but our leader is the liveliest. She leads us to do wild things when we go shopping. Once we played on the escalator and stopped it. We played with spray demonstration perfumes and covered our bodies with suntan lotion, only to find out it wasn't for demonstration, but for sale. We got scolded and ran away. This is the way we get into scrapes.

The training in accommodation, in adjustment and consensus in the friendship groups, complements the training in hierarchy provided by *sempai-kohai* relationships in the formal clubs and activity groups in school.

As we have seen in Chapter 4, an important aspect of school socialization is actually located in peer-run activity groups. These are explicitly hierarchical and extend across all ages within a school, different from friendship groups which are likely to include only same-age children. *Sempai* (seniors), as in traditional apprenticeships, or senior-junior relationships in workplace and family, are seen as responsible for the "upbringing" of the *kōhai* or juniors, and the juniors are to be obedient and diligent in carrying out the wishes of the seniors. *Kōhai* come into a club eager to do well, to pass the test and, after the first year, to be rewarded by being called *sempai* themselves by the new recruits. The structure is predictable and the leader and follower roles clear, unlike those in the less institutionalized age-homogeneous friendship group.

One girl, emphasized the contrast all children come to observe in group friendships: the *tatemae* and *honne* of personal identity and human relationships. She, like many others, has learned to abstract from her experiences—to become a social psychologist as she analyzes the effect of a range of friendships on her self-identity.

Friendship with one friend, for her, is easy: as others said, you can be yourself with one best friend. In a group, you always have to cover up something of yourself, and it makes her feel guilty. She feels, as she puts it, *zurui*, or sneaky, two-faced, hypocritical. Even just noticing that she is uncomfortable with some of the things others do makes her feel awkward and guilty: her *zurui*-threshold is very low.[9]

She, like other teens, has been affected by a new awareness of the distinction between one's personal goals and values, and what one must do to be an accepted member of society. Groups are not like family and not like best friends: you become another person in the group, someone who has accommodated to, or been defined by, a consensus as to what you are. This is, for each teen, the birth of a social self, the price of admission to adult society. When a child says "They just say we're friends: they *pretend* to be friends and then betray each other," it is perhaps an exaggerated response, but it reveals the fact that the young person has only begun to be a *shakaijin* (an adult, member of society), still shocked a bit, still noticing the distinction between her own personal standards and the layers of behavior acceptable and necessary in social life.

One junior-high-school girl, exuberantly close to her "best friends" and proud of her relationships with them, said she was quite different as a friend in a group, a group where she had watched others mistreated, and this led her to some deep thinking about human nature:

> A friend may be someone remote, not a relative, but a real friendship makes him or her more important than a blood relation . . . a friend is the most precious treasure . . . however, I think it is also true to say that man is man's own worst enemy. What is most important to me is a friend—i.e., a human being, and this is also what I am most afraid of.

Personal Identity and the Tests of Friendship

> Now I want only friends I can talk to. I don't really want a group of friends where we call each other all the time. I want to keep my school and private life separate.
>
> —17 year-old high school girl

As teens get older, especially after the rugged friendship trials of middle school, they regularize their friendships and, at the same time, turn more to private, individuated activities. By the college years, the imperative to socialize with friends has diminished even as the opportunities, freedom, and time have increased. A high school senior says, "When I was young, I wanted as many friends as possible, because the more friends I had, the more popular I thought I was. Now I feel it is more important to have a friend I can call a shinyu, and lead a quieter life." Several older teens said they wanted more stability, in themselves and in their close friends, saying that a good friend should be *dosshiri shite hito*, a person who sits solidly, is balanced and stable.[10]

Stability in one's personal identity can be maintained relatively easily where there is no pressure from friendships. Once a child is aware of the dangers of being swallowed up by the group's agenda, all discussions of who he or she is are prefaced by the problem and placed in the context of the problem of locating the "real" self. Most are pragmatic and understand the distinction between private and public selves, and that they are coexistent and complementary. Most are looking not to discard the side where they must be *zurui*, as their American counterparts would feel it necessary to attempt, but to keep a balance.

American teens seemed to feel less need to distinguish a public and private self, assuming no difference. Being "true to oneself" in American terms means never adjusting one's identity to fit different contexts. American teens are, however, like Japanese teens testing the viability of this "true self" in social contexts, and find friendship as test of identity sometimes supportive, sometimes demanding.[11]

Maturity in Japan may seem to an American to mean the acceptance of hypocrisy but, in Japanese terms, it means the cultivation of appropriateness, including situational behaviors that may appear contradictory. A personal identity, American style, totally independent of family and institution is a *new* idea and not, perhaps, one easily accommodated in the deep relational structures of Japanese life. But the ties that bind are also supportive, and what a teen in Japan learns, somewhere between elementary school and adulthood, is that the two are not mutually exclusive. The adolescent moment of awakening to the difference between a private self and a public friendship particularly illuminates the contrast. The teen's self-conscious learning process shows that Japanese young people are by no means seamlessly trained from birth, or genetically programed in what Western observes have called Japan's "situational ethic." In fact, to some like the girl who was so guilty about being *zurui*, the contrast between the safe cocoon of the best-friend relationship and the testing ground of the friendship group provides a very rude awakening to social realities.

Families and Friends

Other discomforts exist as well for the Japanese teen as they do for American adolescents, some less instructive than lessons of friendship groups. Friends and acquaintances also provide a measure against which one's family, home, possession—everything in one's background—are tested. The following scene will resonate for any American teen or parent who has ever said or heard "Oh, Mom, don't do that in front of my friends!" or, "Dad, please drop me off a block before school." Here is a kindred Japanese spirit in Embarrassment City, writing in her dairy.

A high school senior goes with her family to dinner at a Red Lobster, a popular chain family restaurant. She finds a male classmate, M., working there. He brings them all sorts of free snacks and extras and they all have a cheerful time.

> . . . . We laughed as he kept bringing more. But then . . . the worst thing happened. We had a lot of french fries left over, and Mom wanted to take them home for the dog. Dad, to my astonishment, began to pack some of the fries into an empty plastic bag left from a wet towel. I was so embarrassed but tried to calm myself, being encouraged by Mom's saying, "It's just for the dog." We wrapped it then in tissues, and put the packet aside on the table. But Mom completely forgot about it, and left behind the plastic bag stuffed with french fries. Oh, what a disaster! What did M. think when he found the bag after we left? He must have thought our family so crude. He would never have known it was for the dog. Sob, sob . . . It's so embarrassing!!! I may have nightmares about this tonight.

Some children are so embarrassed in a more general way about their parents, or home, or siblings, that they would not bring a friend home. This avoidance is not at all unusual in Japan, where most people only rarely invite non-kin to their homes because living quarters are small and because it is not customary to do so. But teens and even elementary school children now do visit each other, though far less than do American children.

Street addresses for the most part still mean much less in Japan than they do in the United States, since most neighborhoods in large cities house a mixture of socioeconomic levels. However, there are more or less fashionable areas. These differences, revealing differences in family resources, are more apparent among high school children, where children are drawn from a wider geographical area than they are in middle schools, which are usually neighborhood schools.

"Best friends" will often have open access to each other's homes, and they will inevitably know the worst. But it is risky to invite less trustworthy friends, or friends who might make invidious comparisons with their own family or environment. Open

access means revelations about family background and resources. Because of the youth consumer boom, making shopping
a dominant social experience, some teens are left out due to lack
of resources, and there are some on the margins, whose parents
try to make them acceptable by providing more pocket money
than they can actually afford— allowing them to keep up with the
others.

But once a child's friends have entered his or her home, the
fiction of social and economic homogeneity may be exposed,
and a child who knows he or she has less tend to avoid such exposure.

> In elementary school my friends were all in the same apartment
> complex and they used to drop in all the time. We all lived in the
> same way and our mothers knew each other; our fathers all
> worked in the same company. Now that I'm in high school we've
> moved to a small condominium but the neighborhood isn't so good
> and the elevator smells. I think someone pisses in it. I really don't
> want my new friends coming to such a place. I have the same stuff
> they have—a CD player, a VCR, all in my room—but some of them
> live in nice houses in Setagaya-ku . . . If I keep visiting them
> there, they're going to expect to be invited here. I don't know what
> to do.
>
> —1st-year high school boy, Tokyo

Even though there is a similar fiction of classlessness in American ideology, American teens generally have no illusions about
the existence of differences. In urban communities especially
they are not innocent of class: children who attend private
schools tend to speak of others as "public-school kids," and the
latter refer to the former as "private-school snobs" (or a stronger
term). Urban neighborhoods generally are more class homogeneous than in Japan, and children refer to themselves by their
neighborhood identity often. Schools, too, are more class-
segregated in America than in Japan, at least up to high school.
High schools in America tend to be more heterogeneous than in
Japan, where tests admit you to an ability-tracked school.

Friends themselves created moral and situational struggles, independent of the ones naturally arising in the training ground of
the friendship group. Solving the problem of accommodation to
the necessary discrepancy between what you are privately (family
background and personality) and what you are socially (appro-

priate group behavior and priorities) is only one of the tasks of friendship work for teens.

Same Versus Other: Friends and Lovers

Negotiating both heterosexual relationships and same-sex friends may be tricky. A girls' friendship group is particularly alert to a member's inclination toward or involvement with a boy. The close sharing of lore about boy-girl relationships and the romantic fantasies learned from magazines, films, and *manga* and retailed within the group (see Chapter 7) heightens girls' interest in at least the *idea* of having a boyfriend. At the same time, the demands of a friendship group may be, as we've seen, very intense and may make it difficult to spend much time with a boyfriend, either observed or unobserved. While it *may* be a feather in one's cap to have a boyfriend, at least in the abstract, in some girls' circles it may pose a conflict, if the time with a boy interferes with the time-dues owed to the group. When a girl actually does go steady, she may be seen as remote, even unavailable, to her friends who feel betrayed. Of course, the irony is that she is an outsider because she has made the group fantasies and dreams about dating and love a reality; but nothing can make up for the fact that she is absent, in mind or person, and her unavailability is more important than her new status as lover. This paradox between romantic fantasy and the contradictory demands of relationships is not, of course, unknown among American teens.

The terms of endearment in adolescent mating, have reference not to their (sometimes English) origins, but to an elaborated teen code. Words like boyfriend (*boifurendo*), girlfriend (*garufurendo*), steady, lover (*rabaa* or *koibito*), and date (*deito*) are often borrowed from English, but their meanings have usually undergone a sea change. When a teen says she has a lover, it does not inevitably mean that they've gone all the way—more usually, it means they are very close friends and spend *some* time alone together, allowing her, at least, fantasies of a "relationship." As Rohlen points out, in the 1970s, more teens said they had lovers than had experienced even kissing.[12] More common is having a "boifurendo" which usually means a close friend who is a boy, but with a sexual innuendo, so children can use the word to tease each other about a supposed intimacy. As with *shinyū*, a boyfriend can be maintained at a distance[13] and doesn't require what a steady does. Going steady means both partners acknowledge the relationship, and although adults do not favor it, it is a *public* social tie with sexual overtones. As noted in Chapter 7, many teens are sexually active but it is generally kept very private, very removed from the public eye—not because of any moral or cultural puritanism surrounding sex, but because it is simply not to be publicly displayed as an aspect of a social relationship.

Friendship is also a moral testing ground. The negotiation of friendships often entails difficult moral choices and misunderstandings, particularly when love relationships are triangulated with friendship. One girl said confidently, "If my best friend and I were both in love with the same man, we wouldn't hide it. If we were open about our feelings, then we could compete as much as we liked and if one were to win, the one who lost would be happy for the other." This hypothesis had not been tested. Girls confiding in each other often notice they have a conflict of interest, which they try to resolve in a moral way—morality in this case not being an abstract principle but rather an accommodation hurting the least people.

A boy became a confidant to the girlfriend of his close friend, and found himself in a difficult position.

My friend had just told me that someone—a friend of mine—had just told her that he was in love with her. She didn't know what to do, and asked my opinion. . . . Then, for about a month, the girl and I often walked together after school to discuss this. For a while I thought things were going well between them, but soon it was clear that they weren't. Her indecision at the beginning was focused on her not wanting to hurt him by saying no. I though she'd taken my advice to have a moratorium with him to decide her feelings. But he hadn't understood, so they weren't on good terms. . . . He's having a hard time and called me. . . . We're all in the same club and he noticed that we hang around together. . . . He maybe thought I was interfering in their relationship, but he didn't say so, and just told me to explain to other club members that he wouldn't be coming for a while. . . . But in this time, the girl and I became closer as we discussed the matter and I felt maybe I *was* being sneaky, taking advantage. . . . I think the real fact is that I enjoyed being the third person, and watching what was happening . . . the incident made me think about a lot of things.

A girl in one friendship group, awkward in her relationships with boys and apparently insensitive to her girlfriends, recklessly badmouthed her girlfriend in a clumsy attempt to impress the boys. Another in the group recounts the story in her diary, to remind herself of the moral lesson of loyalty and kindness:

> Kumiko had to attract boyfriends by making a fool of Haruko to them. Kumiko was nice to others only superficially and only when it suited her. So when I talk with my friends, I try to avoid malicious gossip or making fun of people, because it hurts them. Why did Kumiko need to get a boyfriend this way? She tries to seem *akarui* (bright, open) but she's really *nekura* (dark, secretive).

Bright and Dark: Personality and the Group

These last terms, *akarui* and *nekura* (roughly, bright spirited and dark spirited), reveal another aspect of peer-group socialization. Japanese teens like American teens whose categories include work, nerd, and jock, focus on personality characteristics. Teens like peer definition, in the same way they like fortune-telling and pop sociology typologies in their magazines. They constantly set up typologies of their own, creating new vocabulary for what's in and what's not in personality and friendship. Teen argot includes some absolute as well as some relative, shaded terms for the range of personalities they observe, condemn, and praise among themselves. A general term of disapproval is *dasai*, meaning uncool, nerdy, out of it. *Utoi* is a more specific word, meaning "trend-insensitive." Often terms are paired, as in *ii ko/warui ko*, good kid, bad kid, or *akaruiko/kuraiko*. These last are in constant use, and are key words in describing teen personalities. Being "bright" is a quality praised in small children[14] in schools and by personnel managers in hiring young women for office staff positions. It means lively and upbeat—positive and even bouncy. Some teens saw it as a necessary quality to show in a group, not so necessary in a best-friend relationship, implying that "brightness" of this kind is related to superficiality. On the other hand, the opposite, *kurai* or *nekura*, is never valued among teens, and may even be suspect as dark, gloomy, and secretive. Usually, though, it only means quiet and not outgoing, perhaps evidence of social insecurity. It does not imply an interesting sort of darkness, rather someone who keeps too much to him or herself, and is not much fun. You want your group to be filled with *akaiuiko* for the outings and entertainment; too serious a personality will not be popular in group activities.

One junior high school girl developed her own theory of *akarui* versus *kurai*. According to her there are two routes to being *kurai*: being born *kurai* and having it thrust upon you. Even if you are born *akarui*, she says, you might become *kurai* if you have no one to bring you out. The difference is friends.

> Those who don't have any friends are the kurai people. There are some people who do have an innate akarui personality but they don't have any friends. They cannot talk to anyone, so they end up being alone and kurai. . . . Those born kurai are quiet from the beginning and don't talk to anyone. . . . Kurai people don't laugh, don't play around . . . they just sit there. And even when someone talks to them, they laugh awkwardly (gikochi nai). . . . They are sometimes disliked but mostly just ignored. Sometimes girls who are kurai are just considered to be feminine and old-fashioned.

Personality types figures very much in group discussions, and they rely heavily on such things as blood type, color preferences, astrological signs, and even which way a person's cowlick bends. The magazines aid and abet such personality parlor games, often with pull-out tests for teens to administer to each other. When the teens in this sample were asked to write a short essay describing themselves, most included their blood type. All included words such as *akarui* and *kurai*, and other qualities that affected their friendships and all described themselves as "a good friend."

American teens, too, develop caste hierarchies of personality— prioritized by the acceptability of types to the dominant caste in a school or neighborhood.[15] Thus, the jock, brain, criminal, princess are categories that have been more or less constant over the past fifty years, but with each fad cycle or generation, the names may change.

Japanese categories, however, are based not on what a person *does*, such as sports or study, as much as on affiliative style—that is, whether a person is bright, active, and engaged appropriately in friendship-group activities or is isolated and private. Of course, *all* middle-class Japanese high schoolers spend more time alone studying than do most Americans, but, what they do with the hours remaining is the question. Most Japanese high schoolers consider themselves good and loyal friends, even under the constraints imposed by study.

A Japanese junior-high-school girl's diary:

> I'm just ordinary, like any girl in junior high school. I've made lots of friends: a selfish friend, a kind and unkind friend, a threatening friend, a cheerful friend, and a crybaby. . . . Without friends, we can't do what we can do. . . . I couldn't live without friends who talk to me and encourage me. I will keep making friends from now on and never lose them. . . . I have no one I hate.
>
> *June 22.* My friends and I all went to the singing competition. . . . It was hard. . . . When we heard we'd won, we hugged each other and shouted for joy.
>
> *June 23.* My friend and I walked to school together, preparing for the exams. We made up memory aids like "the canal that can't drink juice" for the Suez Canal, [*suezu* means cannot drink]. She helps me make these things interesting.
>
> *June 24.* After school my friends and I stopped by a shop near school to buy a diary for us to keep as an exchange diary. . . . After all, all you need are your friends.
>
> *June 25.* My friend gave me a good luck charm she had made by hand. I was very happy.
>
> *June 26.* My friends and I went to painting school today.
>
> *June 27.* After school I called but my friend was out.

Terminal *Kurai:* The Solitary Teen

In small living quarters, creating private space is hard for a teen, and one common mode of separation is reading. Headset on, music video on VCR, and magazine on one knee, the teen has no sensory contact with the crowded home environment. In any case, the hours spent alone, studying or listening to music, create, according to psychologists, solitary habits. One specialist referred to the extreme cases of this as the "distance tribe," young people who don't know how to make contact with others, who suffer from *fureai kyofusho,* or fear of relationships, and who are prevented by study and protected by indulgent parents from learning how to manage socially on their own. A subset of this type has evolved into one of the *maniakku* cultures: the *otakuzoku,* or solitary young people obsesses with comics and soft pornography, who have created their own communication with desktop porn-comic publications. They communicate, but usually by means of computers and telephones, rarely getting together with other young people outside of school.

Otakuzoku are only one type of isolated child. Boys seem especially prone to this lonely behavior, and even children who have full-time housewife mothers behave as though they rarely talk to anyone. Some children are felt to be inadequately socialized for other reasons than fear or avoidance, however. Because the birthrate has fallen to a present average of 1.53 children per household, some commentators predict that many children, with one or no sibling, will suffer from inexperience in human relationships.

Over the Edge: Delinquency and other Teen Social Pathologies

Friendship affiliations in Japan, as in the United States, can cross the line into peer-pressured bad behavior, even perhaps into delinquency. Bad behavior—in the form of the testing of adult and institutional limits—is not, however, encouraged or exaggerated by the availability of drugs and the accompanying acceleration of juvenile crime rates seen in most American cities. Juvenile crime rates in Japan are low—so low that the number of juvenile arrests for one year in Osaka, the second largest city in Japan, is the same as that for one day in New York. The total of juvenile crime cases processed by the police in 1988 was 193,000. The total of juveniles from thirteen to twenty-one years of age involved in stimulant drug use in the same year was 1,273 persons; and in the following year—1989—the total number dropped. Hot-rodders are frequently arrested for a range of crimes, from assault and robbery to extortion and homicide, and these youth are a special category in police records. The number of young people arrested has declined every year since 1983.

Hankōki, or the "rebelliousness of adolescence" is seen mostly as a deviation, not a normal attribute of youth. One researcher, however, noted that one function of the *sempai-kohai* relationship may be to help the teen "pass from the rebelliousness of *hankōki* to the acceptance (of one's position in society) characteristic of a more mature person." In this study, the researcher quoted a teenager who said that the worst thing a *sempai* could say to a *kohai* is "rei shinakatta yo" [you broke with etiquette]. The relationship is then a peer-based mechanism of control.[16]

When such controls have no effect, or when problems have different causes, Japanese youth tend more towards "acting in" than towards "acting out," suffering more from personal pathologies rather than contributing to social disorder. Acting-in leads to psychiatric symptoms, among which most prevalent is school refusal (truancy) due to bullying or to psychosomatic symptoms.[17] These are a subject of great concern but what Japanese officials worry about more is that acting *out* may be on the rise: the ratio of juvenile to adult offenders has increased to the point where juveniles now account for 57.4 percent of all suspects questioned or arrested. And the average age of delinquents has dropped every year for the past decade. Seventy percent of first offenders are now between thirteen and fifteen. Most second offenders were under ten at the time of their first detainment.

The picture of juvenile crime is a complicated one. The offenders come from a wide range of family backgrounds. Eighty percent of those held in juvenile homes were from middle- or upper-middle-class families. Ikuya Sato sees the largely middle-class motorcycle-gang members as adolescents seeking escape from boredom, and a chance for *play,* rather than as alienated dropouts from a class-bound system.[18] Many children arrested for various crimes report that the thrill of risk taking led them on: interviews with the delinquents said their lives are more oriented to friends than to parents, and more to relationships with friends of the opposite sex who apparently goaded them to commit crimes.[19] Many are urged into teen prostitution this way: 60 percent of juvenile arrests are of females involved in some form of sex trade. And yet there is also a strong indication that crimes among some juveniles are also related to economic issues: about one-third of arrested youth are jobless and out of school, between the ages of fourteen to nineteen.

Even among those who have not been led to crime, some young people report a tendency to be pushed to antisocial, or "cool," behavior:

> People conform a lot at my age (15). But in a funny way. It doesn't look good to get too earnest about school events such as the cultural festival, or be too wholehearted about the clean-up brigade: you look foolish. What looks good is to duck out of such things, even though everyone knows that it is good to do the right thing.

Some find just sticking out in gaudy attire or the adjusted school uniform is enough to give them the thrill of being on the edge. Slightly aberrant activity, or just slightly anti-establishment demeanor is one thing, but a sixteen-year-old girl reports that she's at some risk to do more than avoid goody-goody behavior, however mild the risk may look to an American:

> My bad point is that I am easily influenced by my friends. I don't have a strong will of my own. I could easily become delinquent. My friends recently asked me to smoke with them, but since I had as a small child taken a vow, I said no. . . . But in things I don't care much about, I just follow the others.

Many teens smoke (fewer than in the United States, where 1 million teens take up the habit every year), but more problematic for social order is teen drinking. The Japan National Citizens' Association on Alcohol Problems reports from 1990, survey of thirteen to eighteen-year-olds in Tokyo, half were "habitual drinkers," and 56 percent had had their first drink before the end of elementary school. Peer pressure is of course at work here, along with the general availability of beer, wine, whiskey, and sake in sidewalk vending machines. Teens also spend (20 percent spend over 6000 yen per month on average) in bars, and at *karaoke* boxes, where bring-your-own is the rule, and where there is a definite lack of monitoring. Children of hard-drinking fathers can scarcely ignore this role model and even young teens, in an unguarded moment, can tell you their *own* favorite brands: "My beer is Asahi Dry and my whiskey is Suntory White—Oops, what am I telling you!" (a sixteen-year-old high-school student, Chiba Prefecture)

The reporting of alcohol use in both countries is problematic, but interview material in the United States shows similar patterns. Half of all thirteen to eighteen-year-olds in the United States are habitual drinkers, with most of them drinking at least once a week, and half a million drink more than five drinks at a sitting. The rate for young teens has dropped slightly but it is very common for thirteen-year-olds to have a drink. Five percent of eleven-year-olds, for example, regularly attend drinking parties, 61 percent before the end of high school. As in the Japanese study of delinquency, the American study of teen drinking associates alcohol consumption with alienation and lack of parental supervision. Most of these young people come from middle-class homes, but most are alone at home for many hours of the week.

Analysts further say that parental drinking habits as well as peer group drinking are key influences. More important, hard drugs and even marijuana are becoming much less acceptable among American teens, so that alcohol is a replacement.[20]

Drug use is, as any newspaper reader knows, epidemic in America, but Japan has been far more successful in anti-drug enforcement. Dealers, smugglers, and users are arrested. There is aggressive involvement in international drug-control operations. Another difference lies in the drugs of choice: in Japan, amphetamines are popular, rather than cocaine, heroine, marijuana, and psychedelic drugs. But a drug culture is slow to form and there are strong social taboos against drug abuse—excluding, of course, alcohol and smoking, which are approved.[21] *Karaoke* boxes again are one focus for the campaign against all substance abuse by children, for in these private rooms, smoking, drinking, and glue-sniffing are said to be frequent activities.

There has been an increase in delinquent behavior among teenage girls. Their crimes of choice appear to be shoplifting and prostitution. Girls are more frequent repeaters: girls commit another crime within six months of being released from juvenile detention homes and boys within a year.[22]

So-called playful delinquency[23] includes shoplifting and—to some extent—prostitution, engaged in by schoolgirls eager for a thrill and pocket money. Swiping an unlocked bicycle is a favorite sport of some middle-school boys. Defying the police for the thrill of it is part of the pattern of delinquency of the *bōsōzoku*, or motorcycle gangs. Gang membership often emulates participation in adult *yakuza* crime families, with a hierarchical system led by a boss, and rituals of entry and loyalty. Stealing and extortion are often part of the activities of such a group, as are "dare" crimes, in which more junior members of the group are exhorted to prove their stuff by performing a crime.[24]

The problems of teenagers, as noted above, more often turn them in on themselves rather than out into the community. School problems especially bullying and hazing, may create intolerable pressure and even lead in some cases either to violence by the oppressed child, or suicide. Violent crimes are rare, overall, but there is some evidence of violence increasing in schools (against teachers, as well as classmates) and at home (against adult relatives, particularly mothers). Suzanne Vogel notes that where an American child might run away from home if problems become too great, Japanese *parents* have been known to leave the home to the violent or problematic highschooler, who has thrown them out.[25] The discussion of suicide in Japan usually relates it to academic pressure and the potential for failure in the rugged ladder towards the university, but statistics belie this, showing that the higher levels are actually in the twenty to twenty-four age group beyond the age of examination hell.[26]

Remembering that overall the rates of juvenile pathologies and crime are relatively low in Japan, and that deviant-behavior data in general tends to include such violations as those of school regulations—perming one's hair or affixing colored stickers to one's bookbag[27]—places Japanese delinquency in perspective for Americans; but Japanese educators, parents, and social commentators are far from pleased with relativity: they are concerned that any rise in the incidence of problems in any sector of the juvenile population may foretell problems for the future of a generation, and thus for society at large.

The Tokyo Metropolitan Police recently offered parents and teachers a guide to visual indicators that a child might be "going bad," as shown in the accompanying illustration.

This kind of publicity resembles American advertising campaigns aimed at parents, listing signals that children may be taking drugs. In the United States, many such ad campaigns focus on encouraging parents to talk with their children, about drugs and the danger of AIDS. Similar U.S. campaigns are aimed at the children, themselves.

There are larger questions related to the relationship of teen and parent, in terms of friendship and illicit behavior, that inform the contrast between American and Japanese adolescence. At the beginning of this chapter, we noted that American adults are suspicious of teen association, while there is in Japan the notion that children alone or together are not naturally inclined to disobedience or uncontrolled antisocial behavior but are rather inclined naturally and by early training to prosocial behavior. We saw in the discussion of schooling that discipline in the early years of school is rare, and that what would appear to an American to be chaos, rules. Children are certainly expected to be energetic and physical, and to need to use their energies, but the assumption is that children want to do what is right, and confrontation is not

The Tokyo Metropolitan Police Office asks:
Do You Know How Your Children Dress?

Female

1. Light makeup with false eyelashes, eye shadow and lipstick or lipgloss
2. Magnetic earrings
3. Turned-up collar
4. Open jacket with red T-shirt underneath
5. Intentional cigarette burn scar to show toughness
6. Slovenly long skirt with unironed pleats
7. Colored pantyhose
8. Blow-dried hair or straight permanent brushed back
9. Shaved eyebrows
10. No school badge
11. Decorative medal
12. Rolled-up sleeves
13. Large safety pin
14. Ring
15. Keyholder with disco membership card
16. Quilted bag with change of clothes and small candy tin for holding cigarettes
17. Sneakers or deck shoes

Male

18. Forelock
19. Small mustache (if one can be grown)
20. Bright colored T-shirt (usually red)
21. Chain bracelet
22. Beat-up empty school bag
23. Closely shaved hair around temples
24. Shaved eyebrows
25. No school badge
26. Decorative medal
27. Rolled-up sleeves
28. Intentional cigarette burn scar to show toughness
29. Ring
30. Oversized jacket, not too long
31. Long trousers almost covering the feet
32. Black enamel shoes (only gang leaders are allowed to wear these)

This illustration and list is from a police brochure on how to tell a juvenile delinquent when you see one.

necessary, since intentions are good. Parents, too, feel that children do not by nature want or need to oppose them, that "breaking of the will" is not a tenet of childrearing.

Further, age-appropriateness is so strong a value even among delinquent groups, that most rule-breakers are pressured by their peers to "graduate" and settle down to an ordinary life once they have come of age, at twenty.

In America, the conflict between the understanding that children are born naturally good and the notion that given the opportunity, they will misbehave, leads to contradictory parental signals, the contradiction reinforced as well by our philosophic and political ideologies encouraging freedom of choice and the rights of the individual—which, pushed to the extreme in parent-child confrontations, leads to even greater gaps between beliefs and practices in childrearing, discipline, and guidance.

Conclusions

Teen friendship is a test case for our differing ideas about children's behavior and proclivities. If "peer pressure" has strongly negative connotations in the United States, while teen friendship for the most part does not in Japan, this has deep implications for our views of appropriate training and social development. For most Japanese children, priorities are set by family and school, and the remaining uncharted territory is claimed by friends, the media, consumer activities, and goals tying teens simultaneously to friendship and the market.

While parents in Japan, less engaged in monitoring their children's nonschool-related activities, can for the most part count on the congruence between their children's larger goals with their own, parents in America often feel rather more *divergence* than *congruence* between their aims and those of their children, and feel they have less control over their behavior and goals. This problem is exacerbated in America by the often confrontational institutional environment of schools, where it is assumed by many adults that adolescents will try to get away with murder, where classroom management rather than learning may dominate the class hour, and where *parents* and *teachers* confront each other over children's bad behavior. The sense of potential conflict or lack of understanding then comes back home to roost, when parents attempt to control children with threats and punishments, and there remains a gulf between them and their children, a gulf empty of understandable and coherent standards and sympathy.

For most families in America, however, this does not automatically lead to illicit behavior or even to a lack of emotional rapport—or the middle-class delinquency rates would be much higher than they are . The fact that parents and children actually get along much better than our fears and beliefs would indicate, may show that—in our beliefs—we misrepresent our children's capacity to live up to our standards, however mixed they may be.

Our children may not act out our fears for them in overt delinquency as much as may be expected, but they do more frequently confront our concerns in their sexual activity. Here too, as described in the following chapter, we may find surprising contrasts and similarities in the Japanese case.

7
Sexuality

Illusions and Realities

The important thing is for children not to feel confused about sex: if they have information, they can really enjoy it, and they will have a healthy life.

—Japanese psychotherapist

I'm 18, pregnant, with two boyfriends, both without a stable job. I love school and I'm on full scholarship. I don't believe in abortion; now what?

Get unemployed right-to-life roommate to babysit.

Adoption is the only way.

For God's sake, use contraception after this!

Don't criticize. Everyone does dumb things. I wish her luck.

Idiots don't get scholarships. Get a life, love the kid.

It's not as hard as it may seem. I'm 18, have a 4-month old baby girl, full scholarship and everything is working out. It's hard but I would not change a thing. She's all I have.

—Graffiti exchange, women's bathroom stall,
Rider College, New Jersey, noted February 1991.

American young people are surrounded by the most mixed of the messages we have given them, and they create great destruction: "just do it" and "just say no." At a time when AIDS and teen pregnancy rates are high and climbing, the result is that 72 percent of high schoolers have engaged in sexual intercourse, 20 percent of

169

American teens report four or more sexual partners, and 63 per-cent of American teens do not use birth-control measures.[1] One in twenty-five has had a sexually transmitted disease. The birth rate among teens in the United States in 1989 was 58 per 1000, or 11 percent of the fifteen- to nineteen-year-old teen population. Teens account for 25 percent of the total number of abortions performed each year.[2] American data continues to show an increase in all these areas.[3] And indeed, it is all this and more sensational data that draws our attention when we think of adolescent sexuality, far from the sense of the Japanese quotation leading this chapter.

With a backdrop of conflict established as a given between adult authority and youthful independence, the American teen is vulnerable both to the media's sexy messages and to what adults fear more, peer pressure. The freedom we grant teens—some-times under duress—may lead to escalated acting-out, and across all social classes, sexual exploration becomes the freedom of choice.

Becoming adult in Japan, as we have noted, means to most people becoming a responsible member of society, not gaining rights, independence, and freedom as it would appear to many American youth. Becoming twenty-one in Japan does mean being able legally to drink alcohol, and getting a job may mean a somewhat more independent life-style, but legal and economic independence are not critical denominators of maturity in Japan. In the United States, sexual initiation and activity have in the past been part of growing up, and pregnancy has been associated with marriage and parenthood, but neither in today's American nor in Japan is sexual activity linked to full adulthood.

Teens in Japan, to American eyes, seem cute, innocent, per-haps asexual, and serious—they are meant to be tied to their study desks, after all. In public, they appear in single-sex friend-ship groups, girls dressed well but not sexually, in fact exuding giggly virginity. Boys may be scruffy or fashionable in haute punk couture, but they too band together, and may not appear very ex-perienced. As we will see, appearances are deceiving, and it is our own images and practices that delude us in observing Japanese teens. These teens are, nonetheless, experienced. According to data from magazine readership surveys, two-thirds reported sexual activity by the age of fifteen, and over 80 percent reported frequent masturbation. Reporting on sexual activity (not neces-sarily sexual intercourse) is not always reliable and it is hard to generalize from this sample to the wider population of teens. Further, schoolgirl prostitution has become a major crime problem, and many girls engaged in after-school prostitution seem to have little concern about the effects it may have on them emotionally or legally.

When "spring has come" to a young person in Japan, meaning, in teen parlance, when a young person becomes sexually aware, or falls in love, it is exciting and frightening, just as in the United States. Kenichi, a sixteen-year-old living in a provincial town in western Japan, has been seen by his friends with a girl, and his first thought, told to his diary, is "I didn't want it to be obvious to others that 'spring has come to me'." And yet, his primary concern is how he can communicate his attachment to the girl. He relates to his diary how he tried to do this:

> When I was in the chemistry room after school, Y-san came in. . . . I tried to talk with her. Since there were others in the room, however, I just stayed near her but couldn't talk a lot. Then, when some people left, I passed a piece of paper and a red pen, asking her to write whatever she wanted to. . . . She wrote a letter to me, which pleased me. I don't know why, though. In her letter, she wondered if anyone needed her. I am sure I told her before that she was one of the people I needed, so I wondered why. I want to believe that she was talking about someone else but me. But she *might* think I don't need her. That thought is still hanging in my mind. . . .
>
> –diary, July 7, 1990

The tension is high between expressing himself to the object of his affections and being caught in the act by his friends. Peer pressure both encourages and punishes romance, for, while all is permitted in private and in discussion with close friends, the public acting out of individual or group fantasies—being seen paired off, as a couple—may represent a betrayal of the rules of group friendship.

In America, too, being a young teen in a friendship group as well as a "steady girlfriend" may present problems. As a fourteen-year-old junior high school girl said,

> If two people are dating, you leave them alone, and don't interfere with them. If one is your friend, and she's a jerk about it, then it gets in the way of your friendship. Junior high is too young, but people do it, and some adults think it's cute. When you're sixteen, it gets more serious and adults change completely. It's like they're afraid of it, suddenly.

Children in both societies perform mating dances and friend-ship maneuvers and engage in sexual and romantic fantasies through the combined effect of hormones, media, and market-ing—and these are manipulated and amplified in communica-tions between friends. In Japan, romance and sexuality are both approved—Japan is *not* a puritanical society—but usually are kept quite separate. While girls exchange their diaries and rein-force each others' pastel-tinged dreams of romance, boys ex-change pornographic comic books and explicit magazines and sex manuals and tease each other about how far they've gotten with girls. As one young girl said, "It's funny. Boys get a little drunk and they have a lot of stories, sounds like they think about sex all the time. Some say things like, 'I'll do it before the end of this year.' They seem so cute when they say things like that." For the young teen in Japan, sex is a challenge or a lark, a notch on the belt rather than an aspect of a relationship or a source of plea-sure in itself. Information about sex is grist for the mill of friend-ship, and yet first-person experience, potentially alienating the 100 percent commitment of a member to the group, may be a threat to social bonds.

In this chapter, we will look at the images and realities of ro-mance and sexuality among Japanese and American teens, dis-covering themselves both as individuals and as continuing and predictable team players, for whom their bodies are less problem-atic than their affiliations.

Messages and Behavior: You Have to Be Taught

As stated earlier, it is commonplace to note that Americans give their children mixed messages about sex: they dress even small girls in "sexy" halter tops and spandex tights, and market busty Barbie dolls. One Los Angeles father of a elementary school first-grade girl finally had to break down and allow her to play with makeup at home, but drew the line at her desire to bring it to school like the others. He said, "Makeup is now like contraband to these kids. And the girls who have makeup have power over the ones who don't."[5]

A marketing expert in Japan, specialist in children's toys and clothing, noted that when he brought a Japanese Barbie-type doll, together with the doll's kit of clothing and makeup, to the United States to show to American girls, kindergarten girls immediately put the makeup on their own faces, rather than on the doll's, quite different from their Japanese counterparts.

An American marketer defended the trade in fishnet panty hose and dangling earrings for elementary-school children, saying, "The kids look really cute in the stuff. It doesn't have the same connotation that it does on adults. It has a real cute feel to it."[6] But some adults wonder if it isn't playing at sex, rather than playing dress-up in Mom's clothes, and don't see it as so wholesome and innocent.

We continue to confuse children: an adult may slyly ask a nursery school child who his girlfriend is, even as he warns a teenager that sex is an immoral, dangerous, irresponsible activity. At the outer end of the spectrum between encouragement and warning, we find messages directed at girls especially, saying that sex will be punished with pregnancy, which we as a society will neither help you prevent nor help you terminate. And most young teens, especially boys, feel they are pushed unwillingly, to participate in the dating game: it is frightening and, even if girls their age are interested, they often don't feel ready. One American thirteen-year-old boy said, "I don't know about dating. I haven't done it, and I don't want to. You have a lot of nervousness, even nausea, and you never would end up marrying the woman you date as a teenager, so it is pointless."

Sexual activity and delinquency are seen as related in the United States: it is thought that the same children who engage in sex are also engaged in drugs and other criminal pursuits. More directly, the sex-crime nexus is seen to be embodied in teen prostitution, a primary source of income for runaway girls.

Of course it is not only criminally delinquent children who are sexually active in America. Sex and deviance are connected because of an underlying puritanism which acts as a punishing super-ego, demanding payment for pleasure. Americans may for other reasons approve and encourage a superficial sensuality, the use of sex as a public competitive exercise in machismo and power, and marketing and popular culture may also extol romance and sexual expressiveness as a cultural ideal, but at base, we are told to say *no*.

Sex-education programs in the United States exhibit our confusion. Some programs involve the establishment of clinics, school-based or school-linked, to provide contraceptive counseling and to distribute condoms; some curricula give the vaguest of information on sexuality, too little and (often) too late. Only seventeen states now mandate sexuality education, though thirty others recommend it.[7] While 73 percent of adults say that contraception should be available in schools, only about 350 school-linked clinics, and 40 school-based clinics, actually distribute condoms in the United States.[8] There is great diversity among clinics in information and services provided. Some communities have also created teen "hot lines," telephone services for live or recorded information on sex, pregnancy, and sexually transmitted diseases.

Sex-education programs to train *abstinence* are often admonitory, dictatorial, and leave out useful information, such as information on masturbation. Some exhortations from these curricula include:

> Keep ALL of your clothes ALL the way on ALL of the time. Don't let ANY part of ANYone else's body get ANYwhere between you and your clothes. AVOID AROUSAL.[9]

or, moralistic but catchy:

> "Control your urgin'; be a virgin"
> "Don't be a louse; Wait for your spouse"
> "Do the right thing; wait for the ring"[10]

But these messages to say no seem to miss the mark—chiefly because the motivation needed for most children is not provided and because the message may come too late. Street wisdom among teens holds that young girls will not be able to say no, that you won't be popular if you say no, that all your friends are doing it, and that sex is best if it is spontaneous (contraception spoils the mood), and that if you jump up and down after intercourse you won't get pregnant.

Teens' lack of information and direction, in the context of explicitly sexual media and marketing, has produced deep confusion. Pamela Haughton-Denniston, Director of Public Affairs for the Center for Population Options says that behind this confusion are the misplaced priorities of adults: "Our society is tied so much to *adult* success; our individualism and the precariousness of the economy have produced a bad mix in which we only look at the present and we don't see that children are the future."[11]

In Japan, the message about sex is not *mixed* but *compartmen-*

talized: children are never taught that sex is intrinsically immoral or dirty, only that it needs to be in its proper place, not in conflict with social and occupational obligations. Delinquency is not associated with sexuality, though girls even in middle school who need money may become after-school prostitutes, getting into men's cars dressed in their school uniforms, or enlisted by telephone sex lines or kid-porn dealers and pimps. Young girls, age fourteen and fifteen, taken in by the police for prostitution, said "It's fun, and we haven't done anything harmful to others." College call-girl organizations, called *aijin banku* (lovers' banks) have been common since the late 1970s, and are apparently a common form of *arubaito,* or part-time work.

In Japan, as elsewhere, social class determines experience and expectations, and sexuality becomes a commodity in conditions of scarce resources. "Dangerous" sexuality—either in the sense it has come to have in the past decade of American AIDS consciousness—or in the sense it has always had in America of the primrose path of seductive deviance and disorder—has little meaning in Japan.

Historically, the compartmentalization of sexuality in Japan has not meant that either the act itself or the proliferation of services and the growth of a sexual aesthetic represent a moral problem. As a pro-brothel politician proclaimed in the 1930s, licensed prostitution is part of a "beautiful Japanese custom of feelings."[12] Before World War II, Japanese rejected American- and European-style sexual relationships, in which sexuality was seen as a component of a social relationship, and rejected public demonstrativeness in favor of private but separate pleasures. The creation of the art of *shunga,* or erotic woodblock prints, was an aspect of these pleasures, and to some degree the newer tradition of *eromanga* or erotic comics is an extension of this art.

Sex as Information: The Role of Teen Publications

Against this background of relatively unconflicted attitudes towards sexuality and social responsibilities, boys' and girls' inclinations towards each other are, especially recently, the topic of media and marketing interest—most particularly in the magazine industry. The ways in which Japanese editors and marketers sense and develop their audience's proclivities are thorough and subtle, and above all, successful in provoking, engaging, and teaching children about their bodies and themselves as sexual beings.

In Chapter 5, we were introduced to the child as *infomaniakku*, driven to consume information both for its own sake and as the material of exchange in friendship groups. Popular media have exploited this interest and created a voracious market for news on many subjects, from computers to fashions to sex. The comic book industry, *manga*, huge and booming, targets teens as only one of its market segments, which span the entire life course.

Recently, *manga* pornographic on anyone's scale have indeed proliferated. Of 1.9 billion comic books published in 1989, 474 million were explicitly sexual. Japan's obscenity laws are, to American eyes, rather permissive and quirkish: anything goes except pubic hair, adult genitalia, and full depiction of the sexual act. Imports such as *Playboy* can easily be cleaned up by airbrushing out the pubic hair. What can be bought then by anyone with the money—even from sidewalk vending machines offering twenty-four-hour anonymity, includes very explicit material with no warning labels. In many *manga*, male violence against or domination of women is a regular feature, as are sexual scenes with young girls in school uniforms, catering to men who have what in Japan is called the "Lolita Complex."

A grassroots mothers' committee to protest the sale of these comics has produced little but a tentative request to have publishers label comics considered unsuitable for children. Most sexually explicit *manga* do not reveal their contents on their covers, choosing demure drawings of young girls or sketches of sports heroes and vague titles. A few, like "No-Panty Angels," "Rape Man," and "Fresh Slave Dolls" give it all away on the cover and title.[13]

Magazines devoted to teens do not compete with *manga* but rather complement the comics' fantasies with their own practical curriculum in sex. *Manga* are above all *escape;* magazines provide *reinforcement* and *direction* and in the area of sexuality, they are indeed thorough and practical. Magazines are directed at specific audiences, well defined by age and gender, and also by style or social class—this latter especially as the child gets older.

Treatment of sexuality is explicit and straightforward in every age group, from magazines focused on thirteen- to fifteen-year-olds to those for young people in their early twenties. Girls' magazines are no less concerned with sex than are boys', and both take a very practical approach.

A recent American girls' magazine[14] published an article supporting girls who were still virgins and reinforcing the idea of saying no. Most American sex education in schools and in public media have retained the "just say no" message, but limit themselves to the physical risks of sex: pregnancy, AIDS, and other STDS. *Seventeen*, however, pursues several rationales in its attempt to defend girls from peer pressure—pressure from boys who, it is assumed, will push them towards sexual activity.

The mixed message of American popular and consumer culture is embodied in a single issue of such a magazine: on the one hand, titillating stories about sexy pop stars, fashion spreads of revealing prom dresses, tight lycra jeans, makeup articles telling girls how to apply a provocative beauty mark to a cheek, bustline, or shoulder, and of course advertisements which go farther than the text to emphasize sexual allure. On the other hand, articles and editorial responses to readers' letters, with a slightly feminist edge tell girls not to think that because you are short/tall, fat/underdeveloped, have to wear glasses, etc., that you are ugly or abnormal. Articles helping girls to psyche out what boys think (written by young men) about clothes, perfume, kissing, dating—may appear in the same issue with articles directing a girl to stand up to a boy who tells her to lose weight.

The American *Seventeen* tries to cover other bases as well, informing girls that sexual relationships are *relationships* as well as the means for physical pleasure, which they seldom mention. However, over a one-year period (August 1990 to July 1991), articles in *Seventeen* treating sexuality overwhelmingly emphasize the physical aspects (which they take to mean physical dangers and consequences) of sexual activity, rather than the emotional aspects or the pleasures of sexual involvement—except to warn girls that sex might lead to emotional complications.

Articles on physical development and health primarily emphasize the risks of starting sexual activity too young, sexually transmitted diseases, how stress affects your menstrual cycle, how premenstrual tension might affect your relationships. There is, in every issue, whether in an article or in letters, some opportunity provided for supporting a girl who would like to wait to have sex.

In the January 1991 issue, an article titled "The no of the '90s" revealed that 41 percent of the polled readership has had sexual intercourse by the age of seventeen. The article immediately says, "This means, of course, that *59 percent* (italics theirs) of you have not had sex. So there's no reason to feel like an outsider if you're still a virgin at seventeen." Of course, *Seventeen* does not want to be a prude, and so we hear "Sex is a normal, healthy thing, and under the right circumstances, can be one of life's most meaningful experiences."

The annual *Seventeen* survey of teen sexuality is revealing.[15] The summary statement appears to reinforce the idea of confidence and responsibility: "The biggest news isn't that teenagers are having more sex in the '90s than teenagers of the past—even though you are. The real news is that you are . . . thinking about and having sex more responsibly." This study shows that 49 percent of their readership have not had sex, down from 59 percent noted in their January issue. By the age of nineteen, they say, 71 percent of girls have had sex. *Seventeen* points out that girls are now more confident, more "take-charge" in sexual relationships, ask boys out on dates more, and use contraceptives more. Boys more than girls report that they fall in love many times, and both boys and girls say that love should be associated with sex, and that there should be a commitment before there is sexual activity.

But the summary of *Seventeen*'s position must be seen in articles devoted to a series of readers' responses on why they have remained virgins: if you avoid sex, you're "not a slut," "my parents approve," "my church supports me," "you don't get pregnant," "boys will respect you," "you don't feel guilty," and "it will be special if you wait until you get married."

Seventeen does not explicitly prepare teens for sexual activity: there are no instructional articles on birth control or on protection against sexually transmitted diseases, though there are news clips on the frequency of sex and pregnancy among teens (one in twenty fifteen-year-olds is sexually active, one in ten teen girls is pregnant) and on the distribution of condoms in high schools (in the same column, directly following, was a clip on a new kind of frisbee). And there are no instructional articles on the sex act itself, on methods and pleasures.

The level of information on sex available to teens in America is rather low, as noted in the few teen advice columns that treat this issue openly. "Ask Beth" is one such syndicated column in which letters like the following may appear:

I was afraid, and this big older kid got into the car to comfort me and I think he used me for sex. I'm 13 and don't know if I'm pregnant. I did sit-ups everyday like he told me to but I don't know if it worked. Could I be pregnant?[16]

In another column the counselor notes the American double message:

Adolescents see nearly 14,000 instances of sexual material on television each year. Only 165 refer to topics like sex education, STDs, birth control. . . . So kids are having more sex and having it at a steadily dropping age. . . . One in five Americans now loses his or her virginity before the age of 13.[17]

American schools are conflicted about the place and content of sex education, as noted above, but so are Japanese schools, even in a less puritanical culture. It is only now, in 1992, that Japanese grade schools are being provided with a sex-education curriculum, in the fifth and sixth grades. And the texts are rather low on detail on sexual activity, high on the biology of reproduction. Many educators say they don't go far enough.[18]

For clear and unabashed information and instruction, we must look to Japanese teen magazines. Magazines fill the information gap and regularly feature explicit instruction and upbeat, enthusiastic encouragement for sexual activity. Remember that in Japan the basic dilemma in teenage sexuality is between physical and *social*, rather than physical and moral, dimensions of sex. When asked what topics must be avoided in a magazine about pop stars for thirteen- to fifteen-year-old girls in Japan, editors replied that while sex per se is fine; revelations of a pop star's love life are not. This is not because of a taboo on sexual disclosures, but because of the fact that if a star is known to have a girl friend, the reader will feel locked out and cannot fantasize about the star's availability to *her*. For a sexually developing Japanese boy or girl, there is far less of an abstract moral principle of virginity or deep taboo against sexual activity than American teens experience in the ambivalence displayed in their culture and media.

Instead, then, of the American mixed message about sexuality, Japanese teens operate under the notion that sexuality has three arenas of expression: physical passion, socially approved pairing (marriage), and romantic fantasies. The separation of these aspects of sexual consciousness and behavior is culturally approved in Japan. In America, at least ideally, physical passion and the embodiment of a romantic dream are to be found within the permitted, legal, socially-approved bounds of marriage—or a relationship leading to marriage. In Japan, especially for men, there is approval given to different kinds of expression experienced in different arenas of life, sometimes with different people. Extramarital or premarital sexual activity then is not usually a problem as long as it does not become confused with social, publicly approveable relationships. When a teen is sexually active, his or her major concern is not to be public—for when a relationship of this kind is obvious and forces people to acknowledge it, then the criteria for appropriate *social* relationships kick in, which may be different, and which in any case often are subject to adult approval. And for girls especially, the arena of romance is often quite separate from sexual activity or from the realm of marriage dreams or realities. These categories also exist in America and people have such freedoms—but the cultural acceptance of such distinctions is weaker, and the positive ideal of the combination of romance, passion, and socially approved companionship is very strong.

A look at one magazine read by teenage and older girls illustrates this Japanese compartmentalization. *CanCam*, like many other teen and youth magazines, offer pull-out how-to sections each month. In the October 1989 issue appeared a special feature, a manual on arranged marriage, and three months later in February 1990, a similar manual on sex. (See Chapter 5 for further discussion). In all issues, there are also illustrated short stories, whose major theme is romance, poetic stories of unrequited or impossible love, accompanied by misty illustrations of a girl counting daisy petals or writing poetry on a misty hill. Unfulfilled love and what would be to Americans unhappy endings are a feature of these stories.

The *omiai* manual and the sex manual are both about approved, modern, heterosexuality. The juxtaposition of the strategies for achieving a good match, and the strategies for achieving a good orgasm, is not odd in Japan.[19]

Omiai, marriage introductions arranged by relatives or superiors, are still common in Japan, even though many young people say they prefer love marriages. Love marriages, now said to be in the majority, are often the result of an initial introduction of suitable prospects arranged by adults, followed by falling in love before marriage. Many young people, even those with sexual experience, prefer to have an objective mature adult behind an introduction, to take responsibility for an appropriate match. The first statement in the *CanCam omiai* manual is that love is not always a prerequisite to a successful marriage. This is part of a traditional view, which also holds that love may grow better in the context of a mature marriage, than between two people who have nothing in common and no shared responsibilities. If there is love outside this marriage, it is not condemned unless it leads to the destruction of the marriage.

The *CanCam* manual stresses "Arranged Marriage for the '90s"—including new matchmaking agencies, up-to-date with complicated national computer videos (and transmissions direct to one's home computer), and other technologies in service to the arranged marriage. Japanese magazines for all age groups are fond of data (as noted in Chapter 5)—the provision of information is key to the success of a magazine for any age group—and *CanCam* offers pop social science, as in interviews, survey results, and analysis by experts, on what constitutes a good prospective spouse and a good marriage.

The difference, it might be noted, between the process of database matchmaking and traditional parental matchmaking, is that the former elicits information on personality and preferences directly from the young person, whereas parents act as filters and arbiters in the traditional form. Moreover, family background and appropriate social context inform parental choices. However, the agencies themselves act like parental filters as they select "the kind of person your parents would choose," and data collected include social and class context. The *omiai* for the '90s thus preserves some of the intention and responsibility of the older practice, however modern its technology.

From the socially approved matching of people for marriage, *CanCam* turned in February 1990 to sexuality, aimed at present pleasure without future calculation. There is no contradiction between the conservative proprieties necessary for a good marriage and the live-for-the-moment sensuality encouraged in this issue.

The preface sets the tone: "Sex is the most exciting and comfortable stimulation physically as well as psychologically. . . . Good sex makes you more beautiful. Honestly, don't you agree?" Girls are encouraged, it seems, to see sex not as part of a relationship, nor even as the American *Seventeen* concedes, "one of life's most meaningful experiences," but as a technique for individual pleasure and even as a beauty treatment.

Social science encourages the reader: 81.7 percent of unmarried females have intercourse, 44 percent with males who are not steady boyfriends. Thus dispensing with any doubts about what is normal or demographically approved, the pull-out booklet proceeds to its primary topic, the techniques for achieving pleasure. The eight themes are: using massage as foreplay; how to achieve orgasm; how to achieve ecstasy (advice from a famous porn star); how to learn from sex in movies; what men think about sex; how to condition your body for good sex; how to visit a love ("H") hotel (with addresses, price rates, and photographs). (Notes: These hotels are sometimes called "H" hotels, from the teen slang word "H," meaning "horny"—derived, it is said, from the English word "itchy," which sounds like the Japanese pronunciation of the letter H.) A short entry on contraception and abortion leads with pleasure as its main theme, too, as instruction is given in putting on condoms as foreplay to enhance sexual feeling.

The tone and material of this manual are not shocking to any but middle-aged Japanese, for whom not the practice of pleasurable sex but the public discussion of it, especially in a female magazine, seems strange. Older Japanese are likely to find women who *talk* about sex especially forward, but reading about it may not indicate a *public* discourse.

Other media besides *manga* and magazines offer a relatively open and explicit treatment of sex to teenagers. The telephone party lines, discussed in Chapter 5, are similar to American party lines, and are vehicles both of ordinary teen chat and accidental and merchandised pornography. Teen lines offer a kind of teasing intimacy at a distance—you do not have to reveal who you are, since you talk under a nickname you choose for yourself, and you usually do not know any of the five or so other teens on the line.

Some telephone lines encourage girls and boys to talk about sex, by hiring girls to initiate sexual discussions. Some lines, especially late at night, are used by older men who like to engage girls in sexual talk. The teens are usually annoyed and not so interested in these men, and often try to get the men off the line so they can talk about the top hits and where to buy and NFL sweatshirt.

Another offshoot of media-encouraged sexual consciousness

has recently appeared—the *otakuzoku* (the "distant tribe," discussed in Chapter 6) are an object of concern to some adults as some have developed their own pornographic *manga*, produced on their computers and circulated in xeroxed form. More than deploring the sexual turn their hobby has taken, psychologists and commentators are worried about these children's antisocial tendencies, their inability to achieve face to face intimacy with other people.

Getting Together: Dating and Other Proximities

There is no question that the new Japanese teen is sexually sophisticated, if not always sexually experienced. There is a huge gap between today's fifteen-year-old, informed and often experienced, and the fifteen-year-old of only five to ten years ago. Today's twenty-year-old is likely to be shocked by a younger brother or sister's experience and confidence. Social ease with the opposite sex is another matter, and many of the teens in the Japanese sample reported feeling very awkward in a social "dating" situation.

American teens, on the other hand, are very alert, from an early age, to the dating game and its consequence. First, of course, they have more time and access: the teen has both permission and in some cases, and actual *push* from parents to "be popular, socialize, don't be a wallflower." Middle-class teens have enough money and often their own cars, to give them the freedom to plan an extensive social life. While 70 percent of American teens go out from one to three nights per week, 58 percent of Japanese teens go out less than one night per week.

And what does "going out" mean? In Japan, most usually, it means going out in same-sex groups of two to five children, to a movie or to an amusement area, or more rarely to a party. Dating in pairs is an awkward business for Japanese teens, and older teens and those in their twenties rely on friends to introduce them to others or on computer dating services. There are special blind-date clubs, where hundreds of young people play games to sort them into couples, and which arrange matchmaking tours to resorts and sightseeing places.

In the United States, dating depends on the age of the teen: for young teens, it means going out in groups, usually boys and girls together; for older teens it often means dating—going out as a couple—even if the "date" is pizza and a video at one of their houses. Houses are comparatively spacious and parents relatively permissive, or perhaps simply reluctant to resist their children, so that access is simple compared to the case of the Japanese teen. And time is on the side of the American teen, whose homework is light and whose duties are slight. Access to time and privacy for sexual activity is also relatively easy for the American teen whose parents are frequently not at home. Even though teens say that their parents don't know they are sexually active and that they wouldn't approve if they knew, 70 percent of the sexually active teens have sex in the home of one of the partners, 50 percent in the time-honored backseat of a car, with the rest seeking other places, such as motels, woods, and parks.

In Japan, especially, there is a social-class distinction in sexual behavior: young people not continuing to college tend to begin sexual activity earlier than do middle-class college-oriented students. In America, sexual activity is more egalitarian; children of all classes tend to be involved.

How do these teens negotiate the relationships leading to dating? It is scarcely as simple as finding time and access. Meeting someone, sensing availability and suitability—as well as the elusive "chemistry"—becomes a major occupation of the American teen's life. Going out is the end product of much strategizing and anxiety, for many teens.

Some boys put the responsibility for even initial overtures on the girl. But most teenagers prefer traditional roles: many girls said they would *never* ask a boy out: if they did, they wouldn't be sure of his motivation if he said yes; if he asked, then they would be less insecure. Boys feel they should pay for entertainment, and they don't like the riskiness: a sixteen-year-old boy says, "It's tough . . . a lot of time you know the answer is going to be 'no,' and you just don't ask."[20]

While relationships may last only a short time—even a week— they may be experienced as very intense, because so many ego-testing issues are at play. Who likes whom better; how the relationship affects the couple's friends; how ready each is for escalation of the relationship are questions always in the background. Girls seem ready to handle them better than boys: "Guys are not ready for what we think we're ready for, so everything's really messed up. . . . It can't be worth it. . . . It's worth it."[21]

Since dating in couples this young is rare either as entertainment or as mating game in Japan, there are few equivalents to these experiences, and dating in the late teens in Japan has a very different character. Japanese girls in their late teens are very confident of their control of the situation, and they tend to be clear and unequivocal once the boy has expressed his interest. They can be quite assertive, and seem to enjoy having more than one boy on the hook—as "insurance men." One boyfriend can also be called a "horsetail," or do-all-one-can man, someone she may send on errands, and it is helpful to have an *asshi-kun,* or "leg man," who has a car, to drive her around. Not all girls have this full retinue, and some have little contact with boys until college or work years. In any case, dating and its rituals, still forming in Japan, are not a necessary prelude to sexual activity, for the couples who are socially visible as dating are not necessarily the same as those who have a private physical relationship.

Teen girls who are sexually active in Japan tend to have several partners, usually older boys. It is rare for boys and girls of the same age and school in junior and senior high school to have a sexual relationship with each other. Since "giving off the scent" of sexuality is publicly frowned upon, Japanese young people may be in the opposite position to that of the Americans, for the former look quite innocent but may not be, while the latter often affect a sexual sophistication that belies their innocence. American teens may in fact be unhappy with the image they project and the perception adult society has of them.

As one indignant teen wrote to *Newsweek* magazine, protesting articles stating that American teens act out irresponsibly in their sexual relationships,

> The new rules of courtship mock teenagers as we struggle to cope with the adult problem of love. In all my 17 years, I have yet to meet any person, adult or teen, who has it all figured out. Teenagers should not be ridiculed for their identity crises and courtship problems. We are not 'virtual testosterone and estrogen armies primed for battle.' We are developing human beings who have had less time than adults to solve our personal enigmas. Teenagers will catch up with the rest of the world. We always have.[22]

Voices of Japanese Teenagers

Young teens are keenly aware of changes in themselves and their friends, as they mature sexually and socially. Kazuko, a second-year middle school girl, noticed the change between the first and second years in middle school boys and girls:

When we were first year students, boys and girls were just normal friends with each other, but since we became second-year students, it seems like boys and girls are more conscious of each other. Girls act more like *burikko*, (fake innocents, flirtatiously childlike). . . . Boys try to act cool (*kakko tsuketeru*). Girls become simpering *kawaiiko* (cute kids) but when boys aren't around, they revert to normal tomboy gossips.

Girls try to appear cute . . . like, even if they can easily hop over a little stream, they cry out "I can't!" . . . To girls, they look so silly. They sometimes speak in high voices, baby language, very girlish, but when there are only girls around, they are more like "Hey you, what do you think you're doing?" (*Omae, nani yatten no?*) [among older Japanese, this sort of speech sounds rudely masculine when used by girls].

Boys have started to ask girls out, at least during summer vacation. We go to Enoshima to swim. The really precocious girls go out with older boys (*sempai*) but most of us go out in groups of five or six. It's a lot of fun. . . . I don't go out with one person on a date, it seems yucky (*kimochi warui*). Well, maybe not really yucky, but . . . I don't think I really want to do things like that now. . .

In middle school and high school, fully developed, socially recognized sexual relationships are rare: it appears that public friendships and private lovers must be kept in their places, and sometimes choices must be made.

A middle school boy, Ichiro, distances himself from girls:

I'd always choose my best friends over a girl. *Shinyu* (close friends) are more important than girl friends.

A high school sophomore boy, Kazuyuki, talks to his diary:

Tuesday
It's OK not to date. Because, after all, it's a real nuisance to go out on a date. . . . But I think I may be heading toward a girl again. . . . We sometimes go home together. We talk a lot. We call each other. And she likes it. . . . I don't want to go steady this time, though. . . . I won't choose a girl for her appearance; anyone who loves me is welcome. So I won't say I love anyone just now.

Friday
My club went for a weekend excursion with Korean exchange students. . . . Oh those Koreans were wild!. . . . Korean girls were dancing and tried to kiss us. . . . At night, as expected, most didn't sleep at all. . . . The girls were moved to another room but after it became quiet, some girls came to the boys' room and talked and

slipped into our futon (bedding). . . . I met a girl I liked and I would like to go to Korea to see her.

Among non college-oriented high school girls, dating and sexual relationships are usually with older boys, out of school and working or in college.

A senior high school girl, Yuka, describes her sexual jealousy, and a day with her steady boyfriend:

I have a friend who thinks it is all right for her boyfriend to play with other girls just so he likes her best. They aren't just friends; they're thinking of getting married. . . . It's impossible for me. I can't be like her. I don't want my boyfriend to look around for other girls. I may be chicken.

My boyfriend and I went to Maebashi by car. [He is older and works full time]. We shopped and walked around holding hands, feeling like young students again. We went back to his apartment and took a nap together until 8:00 p.m. When I went home, I talked with him on the phone until the middle of the night.

A senior high school boy, Masa, writes to his diary, wishing for a girl who'd meet his needs, as if placing an ad in the personal pages:

I want her to be smart, goodlooking and so gorgeous that my neighbors would envy me. She should be able to cook rice and miso soup and be sensible. She should be an expert housekeeper. If I could find such a partner, that would be great. If you think you are charming, modest, faithful, and interested in being my girlfriend, please send me a letter, and pictures too!!

A high school junior, jerked around by a boy, turns to her best friends for comfort:

I-kun, [-*kun* is the suffix used informally for boys of secondary school age] in our class seemed to like my friend M. She had a boyfriend in another school and I-kun knew this but pursued her anyway—he called her and was nice in class to her. M was very anxious about this relationship and even cried once because of him. But all of a sudden, she saw I-kun speaking intimately with another girl in the classroom during lunch break. M then heard they were going steady and was shocked. I thought M was being played with by I-kun. He tried to call her, but whether or not he thought he had a chance, he changed his attitude 180°. He is the worst. Three of us tried to ease her feelings, but she had tears in her eyes until the fifth class. People can relieve their feelings by telling friends.

Finally, a senior in high school, Yumi, is alienated from her family and turns her dependent feelings to her boyfriend, rather than on friends or family.

> I need someone close to me with whom I can be as I am and on whom I can be emotionally dependent. My boyfriend is the one without question . . . because I have ambivalent feelings about my parents. And friends are just friends. Love means more to me than friendship.
>
> I was a Daddy's girl, but I grew up detached from my parents. While I looked independent, deep down inside I've been looking for someone . . . who really loves me. I can't accept my father but at the same time I feel lonely. That's why my boyfriend is so important to me. . . . I see the ideal image of a father in my boyfriend. Since I met my boyfriend, who is generous to me, I behave like a child when I'm with my friends, for I sometimes find it hard to restrain myself from being dependent and selfish. I'd better be dependent only on my boyfriend. . . . I tend to have everything my own way with him as if I were a child. . . . I like being treated like a pet (*kawaigarareru*) by boys. . . .

The Tatemae and Honne of Sexuality

It is generally thought that sexual activity among young people became widespread after the 1960s in Japan, that Japan's sexual revolution paralleled that of American youth. The student movement of the late 1960s did indeed encourage "free sex." When student occupation of university buildings in Tokyo ended in 1969, faculty and administrators entered the buildings as cleaning teams and found the floors littered with used condoms. Some faculty now remember the "revolution" more for the shock of realizing how liberated the students were sexually than for the political issues that motivated rebellion.

The shock for such people was not the fact of students' sexual activity, but that their elders were forced publicly to acknowledge it. Sex had broken through from the *honne*, the reality, and confounded the *tatemae*, the accepted norm or rule.

What adults who know teenagers well acknowledge is that this generation is more sexually sophisticated and less inhibited than previous generations. They wonder, however, if there might not be a new problem—if young people might not be able to maintain the culturally valued distinction between the approved ideal, or appearance, and the reality, the *tatemae* and *honne*. The *honne* in this case is children's active sexual and emotional expression; the *tatemae* in this case is the socially approved heterosexual relationship of marriage. Like all *tatemae-honne* contrasts, these are both viable if they are kept in balance, in parallel, and in their place. Japanese folk psychology seems to require the distinction, or at least recognizes it as basic to social order and personal emotional adjustment. If, as some adults fear, then, the teens' sexuality (*honne*) comes into conflict with society's norms for public behavior and publicly approved relationships (*tatemae*), an important mechanism for maintaining social stability may be at risk.

A Japanese undergraduate woman, interviewed in Boston, said that she'd had her first sexual experience at the age of fifteen, and that she now, in her early twenties, has many "sex friends": these are friends, not *boifurendo*, (an emotional attachment that may or may not be sexual, like *rabaa* or *koibito* (lover)[23] but men with whom she has sexual relationships. She says, "I do it because it is fun. However, marriage is a totally different story, you know. Marriage should be more realistic and practical. If I can't find a proper prospective husband by the age of 25, I'll try *omiai*. I can always pretend to be innocent, if I must, so there's no problem."[24] The average age of marriage for women is now 25.8 and many now say they will wait even later to marry.[25]

Another twenty-year-old says, "As long as you keep quiet about yourself, it's fine to enjoy sex." And one who is older and closer to marriage is somewhat more cautious: "Many women experience sex before marriage, yet they never talk about it because it is obvious that it will hurt the practical problem of marriage. . . ."[26] As a college student points out, "the sexual relationship is no longer a taboo; what is taboo is the public recognition of the sexual relationship."[27]

Sex and Reproduction: Teen Pregnancy in Japan and the United States

Students in the Somerville High School in Somerville, Massachusetts, were recently questioned on their sexual habits and their states of mind, and a correlation was found between non-use of condoms or other methods of birth control and the frequency of suicidal thoughts: commentators felt that there was a relationship, summed up in the thought that "life is cheap."[28] In a community with poor public-health services, in a context of religious and sexual conservatism, this sounds like blaming the victim.

The ambivalence over teen sexuality in the United States has led to uneven and sparse clinical support and information available to teens, and thus to very difficult conditions and choices for pregnant teenagers. The teenage pregnancy rate is higher in the United States than in any other advanced society, and it is popularly thought that the rate is inflated by an exceptionally high incidence among minority and disadvantaged populations. While the rate among black teenagers is higher (associated with a high value placed on having children and on being a mother),[29] the rate is so high among white teens as well that if black teens are removed from the totals, the United States still leads in teenage pregnancies.

Some commentators have associated the high rate of teen pregnancies with high sexual activity and assume that where there is a high rate, it must be due to high activity, and that to curb teen pregnancy, teens' sexual behavior must be controlled.

However, even accounting for the difficulty of assessing reporting in such cases, the countries reporting highest activity were Sweden and the Netherlands, with the United States rather far behind. Thus the highest rate of sexual activity in the study correlated with *low*—not high—rates of pregnancy. What seems to make the difference is that in the United States, there is rela-

Pregnancy rate per 1000

	15–19	15–17	18–19
U.S. total	96	62	144
U.S. white	83	51	129
England/Wales	45	27	75
France	43	19	79
Canada	44	28	68
Sweden	35	20	59
Netherlands	14	7	25

From: Elise F. Jones, et al., "Teenage Pregnancy in Developed Countries: Determinants and Policy Implications," *Family Planning Perspectives*, vol. 17 (March/April 1985).

tively low openness, there is poor education about sex, and there is very low access to contraception for teens. Sweden and other European countries are far more public and open about sex education and this openness may produce both higher reporting about sexual activity and lower pregnancy rates. Clinics where adolescents feel comfortable are rare in the United States, and in general, sexual conservatism has affected policies and programs that would reduce pregnancies. It appears that it is not sexual activity per se that is the problem, but again, our mixed messages.

> American teenagers seem to have inherited the worst of all possible worlds regarding their exposure to messages about sex: movies, music, radio and TV tell them that sex is romantic, exciting, titillating: premarital sex and cohabitation are visible ways of life among adults they see and hear about; their own parents or their parents' friends are likely to be divorced or separated but involved in sexual relationships. Yet, at the same time, young people get the message that good girls should say no. Almost nothing that they see or hear about sex informs them about contraception or the importance of avoiding pregnancy. . . . [30]

Japan looks more European than American in this regard. Although sex education in the schools in Japan is rather rudimentary, knowledge about sex in the community of teenagers is exchanged in relatively straightforward ways, with, as we have seen, magazines as a major sex educator. Reliability of reporting of sexual activity is difficult to assess in Japan also, but among children interviewed, most at least knew of someone their age with experience. What is significant and surprising to older Japanese, is that most teens (60 percent) approve of sexual relations among their peers—with appropriate contraception.[31] Abortion is the usual outcome of a pregnancy in this age group, and Dr. Yasuo Higashi of Ashiya Counselling Center in Kobe notes that often it is the parents who push children to have an abortion; children may want to keep their babies.[32] One Tokyo sixteen-year-old high school student said that abortions "may not be a big deal [since] many [teenage girls] earn Y20,000 to Y30,000 a month at part times jobs and could afford the cost."[33]

Overall, however, teens account for only 6 percent of Japan's total abortions, and the rates of both pregnancy and abortion in this group are among the lowest in the world. Not content, however, with these low rates, the Japanese Education Ministry has issued guidelines for schools on sex education, including detailed instruction on contraceptive methods.

On the other hand, the Health and Welfare Ministry has also instituted a new course in April 1991, to provide teens with intimate contact with infants. Teens in this class are taken to day-care and public-health centers to work directly with babies. This is intended not as a warning about the outcomes of sexual activity, but to encourage young people to consider having several babies, and to prepare them for parenthood. Demographers are concerned about the dropping birth rate, and an official stated "We hope they will acquire a love for babies after interacting with them."[34]

Toward Healthy Sexuality: Japanese Perspectives

In general, however, clinicians and psychologists in Japan are not primarily worried about pregnancy or sexually transmitted diseases and do not see children's interest in sex per se as evidence of moral decay, perversion, or delinquency. In fact, as the first quotation in this chapter indicates, many want only the "healthy expression" of sexuality to dominate.

Dr. Yasuo Higashi of Kobe began a recent interview[35] by saying that there has been a real decline in young peoples' healthy sexual development, noting that there has been a significant reduction in boys' experience of masturbation. Five years ago, 98 percent of the boys he surveyed had experienced masturbation, while, in 1991, the percentage has fallen to 85 percent. He attributes the drop to the stress caused by a increased focus on examination study, and some of his counseling aims at helping young people relax enough to enjoy their own bodies.

The level of stress he said is related to the educational level and aspirations of parents, for the children who attend high-pressured high schools, such as Nada High School in Kobe, and who attend after-school classes and cram schools, do almost nothing but study. Higashi says this results in a lack of healthy human relationships. He says that the "emotional blockage" that results can lead to sexual problems and that such problems don't end with admission to a good college, for even with a slight easing of pressure in the college years, a success-oriented young person continues in a stress-filled occupation, aiming always at promotion. Stress in the college years, he says is insufficiently studied.

Some students experience problems immediately after admission to college, called "May sickness," in which many students experience disappointment and emptiness: they wonder what all the study was for, and what they have missed, and are paralyzed, not knowing how to proceed with their social and sexual lives. In extreme cases they suffer from *fureai kyofusho*, or fear of relationships.

Dr. Higashi noted that sexuality and mature adulthood are not related in Japan in the same way as they tend to be in the United States. In the United States, he feels, in reality there may be some ambiguity: adolescents may see sexual experiences both as a means to feel more adult, and as a way of rebelling against adult standards. In Japan, where being sexually active doesn't always mean being adult, young people can maintain very childlike qualities, as *kawaikochan*, or "cute kids," and still have very active sex lives. A Mickey Mouse image on a tee-shirt and winsome pigtails caught up with pink-rabbit hairclips does not signify slow sexual development in Japan.

Sex, Responsibility, and Future Lives

While he sees stress as affecting Japanese children's healthy sexual development, he says that sexual anxiety is much greater in America where sexual and social development are closely and explicitly related. In Japan, he notes that one's sexual identity is less an issue than it is in the United States. For both girls and boys in America, becoming sexually active is a very salient part of their maturing identities. In Japan, sexual experience and performance are much less important than friendship and school performance, and even when children are sexually active, this activity does not preoccupy them.

Young people in Japan, then, separate romance, sex, and marriage to a considerable degree. Boys fifteen to eighteen, when interviewed about sex and marriage, consistently say that they look forward to marriage, but that sex is quite a separate thing. Marriage is to them being taken care of, by a motherlike wife. Their fantasy is that marriage will be like being in the family they will leave, but better. The social approval given to male dependency produces in Japan almost the reverse of American fantasies: it is the *man* who looks forward to being taken car of; the *woman* who looks forward to caring for others. Young women, on the other hand, say they'd like to delay marriage, and are increasingly seen to be fussy about whom they will marry. For women, marriage does not represent nurturance and dependency, but rather, high responsibility.

Rather than love and sex, what preoccupies Japanese teens is the need for a predictable future: getting into college and/or getting a good job loom larger than relationships with the opposite sex. One's marriage and family life are more of a given in Japan, or at least, are not generally a focus of anxiety during the teens. Once one's occupational future is determined, except for those who persist on the high-anxiety track to high promotion and status levels, there is relative stability.

Many Japanese compare American and Japanese families and note the strains built into the one and the stability of the other. Stability in middle-class American families is based on the constant need for renewal of attraction and loyalty between a husband and wife, isolated from a larger kin network, whereas stability in the Japanese family is related both to the successful rearing of children and to wider kin ties. The emphasis on sexuality in marriage in the United States confounds Japanese observers. Some women see it as a kind of slavery for the wife, whom they do not envy. One, a sociologist, said, "Why do Americans always have to be in love? It seems such a waste of energy."

At any age then, Americans appear to suffer more stress in sexual relations than do Japanese, because sexual relationships are seen to be the key to emotional fulfillment and satisfaction of dependency needs. In Japan, where a range of more "permanent" relationships—such as parent-child, friendships, and group membership—provide for emotional stability, the search for security does not lie in sexual attraction. Dependent intimacy can be found separate from sexual relationships in Japan, while in the United States, young people separating from dependence on their parents, must seek secure, nurturant intimacy, *and* sexual fulfillment in a sexual partner.

Clearly, however, not all American teens act out their ambivalence over dependency in their sexual relationships, and not all Japanese teens are free from sexual anxiety. The young people in this study exhibit a range of feelings, experiences, and behavior. What we have seen, however, is the role of culture and society in imposing its will on the biological facts of life: What may in Japan surprise an American is the relative lack of moral dicta governing the discourse about adolescent sexuality, as well as the separation between sexual and social relationships—virginity may not be a concern, but social proprieties are. What surprises a Japanese observer of America are both the public moral condemnation of sexuality and the publicly rampant display of sexual activity.

In Japan and America, culture provides young people with guidelines at the extremes—permission and proscription, the outer limits of behavior, as well as the fine-tuning of small acts and the understanding of subtle meanings. Sex is after all sex, but our cultures—in this case, adult values and the messages of the media—teach our teens its place in their lives.

8
Big Thoughts

ADULT VIEWS

. . . A rapidly changing society is creating a generation of youths who are increasingly despondent and lacking in motivation and a proper sense of social responsibility. . . . At the center of the problem is a change in personality of youths toward immature, self-centered persons who are languid and unemotional.

> —Prime Minister's Office, *Annual Report on Youth,*
> *January 1991*, cited in *Japan Report*, March 1991.

. . . There is, finally, the question of their [American youth's] emotional style: here the change has been especially remarkable and disturbing. In a word, the freedom, the openness, the imaginative and expressive range that was so prominent in their early years seem virtually gone; there is something flat, stolid, altogether routinized, about them nowadays. Far from experiencing adolescence as a time of varied opportunity, of experimentation, of flux, of "storm and stress" . . . they have narrowed their sights in a very marked way, and indeed have closed off important options and possibilities . . .

> —John Demos, "The Rise and Fall of Adolescence," *Past, Present*
> *and Personal*, Oxford: Oxford University Press, 1986, page 108.

TEEN VIEWS

A day doesn't go by without happenings. Either something happens, or I *make* it happen, and then I can find a change in me too. So, naturally, I love to go out into the world, because something exciting certainly might happen to me.

> —Fifteen-year-old high school student, Osaka

197

In the future, I see myself being an astronomer or a physicist . . . I will definitely not have more than two children, since I don't want to be responsible for the eventual overpopulation of the earth. . . . I will also be an avid environmentalist, as I am now. I hope to make a great impact on the world, both scientifically and environmentally.

—Fifteen-year-old junior-high-school student, Lawrence, New Jersey

We began this look at American and Japanese teenagers with adult concerns and fears about and for them. We will end with the teens' own concerns and hopes, not just for themselves but for the world. Their broad idealism and sense of responsibility for the future, their "big thoughts," may surprise adults in both countries who have written them off as narrow and self-centered, lacking soul and passion.

There appears to be more than the much-touted generation gap at work in the consideration of adolescence in both the United States and Japan. The perception gap is even greater, and more invidious, as our society's institutions and interventions on behalf of adolescents are based on views *of* teens that differ greatly from the views *from* teens.

The critical task of adolescence is securing a sense of who you are and learning what you can do about who you will be. The process involves trial-and-error experimenting—alone, with adults, with friends, and with what I am calling here "big thoughts"—the ways in which teens try to explain, and place themselves in, a wider world of challenges.

Teenagers, like the rest of us, swing from the trivial obsessions of every day to global thinking about problems beyond their home, school, and sex lives. But teens, just beginning to test their ideas, to try out their cracking new philosophic voices, are both soberly reflective of their environments and wildly iconoclastic. Much of the time, of course, they are reinventing the wheel, but they are sure that they are the very first to have such ideas, and the excitement of discovery is matched by the assertiveness of insecurity. An eighth-grade boy in America, sweating with first-date anxiety, sits on a stoop with his date and looks to the night sky, and says, "Do you ever think how we might just be tiny submicroscopic particles, maybe smaller than cells, in the arm of a huge giant? Maybe our whole universe is such a particle?" "And maybe," she offers, cockily flirtatious, "*you* are just a particle in *my* arm."

The big thoughts these young people experiment with may be thrilling or bleak or upbeat, but they inevitably extend teens' boundaries into a world larger than themselves, moving (sometimes leaping) past the concentric circles of self, family, close friends, and the institutions of school and workplace that surround them. All children in the study had such big thoughts, ranging from concern for the environment and peace in the world (mainly among the Japanese) to concern for the quality of life in a society torn by drugs and crime (mainly among the Americans). Some children had developed critical reflections on their country's political system and leaders, some echoed anti-establishment perspectives from movements and philosophies that had retreated from popular view well before these children were born. Teen concerns about the world today in Japan and the United States focus in part also on what they feel is the most critical relationship: the current uneasy partnership between the United States and Japan.

We have seen how children react to and develop strategies for managing relationships within the family, school, and friendship circles, and more widely, how young people as a cohort are seen and react to as a consumer market. Within this framework, then, we will now look at children's perceptions of themselves, their futures, and finally, look at how they consider the global relationships and the responsibilities they will inherit.

Defining and Refining a Self

Adolescent children reflect on their own development, on how they are learning to be individuals, social people, and members of groups. Learning who you are as an individual is managed through introspection—a well-developed art in both the Japanese and American adolescent. Learning who you are in a social context involves developing relational skills with family and friends while you adjust to the contradictions of rules and practices. Learning who you are in institutional settings—the requirements of the classroom, and for Japanese teens, the stringent demands of peer hierarchies—prepares you for the world of adult work.

Japanese youth learn to consider their feelings and reactions to people in Proustian detail, and they develop concerted programs of self-improvement. American children are also painfully aware of others, but rather than Proust, their literary models may be Charlie Brown or Zippy. In Japan, where child-rearing and educational methods are based on the positive notion that all children can improve, it is expected that all children will have serious personal goals for achievement. American recipes for success— for example, the self-made man or free spirit vs. the traditionally educated woman or classically mentored man—are confused and contradictory. As a result, few teens can clearly formulate the kinds of programs of personal action commonly heard from Japanese teens.

Japanese young people are taught correct behavior early, but the lesson is not top-down commandments. In grade school, besides the usual lessons of appropriate behavior and school customs, such as the proper placement of outdoor shoes, toes pointed in the right direction, in the child's cubbyhole, the first lessons for first graders include understanding one's responsibility for the outcomes of actions and behavior, and learning from other children, through critical reflection (*hansei*) the roots of social and personal acceptability. *Hansei* is not a harsh exercise conducted to attribute blame and label offenders, but to analyze interactions and to establish a framework of practical social ethics.

There are some interesting contrasts with American teens' learning the social and ethical ropes. As we can see from the Japanese diaries and interviews, children in the secondary school years have internalized well the lessons of self-examination. A second-year high school girl in Gumma Prefecture says,

> I am active and take high pride in myself. I like to be a winner . . . but I jump in fast without considering. But, as in a maze, we can take another way when we hit a wall. The more you do, the more walls you may hit, which I think will improve your understanding of who you are.

And another,

> We had swimming in the fifth class for physical education. Since it was just after lunch, I changed into my swim suit early and sat by the pool, chatting with my friends. We didn't enter the water to practice because the swimming club was using the pool. The bell rang and they left, and we went into the water. Our teacher came and . . . sat us next to the pool and said we were too late entering

the pool. . . . Of course, it was impossible to go earlier. The teacher didn't know the swim club had been practicing. We kept quiet and were very upset but we didn't say anything. I thought it would be better to say why we weren't in the pool, but I couldn't. It might have sounded like an excuse. That's what I thought my motivation was, at the time, for keeping quiet, but now I realize, to be honest, that I didn't have enough courage. I think deep down inside that I didn't want to stand up while others kept silent. I should be braver.

Most children believe in self-discipline as the means to self improvement—few believe in luck and opportunity alone—but most have a sense of optimism about outcomes. A senior-high-school boy in Chiba says,

I must discipline myself to be a good man. We have ups and downs in our life. Overcome difficulties, be a man who is respected, and have a good future.

Some children become extremely hard on themselves. A senior-high-school boy in Gumma Prefecture:

I am timid, weak-willed, indecisive, and irresponsible. . . . I have no patience, no willpower, no endurance, no concentration power. I am both optimistic and pessimistic. I have no good points, and I am hard to understand. Most people tend to be hard on themselves when asked to describe themselves. That is because I do not hold any beliefs or ideals so far yet. Generally Japanese are easily molded by others and lose their identities, and therefore it is difficult for me to know what I believe. I, being immature and underdeveloped, still have a long way to go to see my beliefs.

An American teacher reading this essay might be concerned and assume this boy to be seriously depressed. In fact, middle-class American children are not as hard on themselves in their self-descriptions in this study, and overall, are sunny and optimistic, even to the point where Japanese observers found them to be naïve, unrealistic, and unreflective. One American high-school boy says,

What would I like to improve in myself? Not much. I'm doing OK, and I've been pretty lucky, getting teachers who like me and all. Sometimes my parents get at me about grades but I'm doing better than my friends and I'm having a good time.

American ideas about healthy adolescence emphasize positive self-confidence, while Japanese emphasize self-reflection and self-reliance, an emphasis implying more actual responsibility for oneself than the American view, which by contrast, is more about *attitude*.

Self-doubt exists, in America too: A girl focuses her doubts on her appearance:

> If I could change something I'd like to change my hair. My mother says I can't color my hair until I graduate, but I *hate* it. Actually I wish my whole body were different. Sometimes I just wear my raincoat all day because I feel so ugly and fat. I wish I could quit school and get a job.

An African-American boy, whose brother dropped out of school, feels pressure to do better:

> My mother says, "Don't be like Edgar." My teachers warn me that I might go the same way if I don't work hard. I want to stay in school and maybe go to college, but none of my friends will, and with my brother not in school I'd be going too far the other way. And I don't like people pushing me like this.

Another aspect of self-development the boy from Gumma Prefecture reveals is the felt need for core beliefs and ideals among Japanese youth. It was difficult to elicit beliefs and ideals among the American sample, except at the loftiest rhetorical level, such as "I believe in the equality of all people," or "My ideal is to live in a peaceful world." Most Japanese youth, on the other hand, were working to develop functional ideals they could implement in their own lives—perhaps less grand than those of their American counterparts but based on a realistic view of what a person can do. Moreover, the Japanese boy quoted above sees beliefs as something one must create oneself from scratch, not as kits of ideas one can subscribe to simply by choosing from available stock. The Japanese boy seems frustrated that he hasn't yet developed in this direction, but he realizes that it is a long and difficult process.

His remarks, though they appear extreme, reflect the more modest, even self-deprecating tone of a well-socialized, appropriate Japanese, a position of self-presentation required by convention. In fact, one of the signals of deculturation teachers recognize in Japanese children returned from the United States is their lack of *enryo* (hesitation, holding back, modesty), as well as their positive self-promotion—not the same at all as the optimism prevalent among Japanese teens about the distant future and their ability, once mobilized, to reach their goals.

When an American teen reflects on self-development, she might say:

> I wish I could get better grades. I want to go to college and get a job in advertising.

or:

> I want to treat everyone the same way. Remember the Golden Rule. I don't want to be hurt, so I shouldn't be prejudiced against others.

These junior-high-schoolers display some elements of self-reflection common in the group. The first is typical: when asked what changes she'd like to see in herself, she spoke of "wishes" and long-term goals, but without directly mentioning a program of action she herself might take to achieve them. The second demonstrates another common tack American children take, towards abstractions and general principles of behavior. Americans tend to have more universalistic codes of behavior and social performance, and young people's ideals can be readily couched in such terms. Of course, Japanese children too know culturally encoded principles, such as *omoiyari* (sensitivity to others) but they would be less likely to invoke them.

American and Japanese teens both reflect on their moodiness. American children in a bad mood tend to blame something in the environment—friends, parents, school. Japanese children do the same, for transient reactive moods, but recognize a difference between such moments and larger, long-term feelings. Their diaries are particularly instructive on this difference:

> I woke up very angry, remembering that my mother is taking me to a posture specialist today. Why does she do this to me? I was cross at breakfast and wouldn't talk to her.
>   –High school freshman, Cambridge, Massachusetts

> From today, we have only morning classes until the end of school. This makes me very happy. But somehow today I felt more blue than usual. I could not help wanting to be alone. I felt worried about something. Sad at something. Afraid of something. I cannot express it well, but I was pessimistic. So, I wanted to be alone because I couldn't be considerate to those around me, though to be honest I needed so badly to be with them."
>   –High school freshman, Gumma Prefecture

In American terms, again, this Japanese boy seems hyperconscious of his feelings, amazingly sensitive, even in his own unhappiness, of the effect his moods might have on others. The Japanese teen seems more conscious than the American young person that he is a work-in-progress. Of course, since the codification of the idea of adolescence by G. Stanley Hall in 1903, even American teens have referred to themselves as unfinished business—often themselves using the sturm und drang hypothesis as an excuse for moodiness and antisocal behavior, as in

> I'll calm down when my hormones stop raging
> > –Junior high school girl, Lawrence, New Jersey

Another Japanese teen, a girl, reflects on her own difficult feelings related to the realization that she must choose for herself:

> In September of this year I came to the point where I did not go to school. I think the reason undoubtedly was that I could not make friends. . . . I came to feel depressed. Going off track, I was not completely alone. I began to make a way by myself, I wanted to begin to make a way . . . but I did not know what was the right thing to to. . . . I was greatly troubled. I felt remorse. Now I feel only a little remorse. . . . But no matter how much remorse I feel, I myself choose my path.[1]

Friendship, Continuities, and Choices

The confusion over solitary decisions is common to all teens, but in Japan, friends act as guides and fellow travelers on the trip to adulthood. Common also is the inevitability of change and separation, contributing further to the sense of seriousness shared by many Japanese teens.

> While I was at a bus stop, cars were passing in front of me. . . . I wondered what the drivers were thinking about then. . . . I imagined them going along the same road for a while, then some turning to the left, others to the right, each going to his/her own destination. Until they came to the turning point, they all have the same destination but in the end they arrive at different places because of their own goals, thoughts and wills. . . . That's us, now, I think. . . . We have been together so far, but as we each have our own ways, we have to say goodbye someday. That's what I am afraid of. Of course I have to keep going: we have to look ahead and go step by step in the process of growing up.
> > –Senior high school boy, Gumma Prefecture

American teens also face loss while they create deeper affiliations with each other, but passing milestones such as the entrance to junior-high school, or even high-school graduation, evokes only brief expressions of seriousness. One contributing factor is that the role of school and the time spent in educational activities is much less for the American teen than for the Japanese teen, whose affiliations must, as we have seen in Chapter 6, be governed by schedule and geography. American teens have more access to relatively remote friends—even friends who go to different schools or who leave school to work—than do their Japanese counterparts, simply because they have more *time.*

American young people usually have more continuity with their friends. Even wedding bells for American teens don't necessarily break up the gang, as teens who marry tend to maintain their friendships. Of course, both American and Japanese teens who go to college often start from scratch making new friends there, and both noted that going away to school is a real opportunity to *be* someone new, since often one does not bring along friends from one's previous life.

The concerns of the boy without beliefs, that he is influenced by others and has no opinion, are also expressed by a more positive, upbeat girl, a senior in high school in Gumma Prefecture:

> Indecisive as I am, I cannot make a quick choice, especially when I like both alternatives. I am easily influenced by others and I buy things which look cute on them, although I am not too fashion-conscious. I tend to take my friends' advice on what I should get. I'm kind of happy-go-lucky. I don't have much opinion. But that's why I don't get into fights. People say I'm *oraka* (happy, loose). I suppose I could take it to mean *toroi* (slow, dumb), but I'm not bothered. . . . I have some points I don't like about myself, but overall I like the way I am.

In the same vein, a high school boy comments on the pressures to conform leading to school refusal:

> The reason for refusing school has been discussed frequently. . . . But what truly is the reason that there are such children? . . . Without noting the individual character of each person, there is a requirement to be the same as everyone. . . . Without accepting the open self of the child, the school coerces students to make them what the school seeks. In these circumstances, a "loss-of-self" crisis occurs, and it is natural that they do not want to go to school.[2]

Most Japanese teens are not only watching themselves change; they feel they can make a difference in their own development. Many attribute improvements to their dedication to some interest: one boy refers to his karate lessons as having improved his persistence. One girl regretted that she dropped her piano lessons, "I wasn't ever going to be a very talented performer, but you are most confident in yourself if you have one special skill."

Others feel they can change even their personalities: in spite of the teen fads for personality-divination through blood typologies and other "tests," and in spite of the reliance on fortune-telling, spells, and horoscopes, Japanese teens ultimately do not feel their characters are innate or fixed in the stars. As one high school girl said, "I look on the bright side, but I'm not mindless. To resign oneself to one's fate without trying to think on one's own is not the action of a true optimist. A real optimist gives serious thought to things, and understands that we *can* change our personalities."

American children, having learned a mixed message from their elders, reflect it in their views of change: they see a ceiling on their abilities ("I did my best") and view much that is in them as innate and unchangeable. Effort has less of a place in change then, although of course, the American teen at some level knows that is important, too. Many, however, said that they *had* tried hard to *something*, but several had given up (piano, ice hockey, or math), saying "I guess I don't have any talent."

The lesson of *tatemae* and *honne* (the relationship between appearance and reality) learned by teens is perpetuated in interior discussions of the self conducted in the Japanese teens' diaries.

Usually, this lesson is illustrated not in abstractions—but in concrete discussions of the contrast they are learning between what you *can* be with a close friend what you *must* be in a friendship group. The concerns many had about being seen as sneaky or crafty (*zurui*) were fears that they couldn't be whole-hearted: the practical culture of the friendship group, demanding that you behave in an expected way in a group, when at heart you feel different, provides the most clearcut experience yet of the "situational" behavior approved by the *tatemae* of adult culture.

There are few teens who say they are not affected by what people think and say about them, and by the need for correct and approved behavior. But this "public self" is, although important, in children's discussions and diaries to their concern over the "private self"—the honne. High schoolers are especially conscious of the need to find a secure "private self" and to come to terms with their disillusion—or realization that there is, after all, a necessary distinction between these "selves." The private self must be protected,[3] and thus the distinction becomes even more marked, as the teen, only just developing an adult sense of personhood, also must learn the exigencies of social life.

Passages

January 15 is *Seijin no hi,* or Adult Day, Coming-of-Age Day. Every young person who has turned twenty during the year dresses in elaborate kimono or dress clothes and, with families in tow, visits a shrine in the neighborhood—or, for the crowds and glitter, goes to a large shrine such as the Meiji Shrine in Tokyo. Here, a ceremony conducts the new adult into his or her maturity, and afterwards the family has a celebratory meal either at home or at a hotel restaurant. Young people are also given gifts, sometimes of money. Newspapers run editorials about the responsibilities of adulthood, and most young people understand this to be a turning point of some note. Turning sixteen in America is sometimes noted by "Sweet Sixteen" parties, and for prosperous families, sometimes a gift of a car to the young person. Turning twenty-one, a legally sanctioned marker of maturity, is usually noted only as the arrival of the right to drink or to vote. There is no national holiday for youth in America, as there is in Japan for children of three, five, and seven years old on November 15, or for girls on March 3, and all children (formerly just boys) on May 5. Children in American have *individual* passages to adulthood, noted on their own birthdays and are not celebrated as an age cohort together.

Finding an appropriate *model* for adulthood is, however, a very individualized process in both societies.

Role Models and Inspirations

Creating in yourself the person you want to be involves not just self-discipline and a positive outlook, but for many teens, a positive role model. A Gallup poll conducted in 1990 compared American and Japanese teens' role models and found that both groups, in spite of media and expert warnings in both countries about the breakdown in family values, still looked to their parents first.[4]

Parents and grandparents rank high as direct role models in both countries, and yet proximity can cut both ways, as in this Japanese case:

> Above all, I don't want to be like my grandfather. He is the worst kind of person, caring about himself only, and using other people. He is really corrupt.

Japanese boys also often choose a teacher as role model, citing "selflessness," "dedication," "friendliness," and "strictness" as qualities to be emulated. Japanese girls choose their mothers, citing similar qualities in them, even though the self-sacrifices of some mothers appear pointless to their daughters. Some girls noted that their mothers may not have had a choice in their lives: they had to be 100 percent housewives or 200 percent workers and housewives. The first to some seems empty; the second over-full and oppressive. They usually admire their mothers, but wonder if these are the only choices.

American girls also frequently select their mothers, but rather than listing specific traits to be emulated, they draw loving portraits of mothers as supportive companions:

> There's so many people I admire . . . but to make it simple, I'll do my mom. She has brown naturally curly hair, glasses, greenish-blue eyes and is only a little taller than me. She's not exactly pretty, but she has a sort of intelligent, mysterious look. She's very kind and I love her a lot.
>
> –Junior-high-school girl, Lawrence, New Jersey

American boys often choose their fathers as role models. A twelve-year-old said, "I admire my father. He went through that gross process to give me life, I bothered him a lot when I was little, but he stuck around. He's there."

Children's perceptions of heroes in the United States and Japan differ, and are related to their construction of role models. In a recent study,[5] American children were seen as seeking all-around, popular figures, with concrete (usually economic) success stories, while Japanese youth chose heroes with strong aesthetic and emotional values, as well as strong interpersonal skills. Donald Trump and Lee Iacocca were high on the American list, while traditional, nearly mythical, ethical heroes such as Ninomiya Sontoku, the impoverished but dedicated scholar, were on the Japanese. Americans and Japanese both appreciated figures who had won their way through sweat and effort, but Americans chose affluent and establishment figures while Japanese more often chose loners. This finding seems to belie the popular American accusation that Japanese are "economic animals," as well as the Prime Minister's Office Report cited at the beginning of this chapter, stating that Japanese are unemotional and nonidealistic.

American teens in these interviews cited individuals as emblematic, whole role models, without modifications, whereas Japanese teens, more critical and circumspect, usually referred to specific qualities in a person, and discard others they do not want to emulate. And more than Americans who accepted the notion of role model wholeheartedly, Japanese teens sometimes discarded the question altogether:

> I don't want to be like anyone. . . . I want my own self, my own pace. . . . I'd like to emulate qualities in others I admire, but I'd like to be myself.
>
> –High school boy, Osaka

It may be that it is the *Japanese*, not the American youth, who is the greater individualist.

My Future

Adults in Japan complain of low engagement in teens, however. A teacher in Gumma Prefecture complained that today's teens were "small-bore," rather than "large-bore" as he said they were in his youth. He feels they have too narrow a range and shallow ambitions, and that they *have* no heroes and don't make large efforts towards major goals.[6] Other teachers call their students "aliens," "wandering bats," "mental bean sprouts," or even "goldfish excrement."[7]

And others have said that teens are superficial and standardized as the product of media and marketing. Such teens, it is said, shy away from relationships except for shallow ones, and seem "sterilized" (*shodoku*).[8]

It is true that few in the Japanese sample had grand plans for life: most used the word *futsuu* (usual, ordinary) to describe what their futures would be.

> I will just be a small shop owner, just ordinary, not even a salary man.
>
> –High-school senior, Chiba

In the Gallup study, American children were more optimistic about their dreams coming true. In the study, 64 percent of American youth say that school has prepared them very well for life, whereas only 4 percent of Japanese make the same claim.[9] It is important to note that as the high-school boy earlier noted, when asked to comment on any aspect of one's life, Japanese tend to be more critical. And when asked almost any question of opinion, Japanese tend to cluster their responses towards the negative end of the scale, Americans toward the positive end.

Japanese "negativism" has even been made formulaic among teens, according to some media reports. The "three no's" philosophy is said to characterize one slightly deviant adolescent personality type, who as a fashionable pose, tries to look unmotivated. The "three no's" are:

> *mukanshin* (no motivation)
> *mukando* (no impression, can't be moved)
> *musekinin* (no responsibility)

But as we have seen, overall, Japanese youth show an upbeat attitude about their potential and are generally more cheerful about their daily lives as well. Indeed, some Japanese studies show some reluctance among Japanese children to "grow up." The relative joys of childhood outweigh the responsibilities of adulthood. Among high schoolers, 57.2 percent said *no* to "do you want to be grown up?" and 32.9 percent said *yes*.[10]

Being called a "child," *kodomo*, as noted earlier, is not a problem for Japanese teenagers, and knowing the examinations loom makes many yearn for the past days of freedom. Those heading to college, of course, know that they will have a "second childhood" there, a playground time before the seriousness of adult responsibilities.

Choice figures importantly in American teens' ideas about their futures. They count on options, and on not closing down too soon on possibilities. Boys particularly seem to want to keep their options open:

> I may be an engineer, or I could go into computer programming — but I'd also like to be a pilot. I don't have to decide yet — even in college I may not know. Or something else may come along.
> –High-school junior, Lexington, Massachusetts

Some boys were more specific:

I don't have very big plans yet, but I would like to be either a professional baseball player or a writer, probably a sports writer. In ten years, I'll probably be in the start of all that, a steady job and all. And in twenty? Mid-career, with a wife and two kids.
—Fourteen-year-old boy, Newton, Massachusetts

Most Japanese youth, particularly in high school, feel they have only a limited choice, but do not seem frustrated by this. In saying they will have ordinary lives, they do not mean pointless ones. Ordinary may not reflect a feeling of "giving up" ambitions as it might in the United States. It may, in fact, reflect a positive feeling, as the practical understanding of possibilities is the basis of the predictability of one's future, which is at least as important as high ambitions.

Vaulting ambition is not seen in Japanese teens, whereas high-flying goals are part of the rhetoric of American youth. A relatively local and predictably attainable goal is enough for a Japanese child. Girls want to be dressmakers, or work in cosmetic industries, or teach—boys seem interested in small but independent businesses such as shopkeeping and coffeeshop management. Even "delinquent" gang members move on to sober and steady adult lives. As one ex-*bosozoku* youth said,

> "Now I work at a delivery agency . . . from 7 a.m. to 8 p.m., without any leisure time. I went through the coming of age ceremony and became an adult this year. My dream about the future is to become the owner of a small store."[11]

One boy in Saitama Prefecture hopes to be a jazz musician, but this would not be a radical departure for he would be inheriting the family trade, as his father is a very well known jazz musician himself.

Japanese youth were more likely both to follow parental occupations and to seek direction from parents than are American youth. To some American teens, following in their parents' footsteps represents failure. There appears to be a generation gap imperative among United States teens—to compete with and transcend their parents' lives, as though the generation gap in itself meant rejection of the past and improvement toward the future. Japanese teens do want improvement, and indeed sometimes reject their parents' lives, but do not see it as a necessary pose or perspective, prerequisite to becoming adult themselves. And they rarely feel the need for early independence from their parents, most saying that they will continue to live with their parents until they marry.

> I am dependent and I know I'm better off with my mother managing for me.
> —High school senior, girl, Tokyo

> I don't want to live by myself. . . . I just don't think I can take care of myself. . . . I'd be alright emotionally, but from what I hear, you have to do laundry yourself. Clean, cook—all of that.
> —High school senior, girl, Yokohama

But the same teens who seem so physically dependent on their parents may also have very independent plans for their futures. There is no clear correlation between *amaeru* to one's parents (seeking indulgence as a dependent, a positive quality among children and subordinates)[12] and lack of initiative: the same girl who feels she needs to stay at home while she goes to college so that her mother can cook for her says,

> I wouldn't want to be one of those worn-out middle aged women (*tsukareta obasan*). I wouldn't want to be just an ordinary housewife. . . . I just want to be professional enough to be independent. And I would really not like to marry.
> —High school senior, Chiba

Another makes a similar bold statement, with somewhat more detail:

> I don't want marriage, children and housekeeping. I have many friends who want to stay single, and when we write to each other, we talk about living together communally if possible . . . . I might end up living and working just for myself. . . . I like to live the way I like, though I don't know myself well yet.
> —Eighteen-year-old college freshman, girl, Yokohama

Horst Stipp of NBC Research notes that American girls say that they would like to be wives and mothers when they grow up, in a resurgence of traditional values. Japanese girls now say that they want a career and will only marry on their own schedule and terms. As above, it may be that Japanese girls are outstripping their American counterparts in plans for an independent life.

It is hard for Americans to grasp that the high standards and high level of introspection and self-discipline the Japanese child maintains are not tied to high personal-status ambitions and cosmic schemes for success. The "big thoughts" behind a Japanese teen's motivation to work hard are not in terms of a high-profile future, but in terms of being the person he or she wants to be—giving no excuses for oneself, managing relationships, economic goals, and the practical considerations of daily life. They may seem "small-bore" but they also seem realistic. Moreover, most are satisfied with the conditions of their lives at present, in terms of home, school, and work.

Realities

Disatisfaction does, however, exist, and as discussed in Chapter 5, it centers on an increasing sense that economic conditions are unequal. The Prime Minister's Office polls of the past ten years have demonstrated that most Japanese see themselves as middle class. But the distinctions are actually finer than that, and a look at studies considering subtler designations of class identity are more revealing. Over the past fifteen years, there has been an increase in the perception of a gap in income, financial assets, quality of housing, and consumer possessions, and a slight decline among those who call themselves "middle middle class" with a pronounced shift to designations of lower-middle class and lower class.[13]

When specific areas of life are mentioned, most people feel there has been an increase in disparity in the population. If you combine answers in "widened" and "somewhat widened" categories, more than half of Japanese feel that disparities have increased in income, assets, and consumer goods, with 46 percent noting discrepancy in the quality of housing.[14]

Trend of Class Perception of Japanese Households, 1975–1987

Belong to	1975	1978	1981	1984	1987
Upper class	0.8%	0.9%	0.9%	1.1%	1.0%
Upper-middle class	3.0	4.8	4.1	4.3	3.8
Middle class	43.4	49.3	44.3	46.6	40.7
Lower-middle class	35.3	31.7	34.9	35.2	38.7
Lower class	9.8	9.0	11.1	10.5	15.6
Don't know	7.7	4.4	4.7	2.4	0.2

Government of Japan, Economic Planning Agency, November 1989

Public Opinion Survey on People's Perception
of Disparities with Ten Years Ago: Trend of Disparity
Between Income Brackets

	Income	Financial Assets	Spaciousness & Quality of Dwelling	Possession of Durable Consumer Goods
Widened	24.0%	22.3%	16.2%	20.2%
Somewhat widened	36.0	32.3	29.8	37.1
No change	23.5	27.6	35.3	24.9
Somewhat narrowed	12.0	11.4	13.7	13.3
Narrowed	4.0	5.1	4.2	3.7
No answer	0.5	1.3	0.8	0.7

Government of Japan, Economic Planning Agency, November 1989.

How do young people perceive these discrepancies? The obvious and most immediate experience in economic distinctions is apparent to children as consumers, as we noted in Chapter 5. As the targeted audience of consumer industries and the media, youth are actively wooed as purchasers, and wooed through the most powerful agency of all, their friendships. The media providing "shopping training," and the market the most favored form of leisure activity, have teens sewn up as an audience. But the members of the audience are not equally endowed in their ability to spend, and the awareness of these differences becomes painful for many teens. Keeping up with the Satos may lead to embarrassment, and self-ostracism as a last resort. A youth-oriented economy is not a benefit for all youth.

American teens share these problems and experiences. Their communities may be more class-homogeneous than many urban neighborhoods in Japan, but distinctions exist even in an apparently middle-class suburban high school. Noting differences between friends or classmates, American and Japanese kids tend to gravitate towards those who are similar to themselves. Noting broader distinctions—an understanding of the class structure of their societies—is only seldom seen, as the image of both the United States and Japan is that of a "classless" society and the realities form a "dirty secret" behind the public rhetoric.

However, the experience and futures of these teens are tied strongly to these realities. In Japan, youth are said to be strongly materialistic. However, their future projections are relatively humble and responsible, while their larger views of society show a markedly critical perspective and they are not in the least complacent about Japanese economic successes, or Japan's potential for leadership in the world.

Japan, the United States, and The World: Teen Views of Nation and Interdependence

At odds with the apparent domestic and international positions of our two countries, American youth express pride and confidence in our nation and Japanese prefer a more critical position regarding their country's successes. Japanese youth, reflecting the low profile preferred by their elders, do not flaunt Japan's position in the world—in fact, are conscious of a high degree of national vulnerability. Being Japanese is a significant factor in their identity and they feel that Japan and the Japanese are in some ways different or unique.

They speak of the relationship between the United States and Japan as complicated by this unique sense of nationality:

> Rice is Japan's national cultural symbol: therefore, Japan should not import it from abroad. If a war breaks out, foreign nations may refuse to export rice to Japan. If this happens, Japanese people will have to starve.
>
> –Junior high school girl, Yokohama

Boys are more concerned with their identity as Japanese, though in personal, rather than in patriotic, terms. They seem to have adopted some of the media images of national character, connecting their personalities to a "national personality" as does the boy quoted earlier who said that he, like most Japanese, prefers to take a low profile and be self-critical. On the other hand, boys also tend to be somewhat anti-establishment and several, like the following, feel that the Japanese state is based on archaic and feudalistic elements.

I am a person who hates the Emperor. Honorific expressions are always used whenever he is covered on television. I don't understand why he is respected. All men are created equal, so they should use ordinary language to report on him."

–Middle school boy, fifteen, Chiba

Anti-establishment or not, several Japanese girls and boys took a strong position on United States–Japan relations, especially in economic terms, feeling that American demands that Japan open its markets are unfair and unrealistic. These teens are vehement that America is making a scapegoat of Japan in place of treating its own domestic economic problems. But most American teens—even those who said that the Japanese were taking advantage of Americans, and were "buying up our land"—tend to be rather more relaxed about competitiveness and say they would gladly work for a Japanese company. One girl said,

Hey, what's the problem? We need jobs and they offer us jobs. Does it matter whether you work for a Japanese or for an American company? They're helping us out, and they wouldn't hire us if they thought we weren't good workers.

–Senior high school student, Belmont, Massachusetts

Ideas and Ideals

While the Japanese and American student movement peaked in the early 1970s, the political voice of the left in Japan is still strong, and the environmental movement has many followers among young people. Japanese youth are well mobilized in the green movement, and have helped to popularize organic and nonpolluting products in the market. In letters to teen magazines in Japan, there are often comments from readers on ecological issues.

In spite of surveys purporting that Japanese are not interested in public altruism—in giving aid to persons unknown to the giver—Japanese young people are both idealistic in the abstract and interested in taking concrete action. Many expressed an interest in the Japanese Overseas Development Corps, the Japanese version of the Peace Corps, and several wanted to work to improve conditions for *burakumin* and homeless people.

Ideas do not necessarily have a relationship to ideals—formalized philosophic representations of goals—and in fact, it is easier for the teen to espouse an ideal like "individualism" than to take responsibility for an idea. American children, especially, took ideals to be part of the air they breathed, but their ideas needed work—the product of a creative act. One junior high school girl from Vermont said, "I didn't know I *had* ideas until I got to junior high school: before that, I just learned things." Ideals were easier to talk about. A high school boy from Massachusetts said, "Of course I have ideals; my parents are socialists."

American schools seem not to nurture, except indirectly, the independence of spirit that our ideology espouses: one thirteen-year-old boy who said, "My teacher complains that I have 'ideas in my head.' She won't call on me anymore. I'll show her, though: I'm going to grow up to be a genius—there aren't enough of us in the world."

Japanese secondary schools, too, are rarely places where independent thinking and questioning are favored: as we have seen in Chapter 4, the primary task is preparation for a detailed, multiple-choice examination, the parameters of which are known. While elementary schools in Japan do encourage exploration and discovery, "having ideas in your head" or asking a lot of questions are not promoted in secondary schools.

Ideals, however, are available to both groups, and are both thoughtfully and thoughtlessly maintained: American children can always refer to such formulaic but heartfelt phrases as "It's a free country" or "I have a right to do what I want." On a more thoughtful level, American teens refer to racial and gender issues in terms of the ideal of equality and they worry about the problem of the homeless in terms of fairness or unequal distribution. Because of the availability in media and educational rhetoric of the founding ideals of America, American children have a fund from which to draw—at a personal level, when declaring their own independence from their parents, or on a national and global level, when they decry the actions of George Bush or Saddam Hussein.

There were interesting differences between Japanese and American teens' interpretations of the same ideals—particularly the ideal of freedom. American teens, especially those interviewed during and after the Gulf War, were notably convinced that freedom is something to fight for, a legal and political right, as well as an almost religious doctrine. The Japanese teen does not place freedom in such a Manichaean framework of good versus evil, but rather in terms of "doing what you want" and "enjoying life." The Japanese teen, however, sees freedom as something permitted within one's "home quarters" (*kagirareta kuukan no naka de*) and governed by one's sense of responsibility (*sekinin*).[15] This responsibility, and the importance of a boundary within which freedom can be negotiated—situational as opposed to boundless rights—seems to represent a different ideal, more grounded, than that evoked from the American teen.

The ready access to such an ideological framework and phrases, the trusting use of these ideals in adolescent discourse, make American teens look strangely innocent and simplistic, compared to their more cautious, contextualized Japanese counterparts. This contrast is reminiscent of the nineteenth-century European view of Americans—full of optimistic idealism, but naïve and shallow. Japanese youth, while idealistic, are not ideological—they do not have a systematic store of principles that can be trotted out, but they do have ideals that refer to the same concepts—equality, freedom, democracy. And, in spite of the habits of personal humility and self-criticism, and, overall, a more guarded view of their own future than that of American teens, Japanese teens are truly optimistic—upbeat, *akarui*, sunny—but also deeply thoughtful. Believing that hard work, effort, and patience are rewarded by success, and yet also realistic in ambitions and goals, their reach may exceed their grasp; but they know that they can try again with arms lengthened by effort and exercise and the next growth spurt. In short, Japanese youth have strong personal ideals, without a strong sense of ideology, while American teens seem sometimes strongly ideological but uncomfortable in formulating practical, personal ideals.

Whether or not Japanese teens are "small-bore" or "lacking in motivation" and "immature," they do represent a new generation to older Japanese. Are they the new materialists, the new independents, the new individualists? This would not be the first generation thus characterized. Like their American counterparts, they are not as evidently or radically different from their parents as teens of the late 1960s and early 1970s. But they are clearly at a stage of life and a place in history where their differences are exaggerated. Is there *enough* of a difference, rather than too much, is the historical question here. As a social psychologist in Japan said, "The generation gap is *healthy*. If there is no gap, society cannot grow. With a gap, young people can change society in a good direction. But if they just go along with their elders, there is no progress."[16]

Relationships and Relativity

The overwhelming importance of *belonging* in Japanese teen consciousness points to a significant difference from American teens' experience and may help us understand what has happened in both societies to heighten the recognition of the teen—in our society as a present *problem*, in Japan as a focus on the *future*.

In the United States, relationships are indeed key to a teen's life, just as they are in Japan. However, for reasons of history and local psychological interpretation, the American teen's membership in a peer group is seen by society to be a cause of problems rather than a source of valuable social learning, and support of this relational identity is not strong—except for adult-supervised institutions such as Boy Scouts or athletic activities. In Japan, adult society is not as deeply suspicious of "peer-ing"—bonding and group identity among adolescents—and in fact, adult-sponsored but not "managed" relationships abound, as well as the media which feed less formal teen communications.

As the social construction of adolescence in America has emphasized independence and separation on the one hand and conformity to adult standards on the other, the natural tendency to seek an identity in a peer group has represented a threat to adult society. The effect of this has changed over time.

"Acting out" used to be seen as a natural behavior of this stage of life in the West, as in "sowing one's wild oats," and within limits, such "different" behavior would not stigmatize a youth who was merely seen as age-appropriate. As the lines have been drawn more tightly, as we have both feared and provoked our teens, their "acting out," has moved from merely momentary differentness to behavior now labeled as deviant. This has meant that teens are now often very much at risk for becoming the social problem they are feared to be. This does not only apply to social pathologies, for children acting out in less publicly dramatic ways, not stealing, or raping, or killing, are also incurring more permanent labeling than they would have a century ago. A child who is not actively rebeling or committing crimes may still be self-destructive. He may not be performing at capacity at school, he may retreat from relationships at home and with peers. This retreat, often a passive rebellion, of separation and underperformance, is still seen where it is attended to as deviance, and a child may well be labeled as learning-disabled or emotionally disturbed, scarcely better than being called delinquent.

Labeling is not motivating in either society, and we can see tendencies also in Japan toward the creation of a "deviant" population of teenagers. The recent increase in affluence in Japan has had two effects on adolescents. The first, as we have noticed, is to widen the gap between children with money adequate to keep up in the consumer culture and those without such resources. The second is to create a larger pool of candidates for elite and prestigious educational opportunities—forcing the educational system to provide preparation for increasingly competitive examinations at high-school and college entrance levels. This pressured selection system tends to label children by academic achievement at younger and younger ages, in spite of the premise that university entrance is a meritocratic process open to all.

The older stratification system was that of the exams; the new is by "brand identity" and consumer hierarchies. The pressure felt now in middle schools in both these aspects of life has led to a certain degree of acting out among these young teens, and this slight sign of restiveness—in bullying and violence—though statistically very low, is met with an adult-imposed acceleration of school regulation. Like the American labeling of delinquency, there is now a tendency in Japan to create, by noting acts simply intended to be *different*—the perming of bangs, for example—a category of officially *deviant* children. This process, in both societies, may be seen as further construction and codification of the stage of adolescence—but in doing so, we may be removing the possibility of this stage being seen, as it once briefly was, as "normal."

The question of relativism goes deeper. Teens reveal our coded predispositions. Americans give them moral absolutes; Japanese give them a more fluid and relativistic view of propriety, in which even what they would see as contradiction may be tolerable. Both must come to terms with these ideas at a time when physical, moral, and social development converge and when the lesson of their relationships with parents, teachers, and friends often seem at odds with each other.

American teens receive at this time in their lives, and at this time in our history, a bundle of mixed messages; and as a society, American ambivalence towards teens and our lessons for them, has created serious institutional issues:

> Since youths are not adults, concern for their development has always generated the same humanitarian impulses as has concern for children. . . . But . . . we often treat them like adults and deny their development potential.[17]

Japanese youth, too, are considered predictors of the future of their society, somewhat more perhaps than in the United States; yet their fears *for* them may produce problems as much as our fears *of* them. However, institutions and individuals do in Japan mobilize for problems in a population which, as we noted, can still be called "children." High academic performance levels, low juvenile-delinquency rates, and low teen-pregnancy rates are products not of Confucian remnants in a disciplined and controlled society, but are the result of concern on behalf of teens, based in a generally positive view of their development and potential.

But there are new elements in the discussion, and these have come to light not from the statements of social commentators and psychologists, not even by those experts closest to teen consciousness, the marketing and media experts greatly responsible for the experience of "material" adolescents today.

A second-year high school student, in Chiba, says:

> I sometimes feel lonely because I don't feel the same as my classmates but then I wonder if they don't feel the same way I do, that we *aren't* all the same. Does that make us the same, noticing after all that we are different? Wouldn't it be better if we all said that out loud?

It is the teens themselves who have, with some confusion and discomfort, come to terms with a consciousness of diversity and it is this diversity *among* teens themselves, in family life, buying power, sexual and interpersonal experience, political and personal ideas—that will indeed be the basis of new thinking on the nature of Japanese society.

Appendix: School Regulations in Japan

School regulations in Japan are not standardized. Each elementary and secondary school establishes its own. Junior-high schools tend to have the most.

1. Boys' hair should not touch the eyebrows, the ears, or the top of the collar.
2. No one should have a permanent wave, or dye his or her hair. Girls should not wear ribbons or accessories in their hair. Hair dryers should not be used.
3. School uniform skirts should be__centimeters above the ground, no more and no less. (This differs by school and region)
4. Keep your uniform clean and pressed at all times. Girls' middy blouses should have two buttons on the back collar. Boys' pants cuffs should be of the prescribed width. No more than twelve eyelets should be on shoes. The number of buttons on a shirt and tucks in a skirt are also prescribed.

Figure A.1

The top portion of this excerpt from the students' handbook for Hitotsubashi Middle School shows precisely where the pocket and badge should go on a boy's shirt, and how, on the girl's middy blouse, the buttons should be placed and the tie centered.

服装のきまり

男子は黒の学生服，女子は紺のセーラー服，男子は学生帽（校章をつける）を使用する。バッジは図のように，男子は衿，女子は左胸につける。

1．夏の服装について

夏の服装は男子は黒ズボンに，白Yシャツまたは白半袖シャツ。（アイロンマーク）女子は長袖または半袖セーラー服（夏もの）と紺のスカート。（アイロンマーク）

Figure A.2

This page from the handbook for middle school students of Hitotsubashi Middle School shows how the bookbag should be carried, over the right shoulder, resting on left hip as one goes to school, the reverse on the way home.

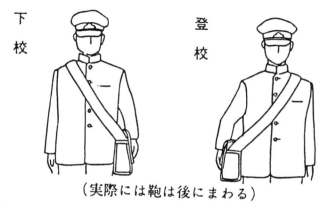

下校　　　　　　　　　　　登校

（実際には鞄は後にまわる）

5. Wear your school badge at all times. It should be positioned exactly.
6. Going to school in the morning, wear your book bag strap on the right shoulder; in the afternoon on the way home, wear it on the left shoulder. Your book case thickness, filled and unfilled, is also prescribed.
7. Girls should wear only regulation white underpants of 100% cotton.
8. When you raise your hand to be called on, your arm should extend forward and up at the angle prescribed in the handbook.
9. Your own route to school is marked in your student rule handbook; observe carefully which side of each street you are to use on the way to and from school.
10. After school you are to go directly home, unless your parent has written a note permitting you to go to another location. Permission will not be granted by the school unless this other location is a suitable one. You must not go to coffee shops. You must be home by——o'clock.
11. It is not permitted to drive or ride a motorcycle, or to have a license to drive one.
12. Before and after school, no matter where you are, you represent our school so you should behave in ways we can all be proud of.

Figure A.3

This map in the students' handbook for Hitotsubashi Middle School shows the routs to and from school as established by the school.

通学路

図中一太線が通学路

最寄駅		所要時間
国電	お茶の水	10分
	水道橋	10分
都新宿線	神保町	3分
	九段下	5分
都三田線	神保町	3分
東西線	竹橋	5分
	九段下	5分

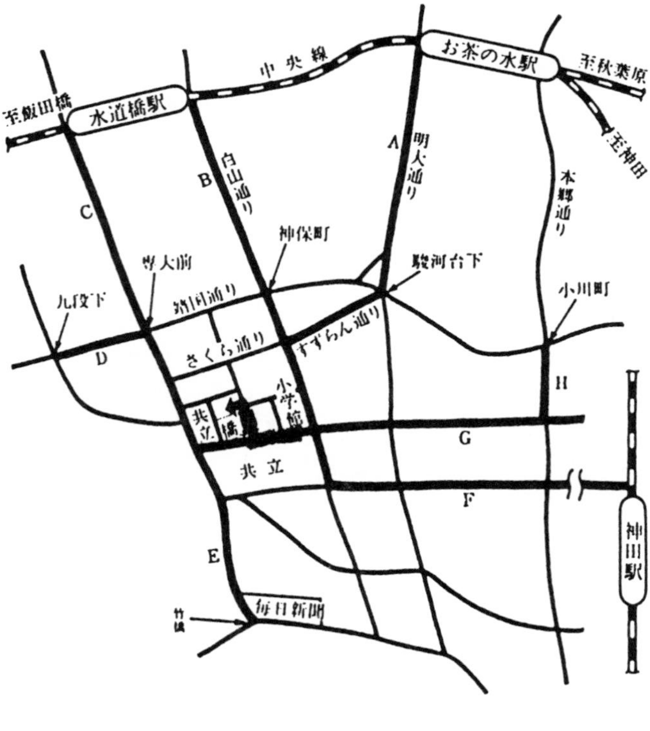

Excerpts from a handbook for students at a Tokyo middle school, are shown in Figures A.1 through A.3. These include dress regulations on how to position badges and tie fasteners on the girls' middy blouse, how to wear the handbag (over right shoulder on the way to school, over left on the way home) and also regulations on the path to take as you near school.

Notes

Introduction

1. Susanna Rodell, personal communication
2. *Youth Indicators*, U.S. Department of Education, Superintendent of Documents, 1988, p. 64.

Chapter 1: Rethinking the Life Course

1. *Japan 1991: An International Comparison*, Institute for Social and Economic Affairs, Tokyo, 1991.
2. Thomas Rohlen, *Japan's High Schools* (Berkeley: University of California Press, 1983), pp. 195–196.
3. Henry Isaacs, personal communication.
4. The masculine and feminine pronouns will both be used generically except where context clearly indicates gender.
5. Ikuya Sato, *Kamikaze Biker* (Chicago: University of Chicago Press, 1991), p. 210ff.
6. *New York Times*, April 13, 1992.

Chapter 2: Youth in Time

1. Takeo Doi, *The Anatomy of Dependence* (Tokyo: Kodansha, 1973).
2. G. Stanley Hall, *Adolescence: Its Psychology and Its Relationship to Physiology, Anthropology, Sex, Crime, Religion and Education* (New York: D. Appleton, 1904).
3. Cited in Howard Chudacoff, *How Old Are You? Age Consciousness in American Culture* (Princeton: Princeton University Press, 1989).
4. John Demos, *Past, Present and Personal* (Oxford: Oxford University Press, 1986), p. 105.
5. Ibid.
6. Morton White and Lucia White, *The Intellectual Versus the City* (Cambridge: Harvard University Press, 1962).
7. Demos, op. cit.

227

8. Ann Swidler, "Love and Adulthood in American Culture," in Robert Bellah et al., *Individualism and Commitment in American Life* (New York: Harper, 1987), p. 113.

9. The doubtful nature of results of reporting of this type makes such studies evocative but not necessarily reliable.

10. See Chapter 7. In data on actual sexual activity, there is a wide range. *Seventeen* magazine in the U.S., reports that 41% of the reporting readership (which includes 11- to 18-year-olds) is sexually experienced. The Guttmacher Institute reports that 20% of 15-year-olds are sexually experienced. Similarly, Japanese media surveys report a higher level of sexual activity than do research institutes.

11. Leah Lefstein, "A Portrait of Young Adolescents in the 1980s" (New York: Lilly Endowment, Center for Early Adolescence, 1986).

12. Gallup Poll, Junior Achievement International Youth Survey, March 1990.

13. Thomas Rohlen, *Japan's High Schools* (Berkeley: University of California Press, 1983), p. 309.

14. Erik Erikson, *Identity, Youth and Crisis* (New York: Norton, 1968).

15. Takeo Doi, *The Anatomy of Self* (Tokyo: Kodansha, 1986).

16. Catherine Lewis, "Cooperation and Control in Japanese Nursery Schools," *Comparative Education Review*, vol. 28, 1984, pp. 69–84.

17. Hiroko Hara and Hiroshi Wagatsuma, *Shitsuke* (Tokyo: Kobundo, 1975).

18. This *sempai-kohai* (senior-junior) relationship prefigures that of contemporary school and college activity groups and clubs. See Chapter 6.

19. Haru Reischauer, *Samurai and Silk*, (Cambridge: Harvard University Press, 1986), pp. 28–32.

20. Fukuzawa Yukichi, *The Autobiography of Fukuzawa Yukichi*, rev. ed., (New York: Schocken Books, 1972).

21. Doi, op. cit., p. 46.

22. Herbert Passin, *Society and Education in Japan* (New York: Columbia University Teachers College Press, 1965), p. 104.

23. Keisuke Kinoshita, Director, 1954.

24. Erikson, op. cit., p. 89.

25. *Kuro saseta hoo ga ii*, it is good to experience hardship, is a byword of traditional Japanese childrearing.

Chapter 3: Family Time and Space

1. AP release, Tokyo, 9/6/91.

2. Ei Rokusuke, "Random Thoughts on Today's Japan," in *Hyoronka Gokko* (Tokyo: Kodansha, 1989).

3. Birth-control pills are still not legally available in Japan except in

rare instances: only 2% of married couples use them for birth control. The reproductive health of women is cited as the reason, but commentators suggest that leaders are worried about declining birth rates. Most adolescents who are sexually active say that they use condoms.

4. Kanagawa Prefecture High School Teachers Union Study, *The Kanagawa*, vol. 33, 1992, pp. 1–8.

5. Gallup Poll, Junior Achievement Study: Youth Attitudes in Japan and the United States, 1990.

6. "Community and the Child and Youth," National Council of Youth Organizations in Japan, *Proceedings*, Sixth Asian Regional Seminar, November 1978, p. 70.

7. Management and Coordination Agency, "International Comparison of Public Opinion: The Ideal Father," Tokyo, 1989.

8. Mariko Sugahara Bando, "Women of Japan," Foreign Press Center, Tokyo, 1978.

9. When there are no available sons to continue the line, it is traditional to have the husband of a daughter formally adopted as *mukoyoshi*, or heir, taking the daughter's family name. It has not been a popular practise among young men, and there is an old saying that you should not become an adopted son-in-law if you have as much as one bowl of rice left.

10. Cyril Simmons and Winnie Wade, "A Comparative Study of Young People's Views of the Family" *Education Studies*, vol. 13, 1987, p. 46.

11. Suzanne Vogel, personal communication.

12. Ezra Vogel, *Japan's New Middle Class* (Berkeley: University of California Press, 1963), p. 27n.

13. Suzanne Vogel, "The Professional Housewife," *Japan Interpreter*, vol. 12, (Autumn 1978), pp. 16–43.

14. Ads for the new double-binned clothes washer emphasize the dirty-slob image of the father: a housewife is shown picking up Dad's underwear with a long tongs and dropping it into one of the two bins, separate from the rest of the family's clothes in the dryer.

15. Michiko Fukuzawa, personal communication.

Chapter 4: School in the Life of the Teen

1. Suzanne Vogel, "The Professional Housewife," *Japan Interpreter*, vol. 12, 1978, 16–43.

2. Merry White, *The Japanese Educational Challenge* (New York: The Free Press, 1987).

3. Thomas Rohlen, presentation at Woodrow Wilson Center, Washington, D.C., April 1992.

4. Ronald Dore, *The Diploma Disease* (Berkeley: University of California Press, 1976).

5. Japan Institute for Social and Economic Affairs, *Japan 1991: An International Comparison,* p. 93.

6. "A Conversation with Deborah Prothrow-Stith," *Harvard Alumni Gazette,* Summer 1992, p. 24.

7. Ikuo Amano, *Education and Examination in Modern Japan* (Tokyo: University of Tokyo Press, 1990)

8. *Pacific Friend,* vol. 18, November 1990.

9. *The Best Teaching Makes Winners* (Tokyo: Yoyogi Preparatory Schools, 1990).

10. Ezra F. Vogel, *Japan's New Middle Class,* 2d ed. (Berkeley: University of California Press, 1991), p. 55.

11. Nana Mizushima Regur, "In The Shadow of Japan's Educational System: Children who Refuse to Go to School," *Japan Society Newsletter,* May 1991, pp. 2–5.

12. Asahi News Service, 12/26/91.

13. Gallup Poll/Junior Achievement International Youth Survey, March 1990.

14. 1990 Report on Children's Health, Nippon College of Physical Education. The report surveyed 1,231 schools from nursery to senior high school levels.

15. *Yomiuri Shimbun,* October 12, 1990.

16. *Japan Times,* August 26, 1989.

17. There is now an unprecedented competition for teaching positions creating a *ronin* category, like that of repeaters in the university entrance exams—the *shoshoku ronin,* or retakers of the appointment exam, waiting another year to retake the exam. Nobuo Shimahara, "Teacher Education in Japan," *Windows on Japanese Education,* ed. by Edward Beauchamp (New York: Greenwood Press, 1991).

18. *New York Times,* July 30, 1992, p. 45.

19. Tamiko Bjerner, "School Violence," *Tokyo Journal,* September 1987, pp. 26–27.

20. Thomas Rohlen, presentation, Woodrow Wilson Center, Washington, D.C., March 23, 1992.

21. Ernest Boyer, *Washington Post,* April 15, 1992, p. A22.

22. Ikuya Sato, *Kamikaze Biker* (Chicago: University of Chicago Press, 1991), p. 116.

23. AP Newswire release, April 30, 1992.

24. Donald Roden, *Schooldays in Imperial Japan* (Berkeley: University of California Press, 1975).

25. Penelope Eckert, *Jocks and Burnouts* (New York: Columbia University Teachers College, 1989).

26. Sachiko Ide, personal communication.

Chapter 5: The Material Child

1. Thomas Rohlen, "Is Japanese Education Becoming Less Egalitarian? Notes on High School Stratification and Reform," *Journal of Japanese Studies*, vol. 3, Winter 1977, pp. 37–70.
2. Seiko Tanabe, "Prodigal Children, Impoverished Parents," in *Bochibochi Zoshi* (Tokyo: Iwanami Shoten, 1988), pp. 129–142.
3. Tamio Takemura, "The Formation of a Mass Consumption Society in Japan in the 1920s," manuscript 1989.
4. George Fields, *From Bonsai to Levis* (New York: New American Library, 1983).
5. Thomas Rohlen, *Japan's High Schools* (Berkeley: University of California Press, 1983), page 279.
6. Wakao Fujioka, "The Rise of the Micromasses," *Japan Echo*, vol. 13, 1986.
7. Ibid., p. 32.
8. Ibid.
9. Howard Chudacoff, *How Old Are You? Age Consciousness in American Culture* (Princeton: Princeton University Press, 1989), p. 117ff.
10. Ibid, p. 157.
11. "The Amount of Pocket Money for Japanese High School Students," NHK Broadcasting Culture Institute, 1985.
12. U.S. Department of Education, *Youth Indicators*, 1988, pp. 86–87.
13. F. Thomas Juster and Frank P. Stafford, *The Allocation of Time: Empirical Findings, Behavioral Models and Problems of Measurement*, Survey Research Center, Institute for Social Research, University of Michigan, 1982.
14. *Maniakku* is an English-derived word from "maniac," but it implies in Japanese only a passion, not usually a pathological mania, for a trend or activity.
15. *Wall Street Journal*, June 28, 1991.
16. Interview, Mr. Kitabatake, Editor, *Duet* magazine, July 1989.
17. "Showering Teenagers Push Family Water Consumption UP," *Japan Times, August 18, 1989.*
18. *The Boston Globe*, July 24, 1991, pp. 71–72.
19. This point will be discussed more thoroughly in Chapter 7.
20. C. Scott Littleton, "Tokyo Rock and Role," *Natural History*, August 1985, pp. 49–57.
21. Interview, Kitabatake, op. cit.
22. Ibid.
23. Keiko Okuda, freelance editor, interview, Tokyo, March 1991.
24. Ikuya Sato, *Kamikaze Biker* (Chicago: University of Chicago Press, 1991), p. 44.
25. AP Newswire release, April 6, 1992.

26. Sumio Kondo, interview, Tokyo, March 1991.
27. Millie Creighton, "Constructing Identity Through Consumer Purchases: Japanese Marketing and the Socialization of a Shopping Identity," paper delivered at Annual Meetings, Association for Asian Studies, Washington, D.C., April 6, 1992.
28. Terry Trucco, "In Japan, Cuteness Counts," *Wall Street Journal*, February 21, 1986.
29. Chiaki Kanda, interview and field notes, 1990. Ms. Kanda's notes have been used extensively in this section.
30. Manami Izumiyama, *Japan Times*, International Weekly, ed., February 16, 1992, p. 13.
31. *Hot Dog*, March 1992.
32. Kanda, field notes.
33. Mary Sanches, "Contemporary Japanese Youth: Mass Media Communication", *Youth and Society*, vol. 8, June 1977.
34. The most famous was Osamu Tezuka, who died in 1989. Tezuka's comics use film techniques, such as three-dimensional perspective, montages, and room closeups, and they often have deep philosophical themes, cosmic struggles of good and evil. See "King of the Toons," *Look Japan*, July 1989, pp. 4–7.
35. *Manga* receive critical attention from many groups. Feminist groups have particularly protested the objectification of women, and mothers' groups protest the east availability of pornographic manga. Recently, unions have protested the depiction of a teacher-turned-school custodian as debased by his new position; and the publisher, *Shonen Jumpu*, has recalled issues and released an apology. *Yomiuri Shimbun*, November 15, 1990.
36. Chiho Nagao, personal communication.
37. Communication from Dr. Horst Stipp, March 1, 1992. Dr. Stipp of NBC Research and Dr. Helen Boehm of Fox Communications were helpful in providing information for this section.
38. Ibid.
39. Sumio Kondo, personal communication 4/10/91.
40. *Seventeen* (Japan), March 1991, pp. 112–113.

Chapter 6: Friendship

1. Among teen motorcycle gang members, the term for "hanging out" is *tamaru*, a word usually used to refer to water standing stagnant, as in puddles on the road. Ikuya Sato, *Kamikaze Biker* (Chicago: University of Chicago Press, 1991), p. 31.
2. "Nihon no kokosei, yujin kankei dorai," *Ashai Shimbun*, February 23, 1992.
3. Ibid.
4. Carol Gilligan, personal communication.

5. Bruce Leigh, "Alienation in the Japanese High School," *Tokyo Journal*, September 1987.
6. From interviews conducted in Gumma Prefecture by Hidetada Shimizu for studies on relationships and identity among adolescents.
7. Ibid.
8. Ibid.
9. Ibid.
10. Ibid.
11. See Chapter 8 for further discussion of "self" and "identity" among adolescents.
12. Thomas Rohlen, *Japan's High Schools* (Berkeley: University of California Press, 1983), p. 290.
13. Ibid., p. 289.
14. Merry White and Robert LeVine, "What Is an Ii Ko?", in *Child Development in Japan*, eds. Hiroshi Azuma, Harold Stevenson and Kenji Hakuta (New York: Freeman, 1985).
15. Penelope Eckert, *Jocks and Burnouts*, New York: Teachers College, Columbia University Press, 1989
16. Katrina Merritt, "The Success of the Japanese Educational System: The Role of the Peer Group in Promoting Student Motivation and Achievement" Undergraduate Senior Honors Thesis, East Asian Studies, Harvard University, April 1992, p. 54.
17. Suzanne Vogel, personal communication.
18. Sato, *op. cit.*, p. 220.
19. "Children and Crime" editorial, *Yomiuri Shimbun*, October 21, 1990.
20. Report on Teen Alcoholism in the United States, *Yomiuri Shimbun*, November 1990.
21. "Japan is successful in containing the drug problem" in *Japan Times*, International Weekly Edition, September 1990.
22. White Paper on Crime, Ministry of Justice, 1990.
23. Tsukasa Kitajima, "The Rise in Juvenile Delinquency," *Japan Echo*, vol. 9, special issue, 1982.
24. Sato, *op. cit.*
25. Suzanne Vogel, personal communication
26. Heisei Gannenchu no Jisatsu no Gaiyo, Report on Suicide in 1989, National Police Agency, Tokyo, 1990.
27. Rosey Clarke, "The New Japanese Teenager," *Winds*, September 1985, pp. 23–30.

Chapter 7: Sexuality, Illusions, and Realities

1. 1991 Report on Teen Sexuality, National Public Radio, April 1992.
2. Brent C. Miller and Kirstin A. Moore, "Adolescent Sexual Behavior,

Pregnancy and Parenting Research through the 1980s," *Journal of Marriage and the Family*, vol. 52, November 1990, p. 1030.

3. "Fact Sheet on Adolescent Sexuality, Pregnancy and Parenthood," Center for Population Options, May 1990.

4. *Poppu Tiinu*, Youth Survey, Tokyo 1981.

5. *Los Angeles Times,* quoted in *Daily Yomiuri*, January 21, 1991, p. 2.

6. Ibid.

7. "Guidelines for Comprehensive Sexuality Education," National Guidelines Task Force, March 1992.

8. Louis Harris Poll, 1988.

9. Susan N. Wilson and Catherine A. Sanderson, "The Sex Respect Curriculum: Is 'Just Say No' Effective?" SIECUS Report, September/October 1988, p. 11.

10. Ibid., p. 10.

11. Pamela Haughton-Denniston, personal communication.

12. Sheldon Garon, "The World's Oldest Debate? Prostitution and the State in Imperial Japan, 1900–1945" manuscript article, 1992.

13. "Angry Mothers Demand Porn Manga Crackdown," *Daily Yomiuri*, March 14, 1991, p. 3.

14. *Seventeen*, January 1991.

15. *Seventeen*, November 1991.

16. "Ask Beth," *The Boston Globe*, October 3, 1991.

17. "Ask Beth," *The Boston Globe*, February 13, 1992.

18. "Textbooks for New School Year Discuss Sex for First Time," Peter Landers, AP Newswire release, April 22, 1992.

19. Kinuko Wakita, "Modern Japanese Women's Concept of Heterosexual Relationships," unpublished paper, Boston University, May 1990.

20. *New York Times*, December 13, 1986, p. 29.

21. Ibid., p. 33.

22. Letter to editors, *Newsweek*, July 30, 1990.

23. Thomas Rohlen, *Japan's High Schools* (Berkeley: University of California Press, 1983), p. 288ff.

24. Wakita, op. cit., p. 3–5.

25. Ibid.

26. Ibid.

27. Ibid.

28. Morning Edition report, National Public Radio, June 6, 1991.

29. Carol Stack, *All Our Kin*, New York: Harper and Row, 1975.

30. Elise F. Jones et al., "Teenage Pregnancy in Developed Countries: Determinants and Policy Implications" *Family Planning Perspectives*, vol. 17 March/April 1985.

31. *Japan Times Weekly*, June 17, 1989, p. 4.

32. Yasuo Higashi, interview, March 1991.

33. *Japan Times* International Weekly Edition, op. cit., p. 4.
34. *Daily Yomiuri*, November 15, 1990, p. 2.
35. Yasuo Higashi, interview, March 1991.

Chapter 8: Big Thoughts

1. From *Wild Sheep Club, vol. 6*, no. 2 in: Katrina Merritt, "The Success of the Japanese Educational System: Role of the Peer Group in Promoting Student Motivation and Achievement," Senior Honors Thesis, Harvard College, April 1992.
2. Ibid., vol. 5, p. 6.
3. Lois Peak and Merry White, "The Anatomy of the Hara," unpublished manuscript, 1981.
4. Gallup Poll, Junior Achievement Study, "Youth Attitudes in Japan and the United States," March 1990.
5. Sengoku Tamotsu, Lois Leiderman Davitz, and Joel Davitz, "Adolescent Perceptions of Heroes in Three Different Cultures: Japan, China and the United States," Japan Youth Research Institute, Tokyo, 1988.
6. M. Higo, Gumma Prefecture, July 1988.
7. *Japan Times*, weekly international ed., May 11–17, 1992, p. 2.
8. Suzanne Vogel, personal communication.
9. Gallup, op. cit.
10. *The Rising Younger Generation in Japan*, National Assembly for Youth Development, Prime Minister's Office, Tokyo 1986.
11. Ikuya Sato, *Kamikaze Biker* (Chicago: University of Chicago Press, 1991), p. 85.
12. Takeo Doi, *The Anatomy of Dependence* (Tokyo: Kodansha, 1973).
13. *Trends in Class Perceptions of Japanese*, Economic Planning Agency, 1975–1987, 1990.
14. "Public Opinion Survey on People's Perception of Disparities with Ten Years Ago," Economic Planning Agency, 1989.
15. Hidetada Shimizu, notes from July 1989 interviews.
16. Keiko Kashiwagi, Shirayuri University, communication.
17. W. Norton Grubb and Marvin Lazerson, *Broken Promises: How Americans Fail their Children* (New York: Basic Books, 1982), p. 156.

Bibliography

Abiko, Tadahiko, and Paul S. George. "Education for Early Adolescents in Japan and the United States: Cross-Cultural Observations." *National Association for Secondary School Principals Bulletin* (December 1986).

Adelson, Joseph. *Handbook of Adolescent Psychology.* New York: Wiley, 1980.

Amano, Ikuo. *Education and Examination in Modern Japan.* Tokyo: University of Tokyo Press, 1990.

Bellah, Robert, ed. *Individualism and Commitment in American Life.* New York: Harper and Row, 1987.

Blos, Peter. *On Adolescence: A Psychoanalytic Interpretation.* New York: Free Press, 1962.

Chudacoff, Howard. *How Old Are You? Age Consciousness in American Culture.* Princeton: Princeton University Press, 1989.

Clarke, Rosey, "The New Japanese Teenager." *Winds*, September 1985, pp. 23–30.

Coleman, James S. *The Adolescent Society.* New York: The Free Press, 1961.

Coleman, James S., and Torsten Husen. *Becoming Adult in a Changing Society.* Paris: OECD, 1985.

Creighton, Millie. "Constructing Identity through Consumer Purchases: Japanese Marketing and the Creation of a Shopping Identity." Paper delivered at annual meeting, Association for Asian Studies, Washington, D.C., April 6, 1992.

Csikszentmihalyi, Mihaly, and Reed Larson. *Being Adolescent: Conflict and Growth in the Teenage Years.* New York: Basic Books, 1984.

Demos, John. *Past, Present and Personal: The Family and the Life Course in American History.* Oxford: Oxford University Press, 1986.

DeVos, George, and Hiroshi Wagatsuma. "Family Life and Delinquency: Some Perspectives from Japanese Research." In *Transcultural Research in Mental Health*, edited by William Lebra. Honolulu: University of Hawaii Press, 1972.

DeVos, George, and Hiroshi Wagatsuma. *Socialization for Achievement*. Berkeley: University of California Press, 1973.

Doi, Takeo. *The Anatomy of Dependence*. Tokyo: Kodansha, 1973.

———. *The Anatomy of Self*. Tokyo: Kodansha, 1986.

———. "Higaishi-ishiki: the Psychology of Revolting Youth." In *Japanese Culture and Behavior*, edited by Takie Lebra and William P. Lebra. Honolulu: University of Hawaii Press, 1974.

———. *The Psychological World of Natsume Soseki*. Cambridge: Harvard University Press, 1976.

Dore, Ronald. *The Diploma Disease*. Berkeley: University of California Press, 1976.

Duke, Benjamin. *The Japanese School*. New York: Praeger, 1986.

Eckert, Penelope. *Jocks and Burnouts*. New York: Teachers College Press, 1989.

Ei Rokusuke. "Random Thoughts on Today's Japan," *Hyoronka Gokko*. Tokyo: Kodansha, 1989.

Erikson, Eric. *Childhood and Society*. New York: Norton, 1963.

———. *Identity: Youth and Crisis*. New York: Norton, 1968.

Fields, George. *From Bonsai to Levis*. New York: Macmillan, 1983.

Friedenberg, Edgar. *The Vanishing Adolescent*. Boston: Beacon Press, 1964.

Fujioka, Wakao. "The Rise of the Micromasses." *Japan Echo*, vol. 13 (1986), pp. 31–38.

Fukuzawa Yukichi. *The Autobiography of Fukuzawa Yukichi*. Rev. ed., New York: Schocken, 1966.

Garon, Sheldon. "The World's Oldest Debate? Prostitution and the State in Imperial Japan, 1900–1945." Unpublished manuscript article.

Gass, William H. "Where East Meets West—to Boogie!" *New York Times Sunday Magazine*, March 4, 1990, p. 63ff.

"Growing Up in Japan." *Japan Echo*. Special issue, vol. 9 (1982).

Grubb, W. Norton, and Marvin Lazerson. *Broken Promises: How Americans Fail Their Children*. New York: Basic Books, 1982.

Hall, G. Stanley. *Adolescence: Its Psychology and Its Relation to Physiology, Anthropology, Sex, Crime, Religion and Education*. New York: Appleton, 1904.

Hendry, Joy. *Becoming Japanese*. Honolulu: University of Hawaii Press, 1986.

Hogan, Dennis. "Issues in Adolescent Development." Paper presented at Conference on Child Development in Japan and the United States. Center for Advanced Study in the Behavioral Sciences, Stanford, Calif., April 6–9, 1983.

Holmstrom, David. "What the Kids Wrote." *Christian Science Monitor*, April 11, 1990, pp. 10–11.

Ito, Shigeyuki. "Future Orientation and Inner Limit of Young Japanese People." *Futures*, February 1987, pp. 82–87.

Japan 1991: An International Comparison. Tokyo: Japan Institute for Social and Economic Affairs, 1991.

"Japan's Troubled Future." Special report, *Fortune*, March 30, 1987, pp. 21–53.

Juster, F. Thomas, and Frank P. Stafford. "The Allocation of Time: Empirical Findings, Behavioral Models and Problems of Measurement." Survey Research Center, Institute for Social Research, University of Michigan, 1982.

Kashiwagi, Keiko. "Issues of Self-Concept in Sex Role Development in Japan." Written for Conference on Child Development in Japan and the United States, Center for Advanced Study in Behavioral Sciences, Stanford, Calif., April 6–9, 1983.

———. "Personality Development of Adolescents." In *Child Development and Education in Japan,* edited by Harold Stevenson, Hiroshi Azuma, and Kenji Hakuta. New York: W. H. Freeman, 1986.

Kett, Joseph. *Rites of Passage: Adolescence in America, 1790 to Present.* New York: Basic Books, 1977.

———. "The History of Age Grading in America." In *Youth: Transition to Adulthood,* edited by James Coleman et al. Chicago: University of Chicago Press, 1974.

Kiefer, Christie. "The Psychological Interdependence of Family, School and Bureaucracy in Japan." In *Japanese Culture and Behavior,* edited by T. S. Lebra and William Lebra. Honolulu: University of Hawaii Press, 1974.

Kitajima Tsukasa. "Rise in Juvenile Delinquency." *Japan Echo.* Special issue, vol. 9 (1982).

Koyama, Takashi, Morioka Kiyomi, and Kumagai Fumie. *Family and Household in Changing Japan.* Tokyo: Japan Society for the Promotion of Science, 1980.

Krauss, Ellis, Thomas Rohlen, and Patricia Steinhoff, eds. *Conflict in Japan.* Honolulu: University of Hawaii Press, 1984.

Lebra, Takie. *Japanese Women.* Honolulu: University of Hawaii Press, 1984.

Lefstein, Leah. "A Portrait of Young Adolescents in the 1980s." Lilly Endowment, Center for Early Adolescence, 1986.

Leigh, Bruce. "Alienation in the Japanese High School." *Tokyo Journal* (September 1987) pp. 14–15.

LeVine, Robert. *Culture, Behavior and Personality.* Chicago: Aldine Press, 1973.

Lewis, Catherine. "Cooperation and Control in Japanese Nursery Schools." *Comparative Education Review* 28 (1984), pp. 69–84.

Lifton, Robert Jay. "Individual Patterns in Historical Change: Imagery of Japanese Youth." *Journal of Social Issues,* vol. 20 (October 1964), pp. 96–111.

———. "Japanese Youth, The Search for the New and the Pure." *The American Scholar,* vol. 30 (Summer 1961), pp. 332–344.

Littleton, C. Scott. "Tokyo Rock and Role." *Natural History*, vol. 94 (August 1985), pp. 48–57.

Lock, Margaret. "Schoolphobia." Unpublished ms.

Mead, Margaret. *Coming of Age in Samoa*. New York: Morrow, 1973.

Merritt, Katrina. "The Success of the Japanese Educational System: Role of the Peer Group in Promoting Student Motivation and Achievement." Senior honors thesis, East Asian Studies, Harvard College, April 1992.

Miller, Brent C., and Kirstin Moore. "Adolescent Sexual Behavior, Pregnancy and Parenting Research through the 1980s." *Journal of Marriage and the Family*, vol. 52 (November 1990), p. 1030.

Morioka, Kiyomi. "Life Course Research." Paper prepared for Conference on Child Development in Japan and the U.S., Center for Advanced Study in the Behavioral Sciences, Stanford, Calif., April 6–9, 1983.

———. "Life Cycle Patterns in Japan, China and the U.S.", *Journal of Marriage and the Family*, vol. 29 (1967), pp. 595–608.

———. "Privatization of Family Life in Japan." In *Child Development and Education in Japan*, edited by Harold Stevenson, Hiroshi Azuma, and Kenji Hakuta. New York: W. H. Freeman, 1986.

National Assembly for Youth Development. *The Rising Younger Generation in Japan*. Tokyo: Prime Minister's Office, 1986.

National Council of Youth Organizations in Japan. *Proceedings*, Sixth Asian Regional Seminar, November 1978.

Nishimura, Kunio. "A Kinder, Gentler Generation." *Look Japan*, April 1991, pp. 4–8.

Offer, Daniel, et al. *The Teenage World: Adolescents' Self-Image in Ten Countries*. New York: Plenum, 1988.

Ono, Yumiko. "Magazine House: Tokyo's Trend Setter." *Wall Street Journal*, June 28, 1991, pp. B1–B4.

Passin, Herbert. *Society and Education in Japan*. New York: Teachers College, 1965.

Peak, Lois, and Merry White. "The Anatomy of the Hara." Unpublished ms.

Petersen, Anne. "Those Gangly Years." *Psychology Today*, September 1987, pp 28–34.

Powers, Richard G., and Hidetoshi Kato, eds. *Handbook of Japanese Popular Culture*. New York: Greenwood Press, 1989.

Prime Minister's Office. *Annual Report on Youth, January 1991*. Cited in *Japan Report*, March 1991.

Regur, Nina Mizushima. "In the Shadow of Japan's Educational System: Children who Refuse to Go to School." *Japan Society Newsletter* (May 1991), pp. 2–5.

Reischauer, Haru. *Samurai and Silk*. Cambridge: Harvard University Press, 1986, pp. 28–32.

Roberts, Kenneth. *Youth and Leisure*. London: George Allen and Unwin, 1983.

Roden, Donald. *Schooldays in Imperial Japan*. Berkeley: University of California Press, 1975.

Rohlen, Thomas. "Is Japanese Education Becoming Less Egalitarian? Notes on High School Stratification and Reform." *Journal of Japanese Studies*, vol. 3 (Winter 1977), pp. 37–70.

———. *Japan's High Schools*. Berkeley: University of California Press, 1983.

Rosenbaum, James E, and Takehiko Kariya. "From High School to Work: Market and Institutional Mechanisms in Japan." *American Journal of Sociology*, vol. 94 (May 1989), pp. 1334–1365.

Rutter, Michael. *Changing Youth in a Changing Society*. Cambridge: Cambridge University Press, 1980.

Sanches, Mary. "Contemporary Japanese Youth: Mass Media and Communication." *Youth and Society*, vol. 8 (June 1977), pp. 389–415.

Sato, Ikuya. *Kamikaze Biker*. Chicago: University of Chicago Press, 1991.

Sengoku Tamotsu, Lois Leiderman Davitz, and Joel R. Davitz. "Adolescents' Perceptions of Heroes in Three Different Cultures: Japan, China and the United States." Tokyo: Japan Youth Research Institute, 1988.

———. "A Study of Senior High School Students in Japan and the United States." Tokyo: Japan Youth Research Institute, 1988.

———. "A Survey of High School Students' Attitudes Toward Friends and Selected Values." Tokyo: Japan Youth Research Institute, 1988.

Shein, Jean-Emmanuel. "Impatience, Immediacy, Superficiality. The Supremacy of Objects in Contemporary Japanese Youth Culture." Unpublished ms.

Simmons, Cyril, and Winnie Wade. "A Comparative Study of Young People's Views of the Family." *Educational Studies*, vol. 13 (1987), pp. 45–56.

Stack, Carol. *All Our Kin*. New York: Harper and Row, 1975.

Swidler, Ann. "Love and Adulthood in American Culture." In *Individualism and Commitment in American Life*, edited by Robert Bellah. New York: Harper and Row, 1987, pp. 107–124.

Takagi, Ryuro. "Suicidal Attempts Among Children in Japan." In *Transcultural Research in Mental Health*, edited by William Lebra. Honolulu: University of Hawaii Press, pp. 88–106.

Takemura, Tamio. "The Formation in Embryo of the Mass Consumption Society and Innovation in the 1920s in Japan." Unpublished ms.

Tanabe, Seiko. "Prodigal Children, Impoverished Parents." *Bochibochi Zoshi*. Tokyo: Iwanami Shoten, 1988, pp. 129–142.

Trucco, Terry. "In Japan, Cuteness Counts." *Wall Street Journal*, February 21, 1986.

Tsurumi, Kazuko. *Social Change and the Individual*. Princeton: Princeton University Press, 1970.

Vogel, Ezra. *Japan's New Middle Class*. Berkeley: University of California Press, 1963.

Vogel, Suzanne. "The Professional Housewife." *Japan Interpreter*, *12*(1978), pp. 16–43.

Wakita Kinuko. "Modern Japanese Women's Concept of Heterosexual Relationships. Unpublished ms., Boston University, May 1990.

White, Merry I. *The Japanese Educational Challenge: A Commitment to Children*. New York: The Free Press, 1987.

———, and Robert A. LeVine. "What Is an Ii Ko?" In *Child Development in Japan*, edited by Hiroshi Azuma, Harold Stevenson, and Kenji Hakuta. New York: W. H. Freeman, 1985.

White, Morton, and Lucia White. *The Intellectual Versus the City*. Cambridge: Harvard University Press, 1962.

Wilson, Susan N., and Catherine A. Sanderson. "The Sex Respect Curriculum: Is 'Just Say No' Effective?" *SIECUS Report*, (September/October 1988).

Winship, Elizabeth. "Ask Beth." *Boston Globe*, October 3, 1991; February 13, 1992.

Youth Indicators. United States Department of Education. Washington D.C.: Superintendent of Documents, 1988.

"Youth Attitudes in Japan and the United States." Gallup Poll and Junior Achievement Report, March 1990.

Japanese and American magazines cited:

Japan

Vivi
Hotdog
Popeye
Mimi
Hanako
Duet
Potato
Shonen Jump
Margaret

Winkup
Olive
CanCam
Non-no
An-an
Seventeen

United States

Seventeen
Sassy

Acknowledgments

As this project expanded across geographical space and generational time, so has my gratitude to those who helped. The teens themselves were generous and thoughtful, and belied negative preconceptions of adolescents in both of their countries. As research assistants, interpreters, and translators, Hidetada Shimizu, Yoshie Nishioka Rice, Chiho Nagao, Hina Hirayama, Mikako Sato, and Yoshi Fujimori were indispensable to the work. Hidetada Shimizu's own research, parallel to this study, was also most useful, and I am grateful for his generosity and friendship over the four years we have worked on this project.

In Japan, many more people supported the study than can be mentioned here. As ever, I have relied on the friendship and help of Sachiko Ide, Wakako Hironaka, Takeo Doi, Mariko Sugahara Bando, Sumiko Iwao, and Mari and Kazutami Yamazaki. My colleague, Professor Keiko Kashiwagi of Shirayuri University in Tokyo, guided the project from its outset. Others in Japan who gave their support were: Sumio Kondo, Mariko Fujiwara, Kunio Wakai, Tamotsu Sengoku, Hiroshi Kida, Akio Nakajima, Masami Kajita, Fukuko Kobayashi, Fumiko Inoue, and Yasuo Higashi. My colleagues at the National Institute of Multimedia Education in Chiba where I spent four months as a Visiting Researcher were also most helpful: Hidetoshi Kato, Kazuyuki Kitamura, Tadahiko Kariya, Noriko Nakamura, Yoko Hirose, and Chieko Mizoue.

In the United States, Leslie Bedford encouraged me with her own enthusiasm for the study of Japanese teens, and the staff at The Children's Museum in Boston were also most helpful. Dan Spock was generous with his photographs of teen street life. Ed Baumeister helped find the sense and the "big points." Mitzi Goheen, Kathleen Hartford, Jean Jackson, Leslie Swartz, Ellen Widmer, Thomas Rohlen, Ezra Vogel, Catherine Lewis, Robert

LeVine, Gerry Lesser, Carol Gilligan, Suzanne Vogel, and Henry Smith, among other friends and colleagues, gave suggestions, sources, and support. Dr. Helen Boehm of Fox Communications and Horst Stipp of NBC Research were both very helpful with data on the media and American teens. Susan Wilson, Pamela Haughton-Denniston, and the staff of the Center for Population Options contributed much to my understanding of issues in adolescent sexuality today. Chiaki Kanda's field study of Japanese teen culture was invaluable for data and perspective. James D. Hoffman of Lawrence Middle School in New Jersey was helpful in arranging meetings with his students. Jennifer White collected data and recorded Japanese teens' lives with her photographs.

This research was assisted by a grant during 1988–1989 from the Joint Committee on Japanese Studies of the Social Science Research Council and the American Council of Learned Societies, with funds provided by the Japan–U.S. Friendship Commission, the Ford Foundation, and the National Endowment for the Humanities. The American Council of Learned Societies also generously provided a fellowship held from 1989 to 1991, enabling me to conduct research and write for an uninterrupted academic term. Boston University provided me with a year's leave of absence in which to collect data and begin to write, and the National Institute of Multimedia Education in Chiba allowed me four months of liberated time and a most hospitable home in Japan. In the Sociology Department at Boston University, Roz Geffen, Angie Milonas, and Sue Spellman picked up the pieces when my teaching and administrative priorities were clearly skewed. The Edwin O. Reischauer Institute of Japanese Studies at Harvard continues to support my frenetic style of work, and I am most grateful to the staff there as well. My patient editor, Susan Arellano, has seen me through the early and necessary confusion to much greater clarity, by asking all the right and difficult questions. Celia Knight directed the painstaking copy editing and clarified many doubtful passages. My gratitude to all does not in any way reduce the responsibility I alone bear for the content of this work.

My family and friends sustained the effort, and me, over the years, and my thanks to them can only be expressed as the *on* I bear to them: the Japanese sense of an obligation that can never be repaid. In Japan, *on* is traditionally owed to parents; in our American generational reversal, I especially give thanks to my children.

Index

245